W9-APM-832

# The Formation of School Subjects

## The Struggle for Creating an American Institution

For my parents who helped me to understand the importance of the past in defining the present.

Studies in Curriculum History:

# The Formation of School Subjects

## The Struggle for Creating an American Institution

*Edited by*
**Thomas S. Popkewitz**
*University of Wisconsin Madison*

 The Falmer Press
(A member of the Taylor & Francis Group)
New York, Philadelphia and London

**UK**      The Falmer Press, Falmer House, Barcombe, Lewes, East Sussex, BN8 5DL

**USA**    The Falmer Press, Taylor & Francis Inc., 242 Cherry Street, Philadelphia, PA 19106-1906

© Selection and editorial material copyright
Thomas S. Popkewitz 1987

*All rights reserved. No part of this publication may be reproduced, stored in a retrieval system, or transmitted in any form or by any means, electronic, mechanical, photocopying, recording or otherwise, without permission in writing from the Publisher.*

First published 1987

**Library of Congress Cataloging in Publication Data**

The formation of school subjects.

    1. Education—United States—Curricula—History.
2. Educational sociology—United States—History.
I. Popkewitz, Thomas S.
LB1570.F66   1987   375′.00973   86-29347
ISBN 1-85000-169-3
ISBN 1-85000-170-7 (pbk.)

Jacket design by Caroline Archer

Jacket illustration by Kerry Freedman

Typeset in 11/13 Garamond by
Imago Publishing Ltd, Thame, Oxon

*Printed in Great Britain by Taylor & Francis (Printers) Ltd, Basingstoke*

# Contents

# Contents

# Series Editor's Preface

The origins of the state school curriculum point to the crucial interaction between schooling and cultural, economic and political history. In seeking to exhume the history of curriculum in the book *The Making of Curriculum* (1987, Falmer Press) I judged that

> If 'class and curriculum' entered educational discourse when school was transformed into a mass activity 'classroom and school subject' were linked at the stage at which that mass activity became a State-subsidised system.

The written curriculum provides a clear guide to the selective history of schooling — a changing testimony of the selected rationales and legitimate rhetorics of schooling. But as a testimony it provides a valuable source for historical study and immediately a range of contradictions then emerge. As Popkewitz notes 'when we look at the formation of the subject matter during the late 1800s and early 1900s the placement of the school curriculum had little to do with inquiry or enlightenment as the conventional rhetoric implies'.

Similar themes have emerged in historical studies of the English curriculum (see Goodson, I.F. (1985) *Social Histories of the Secondary Curriculum*, Falmer Press) or in comparative studies of curriculum history in a range of countries (see Goodson, I.F. (1986) *International Perspectives in Curriculum History*, Croom Helm).

But these studies point to a further salient and critical theme. This is that the battle over the *content* of the curriculum whilst often more visible is in many senses less important than the control over its underlying *form*. In the English context clear continuities can be established between the form of curriculum, particularly examinable curriculum, and particular social groupings and their associated cultural capitals. Indeed it was shown that in one instance the initiation of university examinations for schools came in response to petitions that they should help in the development of 'schools for the middle classes'.

Likewise Popkewitz judges that in the school curriculum 'competence was to be based upon abstract categories rather than upon trust and knowledge built through face-to-face interactions. The legitimacy of the professional was asserted through adopting the ideology of the social sciences located within the university.' We learn that by the first two decades of the twentieth century 'the university had taken a direct role in the forming of the school curriculum' and that 'the required courses provide the university with a direct influence over what was defined as the valued knowledge in the schools'. Popkewitz rightly stresses the underpinning ideology of such a modality of knowledge control 'the school placement stresses the importance of the subject and the experts who "own" that knowledge'.

But such modalities of control have further critical implications for classroom pedagogy. Some of the later chapters deal with this concern eloquently. All the while, however, our attention should be drawn to how particular historical inventions of curriculum, as a concept, particular versions of the social construction which is curriculum, have been institutionalized and rendered normative. These versions represent a particular political 'settlement' with associated priorities and social biases — in this sense they set major parameters for the interactive realization of schooling.

Ivor Goodson
**University of Western Ontario**

# Preface: The Formation of School Subjects. The Struggle for Creating an American Institution

A myth of American public education is the neutrality of schooling. It is believed that there is one common school where all are treated equally and objectively. The ideology is supported by a variety of social rituals: the belief in an objective testing and evaluation process of schooling; the formal organizations of schooling in which all children take the same subjects (science, mathematics, English, art, social studies) and a folklore of rugged individualism, those who work hard and are intelligent will achieve.

When the problem of a common school is considered historically, the myth is challenged. The modern American school was formed with intense debate about its function. The discussions focused upon the role of the schools to socialize the new immigrants, the poor and the minorities; to provide for labor selection; to help create a 'true' democracy in which reason prevailed, and to engage students in learning. The actual direction taken in the curriculum involved negotiation among various groups as schooling responded to the social predicaments it confronted in the larger society.

The intense debate and social interests involved in the formation of American schooling is nowhere as clear as in the development of the subject-matter of the school. The creation of science, social studies, mathematics, reading, English, art or early childhood education, as a school subject-matter, involved the struggle of various social and professional interests who sought to use the school to express particular purpose and value.

The volume focuses upon the emergence of the subject-matter of the American school. The school subject-matter provides entrance to the interplay between social, cultural, economic and professional interests that give form to our contemporary school practices. The historical detail enables us to understand more clearly how school knowledge is shaped and fashioned by issues of structural continuity and social transformation.

By looking at how our practices have been shaped by the particular struggles to define the American school curriculum, we can better understand not only the possibilities open to our predecessors, but the social context of power and discourse which made the actual directions taken as plausible paths to follow. We can appreciate how particular social values are made into ideologies; how the assumptions and debates of a particular segment of American society become taken-for-granted. The study of the past may also enable to consider the possibilities of our own situation.

The contributors to this volume are both curriculum specialists and historians. Their concern is how did our contemporary notions of subject-matter take its form. What were the debates and interests that interacted to give definition to the school content? The discussion provides a unique contribution to the current scholarship on the contemporary organization of school curriculum.

I wish to acknowledge the encouragement of Ivor Goodson to undertake this project.

**Thomas S. Popkewitz**
August 1986
Madison

# 1 The Formation of School Subjects and the Political Context of Schooling

*Thomas S. Popkewitz*

While the issue of social change is historical, many of our theories about change deny an historical consciousness (Popkewitz, 1984). Our current interest in the quality of teaching illustrates this problem. Educational reforms involve a range of proposals to restructure teacher education, the organizational possibilities of teachers' career and student graduation requirements. When we look at these proposals, however, they have been tried and discarded in previous efforts to respond to issues of improving schools. Without going too far into the past, the debates to improve the selection and retention of teachers are very similar to those found in the literature of the late 1960s. The proposals were then called differentiated staffing and merit pay; today, they are called career ladders and varied reward structures. The language has changed, but the institutional concerns and the structure of the discourse remains the same.

One might ask why people believe that such proposals will now work if they were so easily discarded just two decades ago? What is it about the conditions of schooling that made these proposals plausible as rhetoric but implausible as practice? To answer these questions, we need to explore what of the past conditions limited the implementation of these programs, and whether these conditions are still present in contemporary schooling.

Our questions about the present require that we recognize that the present is not just our immediate experiences and practices. Part of our historical consciousness is to recognize that the past is a part of our everyday discourse, structuring what can be said and the possibilities and challenges of our times. The problems of the here and now involve a social dynamic in which elements of transformation confront the structures of our traditions and political interest. The relevances of our predecessors are embedded in our very

*Thomas S. Popkewitz*

conceptions of schools — creating a structure of discourse that enables us to consider certain issues while, at the same time, omitting other concerns as legitimate for action. Classroom transactions, the models of research to study schooling, and our conceptions of children are products of the past as well as the present.

Our patterns of language enable us to lose sight of the socially constructed quality of schooling. What is socially constructed are made to seem natural and inevitable elements. Part of that 'inevitability' is what we have come to accept as talk about schooling: Children are learners, teaching is motivating children, and the curriculum consists of subjects such as science or social studies. Yet in using the language of schooling, we forget that learning, teaching, and the school subjects have particular social histories.[1] They are practices that do not appear until the latter part of the industrial revolution to guide the tasks of modern schooling. The creation of the new school subjects focused the activities of schooling on bourgeois ideologies of individualism, and responded to cultural and economic issues of the immigrations from Eastern and Southern Europe.

The formation of the contemporary school curriculum is the focus of these essays. The histories, however, are not to chronicle the development of schooling. The problem of study is to subject the traditions and customs of our everyday life to scrutiny. It is to make problematic the everyday language and practices of schooling in order to consider how schooling is possible as a social reality. The 'facts' of our everyday institutions are social inventions of people struggling in a world of competing interests and contradictions: The essays seek to understand the social origins, cultural implications and political consequences of our categories and events. The story is of the human hope, interest and fallibility.

## The Science of Schooling and the Removal of an Historical Consciousness

To recognize that the present is a moment in tradition is a reversal of much of our logic about social life and schooling. Our efforts to improve the quality of schooling cannot resist the residues of our past values, remnants in the very patterns that we institute as school change. New programs are continually introduced to individualize instruction, yet as the essays in this book illustrate, the 'new' strategies are designed within an organization of space and time that developed in the past to give specific social form to an emerging common school.

Our separation of the past from the present is related to our models of science. The dominating notion of science places great faith on the rules of data collection and analysis. The rules of science, it is believed, tell us that one should pay attention only to what is or can be observed. History as well as value, it is reasoned, cannot be observed and therefore should not be part of our considerations of science. What emerges is a science that is likened to the rules of administration. Truth is defined as residing in procedures of data collection and focusing attention away from the social horizons in which our discourse has been formed.

While this view is incorrect in its understanding of the relation of history and science, the stance has ideological implications (Popkewitz, 1986). Science *as* rules transforms political, social and economic issues into ones that seem administrative. Illusions of disinterest and efficiency emerge to guide pedagogical practices. Obscured are the ways in which our present is formed by interests of the past. Let me explore this further.

The curriculum of American schools emerges in a period when the United States was reasserting a national confidence and identity through the social, political and educational reforms of the Progressive Era (1880–1920). The reforms ranged from the introduction of civil service in government to the creation of mass schooling for the newly-arrived immigrants from Southern and Eastern Europe. During the periods prior to and during the Progressive Era, the functions of schooling become more complex — the theological purposes of teaching were replaced more forcefully by the secular concerns of socialization and labor selection.

These changes have implications for both the middle classes and the poor/immigrant groups. For the middle classes, school was to provide the taste, aesthetic awareness and cognitions that would enable their children to compete with the older elites. The curriculum was also designed by reformers of the middle and upper classes for the education of the poor, immigrants and generally, non-Protestant groups. The history of school content is an intersection with social, cultural, political and economic interests that underlie the transformations and strains in American institutions.

Most histories of the formation of the school subjects ignore these relations by locating the broadening of the curriculum in the 1890s to the formal functioning of professional committees and administrative problems of schools, such as the articulation between university and high schools.[2] The divisions of schooling into what are now common instructional categories of mathematics, reading, science, social studies, language, and art begin to appear more clearly. Prior instruction, which was defined in relation to the book being studied, such as the reading of a specific Latin book, was replaced by a new category of subjects, such as science or foreign language. Much of the controversy at the time about the changes focused upon whether the high school curriculum was elite oriented and thereby unsuited for the mass of students (see Krug, 1972).

The histories of subjects found in this series of essays focus less on the formal committees and overt events that gave public expression to the organization of schooling. The essays are concerned with the social dynamics that shape the public rhetoric. As the essays indicate, there is no all-inclusive factor that becomes the driving dynamic to the inventions of schooling. Yet, there is a consistent focus upon how the school content is shaped and fashioned by issues located in the larger structure of power. The essays also indicate that those who are favored in society continually use the meaning of schooling to their advantage, such as through the creation of new categories of students (for example, learning disability in the 1960s)[3] and the introduction of computer technology to commodify and control instruction, such as the recent interest given to writing in schools.

In focusing upon the social interests in the formation of the curriculum, the period being examined spans approximately ninety years. The first state mandate requiring drawing curriculum was instituted in 1870; the specialization of learning disability appears in the 1960s. Different interests intersect in each period to shape the curriculum, although the school as a site for contesting interests in society never wanes. These interests can be given focus by attending to certain dynamics that appear in the essays as central to curriculum. These are:

1 The relation of the social and political movement of Progressivism to the creation of mass schooling.
2 Professionalization as a dynamic in creating a social order for schooling, with science serving as a method of administration.
3 The emergence of the university as a dynamic element in the management of society.
4 The invention of psychology for designing curriculum and instruction.

These four dynamics of the curriculum must also be juxtaposed to traditions of curriculum that contained values in opposition to the hegemony. The socialist movement's Sunday schools and Harold Rugg's textbook series provide such a vantage point for understanding the structure of power in the discourse about schooling by focusing upon the structure of omission. In focusing upon these dynamics of tradition and opposition, there is recognition that the changes in school subject-matter involved intense debate in which the outcome was never certain.

### Social Movements and the American Schools: The Late Nineteenth Century America

Much of the abiding interests of American schooling focuses on three related themes.[4] One is the concern with the individual. The language of schooling pays homage to individual creativity, imagination, self development, and personal identity. Pedagogies of individualism value the qualities and states that people bring to situations, not upon the manner in which subjectivities are formed in the social context. Second, school is related to the economy. Career education, curriculum, counseling specialists, as well as the categories of educational sciences provide direction to the ways in which individuals can move into the labor force. A third theme is moral education. Children in school are to learn the appropriate values, habits, taste and manners of the dominant Protestant and business oriented society.

These three themes are influenced by a number of dynamics in American society between 1880 and 1920. First, the moral socialization of schooling was not only for the children of the immigrants and the poor. The middle class also sought to use the school for its own purposes, developing and sustaining theories of pedagogies that would respond to their interests. Second, institutional life was professionalized. Certain professional occupations arose to select, organize and evaluate what was to pass as school curriculum. Whereas school administrators had multiple professions in the early nineteenth century, by 1900 it became a more narrowly focused professional career (Mattingly, 1981). Third, the role of the university as a credentialing agent for both knowledge and people in society emerged (see, for example, Collins, 1979). Each of these dynamics intersect in the formation of the subjects of instruction in American schools.

When we look at the formation of the subject matter during the late

1800s and early 1900s, the placement of the school curriculum had little to do with inquiry or enlightenment as the conventional rhetoric implies. Through the school curriculum, civility was to be brought to those who came from foreign lands. Students would learn to work in an urban environment and ameliorate their immediate surroundings by adopting the values of the democratic, corporate and Protestant nation. School biology, (Rosenthal and Bybee, chapter 5 in this volume) social studies, (Lybarger, chapter 7) art education (Freedman, chapter 3) and early childhood education (Bloch, chapter 2) were to provide moral values to those who did not have the appropriate ones. The early infant schools, for example, were to prevent future vice and crime; the kindergarten was a part of the charity movement. Biology was to teach children about hygiene and, in the 1930s, temperance from alcohol and tobacco. The picture study movement from the late 1890s to the 1920s was to illustrate good and moral character, and God's handiwork in earthly practices.

A socialization through schooling was also to prepare an emerging middle class for its semi-leadership role in society. The dual purposes of schooling can be illustrated by the tensions found in the art curriculum (see, Freedman, chapter 3). At one layer, the art curriculum was to prepare the working classes and immigrant groups for American society. Manners and skills were to be given by others to make the immigrants productive within the scheme of things. The art curriculum was to help students learn how to use everyday objects to decorate their home and, at the same time, learn the craft skills that elites thought were associated with the jobs that the students will have in industry. At a different layer, school art was to develop talent and aesthetic sensitivities for the new middle classes. Art appreciation was brought into schooling — the teaching of art would enable children to have access to what was considered previously only the domain of the very wealthy.

The social and economic themes in the formation of the American schools responded to a structural reorganization of material life and a new collective consciousness associated with the Progressive Era (1880–1920). At one layer, the period under inspection reasserted a national identity and confidence in the progress of the twentieth Century. Prior to the Progressive Era, the well-to-do of the early nineteenth century saw poverty as an embarrassing contradiction to a national identity that defined the United States as a garden of Eden. Individuals were seen as personally responsible for their economic and social existence and for the salvation of the soul. The poor and those who did not succeed, it was thought, were so as the result of their own inadequacies or 'sins.' The view of salvation provided a basis of Anglo Saxon racism, arguing that white persons have the biographical strength of personality and character that enabled them to assume positions of power. The attitude was reinforced by the massive immigration of Slavs and Latins who were Catholic and Jews into urban — industrial areas (Noble, 1970).

By the late 1890s, the beliefs of individualism shifted in the Northern States to one of environmentalism which posited the hope that the uninitiated could be civilized to participate in American society. Immigrants who did not fit the national identity of white, Anglo-Saxon Protestant had access to a second class citizenship (Noble, 1970). The business and political leaders believed that a subordinate democracy could be created within a dominant democracy through changes in politics, social welfare and the schools.

The shift in social consciousness was a part of what came to be called the Progressive Era. The business community saw Progressivism as a new Reformation that would purge the old world traditions and radical ideas by developing more efficient institutions guided by a new elite of political managers (Schiesl, 1977). The Progressive ideology was to incorporate business procedures into government. Corrupt political patronage would be eliminated by business accounting procedures, replacing a system which accommodated corrupt politicians with the older elite structure trained to provide public service. The success of the Progressive Era in government is part of the American legacy of politics and public service to be administered by 'professionals.'

The progressive ideology was given support in the sermons of the Northern Protestant churches. The Churches preached a social gospel that absolved the poor of responsibility of their condition and instead blamed the social system. The muckraking of the period became an accepted way to uncover the evils and tyrannies of social institutions, thus seeking ways to improve the environment of the individual.

The shift in ideology was one in which the process of rationalization of public life was moved into consideration of what has been considered the inner life of individuals. The moral outlook became intertwined with science, religion and commerce. Jackson Lear (1981) argues:

> The cultural dominance of the bourgeoisie was partly an
> unintended consequence of scientific (though often self-

deceiving) efforts to impose moral meaning on a rapidly changing world — efforts led not by bankers and industrialists but by ministers and other moralists. The best term for this process is not social control but cultural hegemony (p. 10).

The cultural definitions of Progressivism made it plausible for the business community to give strong support to the new sociologies, social psychologies and education which emphasized environmentalism. These disciplines sought to understand the ways in which individuals and institutions interacted and provided advice about how welfare policy could be improved (see Haskell, 1977).

In dealing with the social issues, the school was singled out for particular attention. The business community supported the ideas of John Dewey who asserted that the individual could discover and verify truth for him or herself through science and thereby not only direct one's own conduct but become an influential and decisive factor in constructing the environment. The pedagogy was to substitute fixed customs and feudal ideas with a more dynamic vision of social progress and social harmony of interest. The progressive pedagogy of Dewey promised 'to purge the child of the excess social baggage from the past, the erroneous and harmful traditions which kept him from being a cooperative and productive member of society' (Noble, 1970). The pedagogy, Dewey argued, made a contribution to industrialization by developing moral enlightenment and social harmony.

The conception of a social harmony of interests in which the achievement of each individual of his own freedom should contribute to a like perfection of the powers of all through a fraternally organized society is the permanent contribution of the industrial movement to morals (in Noble, 1970, p. 56).

The purpose of progressive pedagogy was not only to purge the child of the 'social baggage' of medieval traditions. It was to help eliminate Marxist and socialist ideas brought from Europe by the new immigrants. Many influential leaders feared that the radical ideas of Europe would find their way into the ghettos of the city and the beliefs of the immigrants children. The pragmatism of Dewey and progressive education, the political and economic leadership believed, would eliminate radical ideas and replace them with a faith in rural democracy, scientific rationality and Protestant conceptions of civility.

The view of environmentalism, however, was not accepted without debate. This conflict is evident in the ways in which the schools responded to its new populations. School leaders invented a notion of 'backwardness' to give focus to the problems confronted in educating the immigrant children (see Franklin, chapter 8). The argument about backwardness gave attention to two different 'causes' of student failure. One was upon physical deficiencies of the children, such as brain damage. The sciences of measurement and testing which developed as an integral part of the eugenics movement was offered as 'proof' of the mental deficiencies of those who came from non-English speaking countries (Gould, 1979). Backwardness was also defined as the product of environmental conditions, producing a psychological debilitating self concept or unsatisfactory school attendance.

Scientific discourse was used in the debate about backwardness to describe and prescribe resolution to the social agendas of moral and economic education. The sciences of testing and environmentalism, in their own irony, drew upon the hegemony to define the categories and offer solutions to the problems, thus reinforcing the existing biases of institutional life. Each offered a functional curriculum to deal with the products of unrestrained immigration, urbanization and industrialization. The tracking in the curriculum could prepare different children for different positions in society.

It is often not emphasized in educational histories that schooling evolved where Northern business interests accepted the new tax burden for schooling to produce mass education. The Northern high school was to socialize the child, teach citizenship and fit the child for an expanding industrial frontier. Whereas the Northern business leaders saw the forces of industrialism and science as a part of a religious crusade; the South maintained earlier notions of individual responsibility for one's social plight. Southern whites used the early nineteenth century view of sin to focus upon the Black as a scapegoat for the plight of the farmers and the white poor, excluding Blacks by the 1890s from even a concept of second class citizenship and education (see Noble, 1970).

## Professionalism as a Dynamic in Creating a the Social Order for Schooling

Central to the emerging strategies of schooling was the use of science to create a feeling of a common school where all social classes could mingle freely and harmoniously. The Carnegie Commission on Higher Education, for example, asserted in 1927 that the schools 'consolidate and advance' the American civilization. '... [B]oth American theory and American practice have furnished a powerful antidote to the class discrimination long characteristic of European procedure is beyond dispute ...' (Learned, 1927, p. 3). But it is the coupling of the American situation with education that brings a 'full return for every child concerned ...'.

Important to the development of an American school was its science. Science would identify those individuals who should be supported in their occupational pursuits. At the same time, the scientific curriculum would help to provide the mechanisms to maintain social order and consensus among classes.

The faith in a science of schooling was part of a discourse related to the professionalization occurring in the social and economic structures of American society.[5] The Progressive Era is one manifestation of a larger change in the social organization of work and the commodification of knowledge through the formation of structured communities of experts.

The development of new occupations with social and cultural authority emerged after the American Civil War (1865). These occupations of teaching, social work and social sciences were a response to fundamental social, economic and cultural transformations. Technological changes in transportation and industrialization created new sets of material dependency. It became difficult for people to understand the interrelationship of decisions made in far away places with their personal situation. New occupations developed among the gentry and middle classes to interpret the more complex social relations and interdependence among communities.

There was a fundamental redefinition of individualism among the American middle class. The democratic ideals of self development and fulfillment were to be tied to participation in structured communities. Competence was to be based upon abstract categories rather than upon trust and knowledge built through face-to-face interactions. The legitimacy of the professional was asserted through adopting the ideology of the social sciences located within the university (Silva and Slaughter, 1984). The ideology maintained that academics were experts to policy-makers. Professional work by the early twentieth century was defined as disinterested in its approach to problems of social amelioration.

Social science was thought of as an instrument of control.

'Central was the vision of a science which would make society as amenable to analysis and certain kinds of mastery and reform as was the world investigated by the natural sciences' (Silver, 1983, p. 104). American social scientists, journalists and clergy began to incorporate a positivism which was less a systematic philosophy of Auguste Comte or the logical positivism of twentieth century analytical philosophies, than a cultural tendency that the entire world was 'governed by deterministic laws discovered only through scientific inquiry' (Lear, 1981, p. 21).

The manner of response can be illustrated in the changing conception of the family occurring in the United States, France, Britain, and Australia (see, Donzelot, 1979; Lasch, 1977; Poster, 1978; Reiger, 1985; Shorter, 1975). Influences of technology were brought into the home; material production was moved away from the home. With urbanization, there was growth in suburban areas that combined to alter the patterns of the private world of the home and family.

The professionals' agendas were to ameliorate these conditions, but their programs in fact had conflicting consequences. Changes in the home were initiated by reform groups outside the home. An emergent class of professionals set in motion contradictions between the dominant, bourgeois ideological constructions and the experts' view of the family as organized around a set of rational, manipulable social practices. The dominant bourgeois familial ideology was that the family and home were to be characterized by intimate and personal relationships that were inappropriate to the world of industry and commerce. For men, the home was to be a place of rest, a way of maintaining an expressive relationship that was not permissible in the rational world of business. For women, the home was to provide the formative influence on their children's character. The principles of the emerging domestic economy movement, in contrast, stressed scientific housewifery which taught domestic skills of planning, preparation and execution of meals, proper hygiene, nutrition and care of domestic housing. The new professionals invaded at every point the separation of sexual spheres and the privacy of the home by '... demanding that women learn and apply the principles of the capitalist industrial world' (Reiger, 1985, p. 55).

The new sciences tended to erode the older values in the name of preserving the ideals of the home and family. Social science was used as a means to establish a social policy in which professional expertise became part of the social agenda itself. Various techniques of intimidation, rational and irrational propaganda, mystifications and manipulations developed to maintain the special social and cultural authority of the expert.[6]

The cultural and ideological conflict provided background assumptions to the formation of the school subjects. The changing definitions of the family were incorporated into the subject matter of the schools. Nutritional science, hygiene, and sex became topics of school curriculum. But more significant was the incorporation of the ideologies of the family into theories of pedagogy. The work of Bobbitt, Charters, Dewey, Thorndike or G. Stanley Hall, while at one level different from each other, can be read as influenced by the debates about the family and the changing conceptions of social organization that were being borrowed from industry for public administration.

An essential element in the transformation of the school was the professionalization of social knowledge. More and more of public and private life tended to be defined through patterns of discourse developed for technological production and bureaucratic organizations (see Berger *et al.*, 1973). A social consciousness began to reflect a particular structure which defined the social world as logical, linear and progressive. Social life was divided into discrete, manageable and taxonomic categories. The social, political and economic issues in schooling were transposed into issues of efficiency and administration.

To this point, I have juxtaposed business, political ideologies, science with the social gospel movement in Progressivism. The religious motif was an important element of the early social science movement and in the theories of pedagogy. The school reformers had the missionary zeal of clerics.[7] The problems of an urban society were related to the problem of salvation and the means by which the secular expert could help those below expunge the evil within. It is more than a coincidence that the first teaching of reading was to learn the bible and that much of the efforts at civic reform was approached with the same religious quality that previous generations approached the tasks of conversion for the heathens in the European colonies.

In arguing a relation between capitalism, politics, religion and science, we need to be aware that there are many Protestant denominations within the United States, including the evangelical Churches of the South and West (see, Hofstadter 1962). Yet, the divergence should not take away from the importance of the interplay of religious conceptions with our secular world. (For a classical study of this relation, see Weber, 1920/1930; for the ties of science to utopian thought, see Manuel and Manuel, 1979.) The notion of science, technology and progress that direct our modern institutions have religious assumptions that emerged with the Protestant Reformation.

## The University and the Management of Society

Professionalization and social science converged through the expanding role of the university in managing society. New research and graduate programs were to mediate social and economic agendas. The university social functions evolved around at least two related dynamics.

One dynamic was the part of the university in defining what society was to value as its sacred knowledge. Prior to the industrial revolution, the university was a place where elite men learned the character and the habits of mind that would prepare them for their station in life. With the industrial revolution, the function of the university became multiple. It prepared the elites to the sensitivities, awarenesses and taste of those who would have the social and cultural authority to rule. The categories of 'high culture' were to establish an hegemony of those who had power.

A second dynamic was the responsibility of the university for the productive elements related to an industrial society. Through the philanthropy of the new industrial barons, professional education was brought into the American university by the turn of the century (Curti and Nash, 1965). Practical knowledge was to provide the foundation for corporate development and social betterment. The argument of business leaders for their expanding role was that capitalism could provide for the public welfare as well as could socialism. It was thought that useful knowledge was necessary for an enlightened citizenry.

The practical purpose of the university was to provide expert knowledge about how society was to be managed. A direct relation between the university and the state, economy and public affairs was established in the Progressive Era. Sometimes referred to 'the Wisconsin idea' (Curti and Carstensen, 1949), the university was to provide the expertise necessary to make government and social amelioration efficient and modern. The emphasis was upon practical and useful knowledge — to assist commerce, industry, agriculture, and government through the offering of expert advice and the creation of symbolic canopies to form and give direction. University graduate research programs became an essential element in social production.

The effort of the university had twin motifs. It established business ideologies of efficiency and accountability in the organization of the state and its multiple institutions, such as the school. At the same time, the university expertise guided social welfare programs that would help maintain social order, as American leaders feared the importation of the unrest and revolution occurring in European societies. Scientists were to do research, plan programs and evaluate the consequences of programs for implementing political agendas.

These motifs can be seen in the development of mathematics education (see Stanic, chapter 6). Central in the debate about the purpose and organization of mathematics were university professors. The debate evolved around at least two types of instruction. One concerned instruction that would teach children how to think and reason properly. It was assumed that mathematics in public schooling would prepare the mental discipline and character of mind appropriate for university study and eventual leadership in social and economic institutions. A second curriculum focus was on the functional requirements of the subject for those who would never go to college. These curricula provided practice for the managing of everyday life, such as using mathematics for household budgets. For each type of instruction, research programs developed to justify and organize teaching.

By the first two decades of the twentieth century the universities had taken a direct role in the forming of the school curriculum. The 1893 recommendations of The Committee of Ten for modern academic subjects in the high school were included in the pattern of college admissions (Krug, 1972). The required courses provide the university with a direct influence over what was defined as the valued knowledge in the schools. University schools of education also began to replace the normal schools in defining the careers of school administrators and teachers. As part of the university occupational structure, there were research careers in the new experimental and organizational sciences, an issue to be considered in the following section.

While the debates about curriculum continue, the inclusion of university categories of knowledge into schools had a consequence of legitimating both the knowledge and its 'holders'. By making particular occupational work a subject of schooling, an occupation is given status. The sacred quality is important not only for those who take and 'pass' the subjects. It is also important to those who may not study a subject, for the school placement stresses the importance of the subject and the experts who 'own' that knowledge.

The professionalization of knowledge is an horizon to locate in the United States school reforms of the 1960s. The reforms were to introduce the structure of knowledge and practice found in the social and physical sciences. The categories of teaching shifted from general categories of history or science to specific disciplines, such as political science, anthropology, economics or physics. Instruction concerned teaching the definitions (concepts) of these fields and indirectly, national ideologies, such as economics as the division of labor, profit, capital investment, or democracy as the American system and totalitarianism as the Soviet system.

The centrality of the university in legitimating the social order is apparent when we consider the degree to which American society is based upon credentialing (see, Collins, 1979). Americans take for granted that a doctor needs twenty-two years of education, that a teacher should have a college degree, and that lawyers require seven years of university education. Current reforms in teacher education accept the premise of credentialing by moving into programs that will require five and six years of university schooling before certification.

While the social function of the university was utilitarian, it also had its own contradictions. One relates to the principle of academic freedom. Developed during the Progressive Era to protect the expert role of the new academic, it became a principle that permitted a dissenting academy to maintain legitimacy within certain general social boundaries. Economic beliefs in a market place were incorporated into academic life, as is evident in recent histories and sociologies of science which emphasize competition and 'a market place of ideas'.

## The Invention of Psychology for Curriculum Design

An important element in the development of pedagogy was the psychologization of social phenomena (see, for example, Sennett, 1978; Lear, 1981). The corporate drive for efficiency intensified the Victorian ethic of self-control and extended the process of rationalization into new areas of personal conduct. The sciences of industrialization pressed for 'systematic methods of self-control ... beyond the work place into the most intimate areas of daily experience — perhaps even into unconscious wishes, dreams, and fantasies' (Lear, 1981, p. 13). In literature, art as well as the methods of social

*Thomas S. Popkewitz*

science was a denial of the conflicts in a modern capitalist society and an affirmation of continual harmony and progress through the efforts of individuals. The key to progress was the disciplined, autonomous self that emerged from the proper bourgeois family upbringing.

The search for a rationalization of personal conduct extended into the conduct of schooling. Much of the school discourse after the turn of the century was organized around principles of educational psychology. The language of psychology created a way to reason about social conduct as defined tasks to be evaluated in relation to universal attributes of individuals and notions of efficiency.

To understand the psychologization of curriculum, we need to consider that psychology is not 'natural' to the selection and organization of school knowledge. Questions about school knowledge cannot be derived from questions of psychology or social science. The choice of curriculum involves philosophical, political and ethical questions (see Popkewitz, 1982; Soltis, 1968). Yet, by the 1930s, the dominant paradigm in curriculum is one that was articulated by psychological and social-psychological perspectives (see Franklin, 1986).

Educational research developed within university departments to provide management of the knowledge and of the people processed in schools. The experimental, psychological studies were consistent with the new role of the social scientists within the university, that of providing expert advice about the formation and implementation of policy. Research was to be 'a professional tool for all responsible school officers' (Powell, 1980, p. 103). Much of the early research sought to establish 'an inductive approach' to curriculum, based upon the regularities of existing patterns of behavior found in schooling (Powell, 1980). Quantitative measures were used as a means 'for establishing unchallengeable administrative authority in a time of growing school enrollments and expenditure' (Powell, 1980, p. 10). Hanus and Lowell, Professors at Harvard, saw educational science as a contribution to professional authority rather than a scholarly activity. Thorndike argued that the human mind is given to exact measurement similar to that of the natural sciences, that such measurement is beyond the capacity of kindergarten teachers, and that the formation of curriculum should be left in the hands of experimental psychologists (Bloch, chapter 2).

The various approaches to organizing the curriculum have been considered as related to different psychological perspectives — mental discipline, scientific curriculum, humanism and development. Each approach contains a different orientation to knowledge, society,

16

and individuality. Yet the variations are in fact themes in a complementary structure, as the pedagogies are located in society. The psychologies supported the hegemony about the nature of the social organization. The 'scientific' curriculum of Thorndike and the progressive theories of Dewey were different, but not oppositional, strategies for considering the issues of urbanization and industrialization. Each perspective maintained a posture about individualism and science as creating a new millennium of harmony and consensus among all groups.

The assumption was that children grew universally in relation to a normative progression. In art education, developmentally-based arguments emerged to allow children to learn how to represent objects according to certain adult standards (see Freedman, chapter 3). The psychologies supported the belief in individual creativity and talent that was shaped and fashioned by middle-class notions of taste and aesthetics. The Child Study Movement of G. Stanley Hall, for example, adopted conceptions of psychology and biological evolution (a form of social Darwinism) for constructing a scientific curriculum. Hall's work influenced much curriculum work in the United States by emphasizing testing and observable growth of children. The problem of curriculum was to identify and nurture individual talent.

The purposes of psychology must also be considered in relation to prevalent ideologies in the American society. Psychology emphasized individual ability and social development based upon merit. The discourse responded directly to concerns about moral upbringing and labor socialization by focusing upon the thoughts and attitudes of individuals. In the 1920s, psychology offered a seemingly objective way to monitor the upbringing tasks of modern schooling.

The psychological basis for curriculum is a mechanism of social control in schooling. The sciences of school knowledge and children's development introduced the mental structure associated with technological production and bureaucracy. More compelling than overt propaganda, the new ways of constructing consciousness set forth patterns of thinking, reasoning, acting, feeling and talking that made elite social agendas into patterns of children's socialization. The logic of the machine as orderliness, hierarchy and taxonomic thought was brought into the organization of school knowledge. School work and social organization were defined as being independent, maintaining a discrete and fragmentary existence. Abstraction, anonymity and prediction were made central to the domains of schooling.[8]

The psychologies decontextualized curriculum issues and reformulated them as those of administration and efficiency. The sciences mobilized a bias that obscured the social and class struggles that underlie the formation of schooling. The decontextualization and reformulation of social interest through school psychologies can be understood focusing upon the notion of 'need' (Lybarger, chapter 7). In the late 1800s, the leaders of the charity movement were concerned with the abuse of government expenditures for relief and political corruption. They sought to give the unfortunate city dwellers new forms of organization that would provide something more precious than money, food and clothes. Charity was to bring character, self-respect, and ambition to the poor. The Settlement House Movement, as well, sought to instill character, virtue and social unity through learning about American social institutions and customs.

The educational activities of these groups were structured around what they thought the immigrants 'needed' to know. This included recognizing the purpose and utility of one's work, ways by which social betterment of one's conditions could be achieved, and the 'larger visions and higher ideals of Anglo-Saxon culture that could be given by the leadership of the Charity/Settlement house workers' (Lybarger, chapter 7).

The reformers, social scientists, and women saw their mission as bringing the best possible methods by which the poor could emulate the wealthy. They were joined by labor unions and ethnic welfare organizations who saw the school as a way to improve their social conditions. Having some similarity to Adam Smith's notion of education as emulation and sympathy (Hamilton, 1980), the curriculum was to help the poor and immigrants assume a productive and rewarding life within a scheme organized by American Protestant values and scientific reasoning. To teach children proper sanitation, nutrition and habits of daily routine would uplift the lower classes, and thereby improve the society as a whole. The motivation was uplifting and noble; the consequences often contained contradictions as the knowledge of schooling reproduced the stratifications and inequities of the larger society.

The notion of 'need' implied dependency and defects in moral, intellectual and personal make-up of segments of the school clientele. Yet, it was this notion of need that was incorporated into the work of the Committee of the Social Studies in 1915. The conception of need underlies the strategies for selection and organization of curriculum today.

## The Structure of Omission:
## Socialist and Critical Traditions

While pursuing the social and intellectual setting in which the American curriculum developed, the structure of omission needs also to be considered. The subjects of school instruction represent those who have power to give definition to reality. Yet, the history of the United States in the years preceding and after the turn of the century is one in which strong socialist movements existed (see Teitelbaum, chapter 10). In the 1908 Presidential campaign, the Socialist candidate Eugene V. Debs won 897,000 votes; in 1910, Milwaukee elected a Socialist mayor, and both Milwaukee and New York's lower East Side elected a Socialist Congressman. In addition, from the turn of the century to the 1930s, American socialists published hundreds of newspapers, magazines and journals. The socialist movements also developed Sunday schools in which different categories of instruction emerged than those found in public education. The curriculum stress the development of a collective commitment to social improvement and,institutional critique. Oppositional notions of curriculum were considered an option for the immigrant and American-born for many years, yet there are few, if any, discussions of these experiments in relation to the organization of schooling.

The development of textbooks during the late 1930s also indicate a pedagogical stance that runs counter to the hegemony posited in schooling. It was a period where many American institutions were receiving critical scrutiny in intellectual circles, particularly in the East Coast. Harold Rugg, who came to Teachers College in New York during the 1920s, for example, began to affiliate with sentiments being offered in New York intellectual circles and wrote a textbook series that was very critical of the role of the United States in world affairs. The text book brought a vision of a new America and world to schools. These books were sold to many school districts around the United States. By the 1940s, with the end of World War II and the rise of American nationalism and anti-communism, however, the books fell into disuse. Their appearance and disappearance, as Kliebard and Wegner argue (chapter 10 in this volume), tend to be silences in curriculum history.

The pressure and struggles that omit possibilities in our institutions permit an understanding of structures of power that make schooling a social fact. The discussions of Teitlebaum, and Kliebard and Wegner enable us to consider that it is not only what is made into schooling that 'tells' us its history. The silences of the school curriculum focus attention on how organization creates a mobilization of bias. The individualism, corporatism and moralism of the main strands of American pedagogy are more clearly illuminated when juxtaposed to the alternative and oppositional forms of curriculum.

## Conclusions

Too often, the problem of study takes-for-granted the development of the school as a normal evolution in societies. History is most often that of exemplars, selecting the relevant examples to illustrate the growth of a civilization. The function of the history is didactic, illustrating the traditional pieties or the general and natural laws that underlie human development.

The difficulty of the pieties and laws of development is that they are neither. The 'natural' histories were inventions of those who were able to exercise power in giving moral direction and will to a society. The eighteenth century notion of Natural History, for example, offered an ideology of 'manifest destiny' for those European nations who were in the business of colonizing (see, for example, Nisbet, 1980). The Natural History justified the position of the white man in Africa and Asia, made plausible the tenets of a market economy, and gave the importance to change guided by the new mandarins. To accept uncritically the histories of school development is to obscure the biases of its social organization of its discourse.

Central to the formation of the school has been the tension of individualism and social order. This tension is one of contemporary society. Individualism responds to what Niklas Luhmann (1982) calls the differentiated society. The concern for individuality in the modern nation-state becomes a necessity to counter threats posed by the expansion of political authority and the consequences of multiple channels of communication.

But the focus on individualism is given meaning and interpretation through social struggle. The discourse about learning and teaching is an invention which takes social interests and normalizes them through sciences that portray an objective and common school. The curriculum is neither objective nor free of interest. It was formed by segments of the middle and upper classes for multiple purposes: the middle classes were to use the school for their own children. Also, school was to be organized for 'other' children who were in need of moral uplifting.

The discourse of schooling ignores the functions assumed by the early twentieth century; that of socialization, labor selection and institutional legitimation. It removes from scrutiny the tensions of individual and community. The individual is seen to exist as separate from a social world which contains inequities, differential power arrangements and competing conceptions of knowledge.

The essays that follow are grouped into three categories. The first focuses upon the curriculum subjects: art, biology, mathematics, social studies, reading and writing. Included in the section is a discussion of early childhood education. While early childhood education was originally conceived as separate from the demands of public schooling, it responded, in fact, to the same social, cultural and economic pressures as the school curriculum.

The second section considers the problem of those children who are defined by the school as failure or backward. The inclusion of histories of special education enables us to consider how issues of deviance were created and treated within the school. The discussion leads to a recent history of special education, giving focus to how the terrain of debate shifts in contemporary discourse while preserving the ability of those who have cultural and social power to create and modify pedagogy for their purposes.

The final section is concerned with the silences of the school curriculum. The two essays focus upon meanings of social studies, and the social contexts that influences the curriculum.

The essays do not provide a history of all the curriculum subjects in the American schools. The essays enable us to gain details of the interrelation of schooling to its social, cultural political and economic contexts through selected examinations of schooling. The issues raised, however, are not only those of the past. The past is sedimented into the present, only the social assumptions are more compelling as the social histories of schooling are obscured by our contemporary discourse.

Two further notes. The range of time considered varies in the essays. This occurs because each author had to follow the specific debates that informed school subjects. Reading, for example, needs to be understood in relation to its religious function in colonial times to learning biblical texts; social studies as a response to urbanization and industrialization. While the years differ, the central issues of schooling as a social and political institution remains. A different issue relates to the problem of curriculum history itself. It is only within the past two or three years have there been people in America who are educated in the field of curriculum and who consider the issue of social histories of school knowledge important. Hopefully, their work will enable us to confront the social amnesia of schooling.

## Acknowledgements

I wish to thank Kerry Freedman, Barry Franklin, Ivor Goodson and Catherine Cornbleth for their thoughtful comments to previous drafts of this chapter.

## Notes

1 See GOODSON (1985) for discussion of this issue and comparable studies of the British school curriculum.
2 There is a specific tradition of school histories that focuses upon problems of knowledge and culture, for example, KLIEBARD, 1986; DURKHEIM, 1936/1977; FRANKLIN, 1986; and HAMILTON, 1980.
3 See SLEETER, chapter 9 in this volume.
4 See, POPKEWITZ (1986) for a discussion of the issues that follow. Also, see FRANKLIN (1986); KLIEBARD (1986) and DURKHEIM (1977).
5 For a sociological treatise of professionalism, see LARSON, 1977.
6 See BERGER, P. and LUCKMANN, T., 1967, for a discussion of the development of experts in institutions.
7 See, for example, Noble's 1970 discussion of Dewey; JONCICH'S (1968) bibliography of Thorndike.
8 For an example about how this style of thought has become a part of contemporary models of change and reform, see POPKEWITZ, *et al.*, 1982.

## References

BERGER, P., BERGER, B. and KELLNER, H. *The Homeless Mind, Modernization and Consciousness.* New York: Vintage Books, 1973.

BERGER, P. and LUCKMAN, T. *The Social Construction of Reality: A Treatise in the Sociology of Knowledge.* Garden City, New York, Anchor Books, 1967.

COLLINS, R. *The Credential Society, An Historical Sociology of Education and Stratification.* New York: Academic Press, 1979.

CURTI, M. and CARSTENSEN, V. *University of Wisconsin, A History, 1848–1925,* Vol. 1. Madison, WI., University of Wisconsin, 1949.

CURTI, M. and NASH, R. *Philanthropy in the Shaping of American Higher Education.* New Brunswick, N.J.: Rutgers University Press, 1965.

DONZELOT, J. *The Policing of the Family*. New York: Pantheon Books, 1979.

DURKHEIM, E. *The Evolution Of Educational Thought: Lectures On The Formation And Development Of Secondary Education In France*. P. COLLINS (trans.) originally published 1938. London: Routledge and Kegan Paul 1977.

FRANKLIN, B. *Building The American Community: The School Curriculum And The Search For Social Control*. London: Falmer Press, 1986.

GOODSON, I. *Social Histories of the Secondary Curriculum, Subjects for Study*. London: Falmer Press, 1985.

GOULD, S. *The Mismeasure of Man*. New York: Norton, 1979.

HAMILTON, D. 'Adam Smith and the moral economy of the classroom system', *Journal of Curriculum Studies*, *12*, (4) 1980, pp. 78–98.

HASKELL, T. *The Emergence of Professional Social Science: The American Social Science Association and the Nineteenth-Century Crisis of Authority*. Urbana, IL: University of Illinois Press, 1977.

HOFSTADTER, R. *Anti-Intellectualism in American Life*. New York: Vintage Books, 1962.

JONCICH, G. *The Sane Positivist, A Bibliography of Edward Thorndike*. Middleton, CT: Wesleyan University Press, 1968.

KLIEBARD, H. *Struggle For The American Curriculum*. London: Routledge and Kegan Paul, 1986.

KRUG, E. *The Shaping of the American High School, 1920–1941*. Madison, WI: University of Wisconsin Press, 1972.

LARSON, M. *The Rise of Professionalism: A Sociological Analysis*. Berkeley: University of California Press, 1977.

LASCH, C. *Haven in a Heartless World: The Family Besieged*. N.Y.: Basic Books, 1977.

LEAR, J. *No Place of Grace, Antimodernism and the Transformation of American Culture. 1880–1920*. New York: Pantheon, 1981.

LEARNED, W. 'The quality of the educational process in the United States and in Europe', *The Carnegie Commission on Higher Education*. Boston: P.B. Updike, The Merrymount Press, 1927.

LUHMANN, N. *The Differentiation of Society*. S. HOLMES and C. LARMORE (trans.) New York: Columbia University Press, 1982.

MANUEL, F., and MANUEL, F. *Utopian Thought in the Western World*. Cambridge, MA: Harvard University Press, 1979.

MATTINGLY, P. 'Academia and professional school careers, 1840–1900', *Teachers College Record*. 83(2), 1981, pp. 219–233.

NISBET, R. *History of the Idea of Progress*. N.Y.: Basic Books, 1980.

NOBLE, D. *The Progressive Mind, 1890–1917*. Chicago: Rand McNally, 1970.

POPKEWITZ, T. 'History in educational science: Educational science as History,' in PITMAN, A. (ed.) *Educational Inquiry: Approaches to Research*. Geelong, Australia: Deakin University Press, 1986.

*Thomas S. Popkewitz*

POPKEWITZ, T. *Paradigm and Ideology in Educational Research: The Social Functions of the Intellectual.* London: Falmer Press, 1984.

POPKEWITZ, T. 'Whither, wither the curriculum field?' *Contemporary Educational Review.* 1, (1), 1982, pp. 15–22.

POPKEWITZ, T., TABACHNICK, R. and WEHLAGE, G. *The Myth of Educational Reform: A Study of Planned Change.* Madison, WI: University of Wisconsin Press, 1982.

POSTER, M. *Critical Theory of the Family.* London: Pluto Press, 1978.

POWELL, A. *The Uncertain Profession.* Cambridge: Harvard University Press, 1980.

REIGER, K. *The Disenchantment of the Home, Modernizing the Australian Family 1880–1914.* New York: Oxford University Press, 1985.

SCHIESL, M. *The Politics of Efficiency, Municipal Administration and Reform in America, 1880–1920.* Berkeley, CA: University of California Press, 1977.

SENNETT, R. *The Fall of Public Man: On the Social Psychology of Capitalism.* New York: Random House, 1978.

SHORTER, E. *The Making of the Modern Family.* New York: Basic Books, 1975.

SILVA, E., and SLAUGHTER, S. *Serving power; the making of the academic social science expert.* Westport, CT: Greenwood Press, 1984.

SILVER, H. *Education As History: Interpreting Nineteenth and Twentieth Century Education.* London: Methuen, 1983.

SOLTIS, J. *An Introduction to the Analysis of Educational Concepts.* Reading, MA: Addison-Wesley Publishing Co., 1968.

WEBER, M. *The Protestant Ethic and the Spirit of Capitalism.* T. PARSONS (trans.) New York: Charles Scribner's and Son, 1920/1930.

## 2 Becoming Scientific and Professional: An Historical Perspective on the Aims and Effects of Early Education[1]

*Marianne N. Bloch*

### Abstract

This chapter analyzes the history of educators' reports about the aims and effects of early education and child care programs in the United States from the eighteenth century through the early 1930s when the three current forms of US early education and care programs (kindergarten, pre-school, day care) were in place. The chapter emphasizes the influence of the sociohistorical context on the content of educators' statements and on the form and content of early education/care programs as they developed in the United States. The analyses of educators' statements suggest that class, ethnic, and gender-related assumptions have had a strong influence on the way aims and effects were stated in the past, and that similar assumptions shape the policies and practices in the field today. The historical analysis also shows that kindergarten and, eventually, nursery school, leaders' attempts to professionalize the field of early education, to make it be or appear to be scientific, and to affiliate with other professional and scientific organizations resulted in costs as well as benefits to early childhood education and child care programs as they developed. In the summary of the paper, persistent aims, effects, and cultural and socioeconomic factors that have affected educators' reports as well as the the American early education field are summarized and discussed.

For the past twenty years, American researchers in the field of early education and child care have benefited from both public and private funding for educational research and program development. Substantial federal funding for Head Start and Follow Through research began in 1965 during Johnson's War on Poverty (Ross, 1979; Takanishi, 1979; Zigler and Valentine, 1979). Day-care research and high quality program development were initiated during the 1970s as the call for good day care grew concomitant with the women's liberation movement, the rise in female-headed households, and the maternal employment rate (Clarke-Stewart, 1982).

Two decades of research by leaders in the fields of psychology, child development, and education have resulted in more 'scientifically proven' knowledge about how different programs affect young American children than has ever been available (for example, Belsky and Steinberg, 1978; Clarke-Stewart and Fein, 1983; Lazar, Darlington, Murray, Royce and Snipper, 1982; Berrueta-Clement, Schweinhart, Barnett, Epstein, and Weikart, 1984). The results of this research effort have been publicized internationally, both by professionals and by the press (for example, *Time*, 1981), and reports have been used, in part, to bolster continuing intellectual and financial support for pre-school and day-care programs and research in the United States and abroad. These reports stress the short- and long-term positive effects high quality pre-school and day-care programs have, in particular, on low income children's achievement and their progress in school (Belsky and Steinberg, 1978; Clarke-Stewart and Fein, 1983; Lazar *et al.*, 1982; Berrueta, *et al.*, 1984). Recent studies have also focused on the reduced economic and social costs for society that are associated with pre-school attendance (Lazar *et al.*, 1982; Berrueta, *et al.*, 1984). While research on pre-school and day-care has also shown that programs may have some negative effects (for example, day-care's impact on children's health and social interaction), these findings are generally overshadowed by the positive reports concerning children's school achievement, progress in school, and the relationships between pre-school attendance and long-term benefits for society.

## Reports of the Aims and Effects of Early Education and Care in their Sociohistorical Context

While program and research developments in early education (now defined to include pre-school, kindergarten, and day-care programs) have been rapid and significant during the past two decades, only a few have attempted to write about the sociohistorical context in which these developments and reports have occurred (for example, Ross, 1979; Takanishi, 1979; Zigler and Valentine, 1979). With rare exception (for example, Kaestle and Vinovskis, 1980; Ross, 1979; Steinfels, 1973; Takanishi, 1979), the similarity between current movements and ideas and those of past periods has not been acknowledged. Some of the major historical analyses (for example, Zigler and Valentine, 1979) have also celebrated past and present achievements. Only rarely has critical analysis focused on the political and social assumptions that have guided this field.

The primary purpose of this chapter is to examine the ideological, political, and social contexts which have shaped many of the developments in early childhood education. A second purpose is to examine the similarities and differences between current and past ideas of the aims and effects of early education programs, and to provide a social history of the context in which these ideas have developed. A final purpose is to illuminate contextual factors that may be affecting current research and development in the field today.

This chapter provides a sense of many of the historical developments in the field of early childhood education as it emerged during the nineteenth and early twentieth centuries. To provide a context for analysis, observations and perceptions of influential educators and professionals during this period (approximately 1800–1935) were reviewed and their perceptions of the field are selectively described and analyzed. The review includes major educational reports as well as secondary documents concerning early education and child-care programs, and it focuses on educators' perceptions of the aims and effects of different programs as well as on factors affecting these perceptions.[2]

The extensive period selected for study in this chapter was chosen because it was during this time that ideas about the institutional forms and alliances of programs and social assumptions about the purposes, goals, and content of early education were debated and formulated. It was also a period when notions of science and scientific methodology, and their relationship to education were taking form and beginning to influence the way educational ideas were presented (see Schlossman, 1981; Sears, 1975; Takanishi, 1979). Despite its breadth, a number of important events and movements that took place during the period and many, although not all, of the factors affecting past and current program development and educators' perceptions will be highlighted.

*Marianne N. Bloch*

## Early Education and Care for Young Children: An Overview of Themes and Issues

In the United States, the dominant form of care and education for young children (those under 7 years of age) has been care by parents (primarily mothers), siblings, other relatives and caretakers within a home setting (Bane, Lein, O'Donnell, Steuve, and Wells, 1980). While at-home care has been most prevalent, out-of-home care and education for young children has been available in various forms and for particular groups since at least the latter part of the seventeenth century (for example, Demos, 1970).

Social assumptions about who provides 'good' education and child care have influenced the development of new out-of-home forms of care and education for young children. During the colonial era, for example, communities provided care (for example, foster parents) and education (for example, dame schools) for orphaned children or those from families who were perceived unable to provide necessary or 'appropriate' education for their children. During the late eighteenth and early nineteenth centuries, most rural families made use of district, dame, or petty schools. In urbanizing areas, free schools were open to young children only if they were from poor, immigrant, or less well-educated working class backgrounds; while the children of the well-to-do were educated at home by tutors or in private schools. Urban working-class children attended primary schools (open to children of 2 or 3 and older) or infant schools (open to children 18 months to 6 years) (see Finkelstein, 1979; Kaestle and Vinovskis, 1980). As the infant school movement declined during the mid-1800s, kindergartens were started for children ranging from 3 to 7 years. While the original American kindergartens were largely for the children of well-educated German immigrants, they soon became an instrument of philanthropists and well-intentioned reformers who, from 1870 to approximately 1913, supported them to give moral and 'American' education to children from minority, poor, or immigrant families.

During the early twentieth century, class assumptions continued to influence the form of care and education parents used for their children. While young rural children were still cared for at home or in multi-age district classrooms, working-class and immigrant urban children were cared for at home, in the streets, or in 'charity' kindergartens and full-day day nurseries affiliated with the urban settlement house movement (Steinfels, 1973). Before the early 1920s, with the advent of the American nursery school movement, the 'proper' education for young children from wealthier homes took place at home, usually with their 'educated' mother and servants (for example, see Rothman, 1980).

While social assumptions have continued to influence both the form and content of programs for young children in the United States, other economic, scientific, educational, and ideological changes in the first third of the twentieth century influenced the emergence of early education as a field or 'profession'. As the number of kindergartens grew during the nineteenth century, teachers and other kindergarten advocates wanted to be viewed as professionals. Their efforts, similar to those in many other fields at the time, focused on the institutionalization of the kindergarten in publicly financed schools and on the acquisition of status through increased training, allegiance with other 'professionals', and by showing that they were 'scientific'. By 1930, the majority of kindergarten teachers and professionals affiliated with the kindergarten had achieved their goals: they were increasingly viewed as professionals and were linked in curricular orientation, scientific rationale, and physically to public primary schools. They also had narrowed and decontextualized their curricular focus and made it an age-graded program for 5 and 6 year olds that was separate in alliance and form from other modes of out-of home care for young children in the United States. Pre-kindergarten age children (under 5) were cared for at home, in middle-class oriented nursery schools frequently affiliated with the growing professional child development research community, or in welfare supported day nurseries. By 1930, the separate forms, populations, and alliances of the majority of the early educational programs that are now current in the United States had taken shape.

### Character Development and Moral Education: Aims and Perceived Effects of Early Education in the Eighteenth and Nineteenth Century

*District Schools*

Rural members of colonial communities expected that parents would teach their young children to read in order to ensure their later salvation from the devil. Young children were considered to be born with original sin and to be evil in nature; parents were expected to teach children to be quiet, to obey adults, and to believe in and follow the religious beliefs of their parents (Demos, 1970; Kaestle and Vinovskis, 1980). When communities perceived that some children were not learning these skills at home, they assumed the responsibility. Schools were gradually developed to ensure children's spiritual salvation and ultimately to save the communities from immoral and viceful members (Demos, 1970). Although some communities had no schools, and not all 'needy' children attended the schools that existed, the first American schools that included young children were district schools, with children as young as 2–3 years in them, and petty or dame schools, run by women in rural villages who were capable of elementary reading instruction.

The short-term effects of these schools on moral behavior are recorded in autobiographies describing the harsh discipline and tedium of the school, while the long-term effects on community morality and vice are difficult to document. The benefits of reading instruction were claimed by the more literate writers of the period in their autobiographies. Kaestle and Vinovskis (1980) cite one person who said he learned to read by age 3 or 4 and speak Latin by 5 or 6. Kaestle (1983, p. 15–16) qualified this report, however, by quoting William Mowry of Rhode Island who 'wrote that learning the whole alphabet "would take probably the entire summer term," and for some children "a whole year would pass before this task was successfully accomplished"'.

### The Sunday School, Infant School and Primary School Movement: 1800–1870

As more people began to migrate to urban towns and cities in the early 1800s and as new forms of industry, trade and commerce developed, several new types of schooling for young children emerged. These schools were designed for children from poor families or from new immigrant or culturally 'different' families. Such schools were based on the assumption that the home environment and training of these children were deficient and that they needed educational training as well as moral guidance to become good American citizens. It was assumed that new forms of school-based education could rectify deficiencies of the home. No schools were originally designed for children from wealthier, western European family backgrounds because it was assumed that, first, these children received satisfactory training within the home, and, second, that people were at home to provide the necessary education.

*Sunday Schools*, a form of charity school, were developed in rural and urban areas largely for children from the poorer and newer immigrant families. It was perceived that such children spent their

Sundays idly, and the schools were developed to rectify this problem. Young children were included to provide child care for them while their parents attended church and to 'catch children when they were young', before they formed bad habits. The principal purpose of these schools seemed to be to teach virtuous behavior and prevent future vice.

In the early nineteenth century, urban private and public *primary schools* included children as young as three years of age. In Boston, for example, publicly-funded primary schooling for 4–6 year olds was guaranteed by law in 1817 (Kaestle and Vinovskis, 1980). Particularly in the public schools, large gallery classrooms, modeled on the British Lancaster monitorial system, were used with poor urban, frequently immigrant, children; in these, older children served as monitors and instructors in the rudiments of reading and writing for younger children. In addition to reading and beginning writing, the primary aims of these early schools were to teach conformity, silence, and obedience to children (Finkelstein, 1979); initiative and curiosity were not goals of the public school curriculum for poor children.

From 1827 to 1870, charitable ladies' organizations and educators promoted and sponsored the development of an alternative to the public primary school for poor young urban children. The *infant schools*, open to children between the ages of 18 months and 7 years (depending on locale), were modeled after those started by Robert Owen and Samuel Wilderspin in England in the early 1800s, and they were designed to include informal instruction, sensory-oriented object lessons, and play. Originally promoted by William Russell, the influential editor of the *American Journal of Education*, and other educators who were influenced by the new European Romantic conception of the child as good rather than evil, these schools provided educational environments for young children that were more natural, nurturant, and informal than the rigid, harsh, and formal primary schools.

Debates centered on the value of out-of-home education for young children with the assumption that a good home was the most natural environment for young children and a good mother was the best trainer. Russell promoted infant schools for children who he assumed did not have a good home environment and mother to care for them. He also promoted infant school pedagogy in the hope that the informal curriculum might promote reform in the formal, didactic, and relatively harsh primary school curriculum of the day. Russell's views on reform and his perception of the differences between the two kinds of schools can be seen in the following statement from Kaestle and Vinovskis (1980). Some of the perceived effects of infant schools are also suggested:

> Infants, taken from the most unfavorable situation in which they are ever placed, from the abodes of poverty and vice, are capable of learning at least a hundred times as much, a hundred times as well, and of being a hundred times as happy, by the system adopted in infant schools, as by that which prevails in the common schools throughout the country. (p. 53)

Russell and others were very convincing. Elite urban women influenced by his articles funded the infant schools as a popular philanthropic move and to provide better moral education for the infants of the poor than they thought children would receive at home. Again, prevention of future vice and crime seemed to be an unstated but critical aspect of this movement.

For approximately two decades, from 1820 to 1840, infant schools were very popular for children from poorer classes. In fact, arguments in their favor were so strong that they even began to attract children from wealthier families. The following quotation, from May and Vinovskis (1977), attests to this and also illuminates some of the complex issues involved in this debate.

> The interesting subject of infant schools is becoming more and more fashionable ... We have been told that it is now in contemplation, to open a school for the infants of others besides the poor. If such a course be not soon adopted, at the age for entering primary schools those poor children will assuredly be the richest scholars. And why should a plan which promises so many advantages, independent of merely relieving the mother from her charge, be confined to children of the indigent? (*Ladies' Magazine*, February 1829).

By the 1840s, then, in many urban areas children from wealthy as well as poor families were attending infant schools. But the goals for the infant schools, originally promoted by Russell and others — to remove rigid instruction and memorization from schools for young children — had been transformed. As the passage from the *Ladies' Magazine* article cited above suggests 'scholarship' of children in infant schools was envied, not the playful, more healthful atmosphere that Russell had originally advocated and that many schools did embody; infant schools for children as young as 18 months were perceived to offer better and earlier instruction than the primary school alternatives. Although relief for mothers seemed of minor importance to those who wrote about infant schools, they did provide some relief from child care for mothers who worked outside their home as well as for those who stayed at home.

Infant schooling was, however, a fad to the philanthropists who supported it. As long as it was popular, represented current or new pedagogical ideas, and provided instruction perceived as necessary, it was funded. By the 1840s, however, some writers suggested that out-of-home education for young children· was damaging to them and that it undermined the home and motherhood as the primary basis of education for the young. Magazines such as the *Ladies' Magazine* suggested the *best* and most natural place for a child to receive education was in the home by the mother; there was little recognition of the fact that poor working mothers required care for their children.

To support their arguments, some suggested that early instruction was dangerous to children, while others maintained that the infant school hurt rather than helped the transition to primary schools. Kaestle and Vinovskis (1980, pp. 58–9), for example, cite Samuel Woodward's remarks to Horace Mann in 1840, 'warning of the dangers of confining children under the age of eight in school for more than one hour at a time, because "intensity" might lead to precocity, which was a "morbid condition" of the brain that might lead to "epilepsy, insanity, or imbecility"'. A report by John P. Bigelow to the Primary School Board in 1830, based upon a survey of teachers who had accepted infant school graduates into their primary school classes, also indicated that teachers were less pleased by the effects of early education in infant schools than they perhaps had expected to be.

> With regard to children from 'infant schools', it is the decided opinion of every instructress in the district, who had had any experience on the subject, that it is better to receive children into the primary schools who have had no instruction whatever, than those who have graduated with the highest honors of the infant seminaries. It is stated that these children are peculiarly restless in their habits, and are thereby the cause of restlessness and disorder among the other children; and it does not appear that their previous instruction renders them,

in any respect, peculiarly proficient or forward in the studies of the primary schools. (in J.M. Wightman, *Annals of the Boston Primary School Committee*, 1860, quoted in May and Vinovskis, 1977, p. 80).

### The Kindergarten: 1856–1913

The decline of infant schooling after 1840 was related to arguments that suggested that the home was the best place for young children to be educated. As infant schooling declined, however, new ideas about educating young children emerged in Europe. The philosophies and kindergarten methods developed by the German educator, Friedrich Froebel in the first half of the nineteenth century were imported to the United States in 1856 by Margarethe Schurz.

Schurz, a German immigrant to America, started one kindergarten in 1856 in Wisconsin for her own children. Shortly, thereafter, the kindergarten began to attract attention, especially that of influential 'idealist' educators, including Elizabeth Peabody, Henry Barnard, William Harrison, and Susan Blow. Some of the same changes in intellectual and pedagogical philosophies of education for young children which had originally influenced Russell's promotion of the infant school also influenced the development of the kindergarten in the US. While these pedagogical ideas remained important influences, the growth of the kindergarten and changes in its aims and support over time are also related to the continuing assumption that early education could especially be used to rectify moral deficiencies in the homes of poor and immigrant children. Ultimately, the growth of the kindergarten and its attachment in pedagogy and practice to primary schools became associated with the new movement for professional status affecting all segments of education by the turn of the century.

Vandewalker documents some of the changes taking place in early childhood education in one passage of her 1908 book on the history of the kindergarten:

In 1870 there were less than a dozen kindergartens in existence, all save one established by Germans and conducted in the German language; in 1880 there were no less than 400 scattered over thirty states. In 1870 there was one kindergarten training school in the United States; in 1880 such schools had been established in the ten largest cities of the country and in many smaller ones. The year 1870 saw the establishment of the first charity kindergarten; in 1880 the new institution had become recognized as the most valuable of child-saving agencies, and mission kindergarten work had become so popular among wealthy young women as to be almost a fad. The practicability of the kindergarten as a part of the school system had been successfully demonstrated and the logical sequence of its future relation to the school had been recognized by the establishment of kindergarten training departments in the normal school systems of two great states. The National Educational Association had set the seal of its approval upon the principles which the kindergarten embodied, and had commended the institution to the school men of the country for experiment and consideration. (p. 23)

Vandewalker suggests, therefore, that the kindergarten was well established by 1880 and, until 1900, was a central part of the charity school movement, generally financed by social reformers and philanthropists, in the growing urban areas of the United States.

Kindergarten curriculum was also influenced by scientific and institutional changes occurring in Europe and in the United States during this same period, and because of this the curriculum came under scrutiny as the kindergarten movement grew. New concepts of scientific research (for example, Darwin, 1859), theory, philosophies (including those promoted by Social Darwinists), and research concerned with educational and psychological development in children were espoused. G. Stanley Hall, Edward Thorndike, John Dewey, and Patty Smith Hill became the new leaders of experimental and scientific movements in education and psychology. In addition, new ideas about the relationship between the kindergarten and primary schooling were suggested. Beginning with the 1890s, various anti-Froebelian, experimental curricula were explored, and by 1920, a new 'liberal' kindergarten curriculum had gained favor and began to be used in private kindergartens as well as in the increasing numbers of kindergartens attached to public primary schools (The Committee of Nineteen, 1913; Burke, 1923; Weber, 1969).

### Aims of the Froebelian Kindergarten

The 'pure' Froebelian philosophy in American schools was best described by Susan Blow (for example, see her articles in H. Barnard, (Ed) *Kindergarten and Child Culture Papers*, 1890). The Froebelian method, according to Blow, rested on the Romantic assumption of the innate goodness of young children and the necessity of an educational environment that better suited the natural inclinations of children at different stages. The Froebelian emphasis on a female instructor for young children and a home-like nurturing environment filled with songs, play, object lessons, and games stemmed from Froebel's contact with the philosophy of Rousseau and the methods of Pestalozzi. Conceived during the era of German political debates about unifying the many separate German states into one centralized unit, Froebel's philosophy also reflected his strong religious background and his interpretation of Schelling's and Fichte's idealist philosophies, particularly the overriding unity between external sensory perception and inner knowledge. These various influences led Froebel to develop a method that focused on the unification of man with God. His pedagogy centered on a set of sequenced 'gifts', 'occupations', songs, and 'plays' that would gradually help children gain knowledge of unity (between objects, with nature, and with God) and of the inner connectedness of all things, man, and God. The geometric spheres, cubes, and cylinders that made up the gifts and occupations were supposed to be studied by children, and the constructions they made with the objects were to give them inner knowledge of Froebel's 'truths' (unity, inner connectedness, and an ordered whole). The Froebelian philosophy also assumed that through self-active study children would learn the language, form, and number of the objects.

The popularity of the American Froebelian kindergarten, which spanned more than fifty years, was related to a variety of different perceptions of its aims and accomplishments. The following examples of these different perspectives provide some idea of the central aims and effects attributed to the program up to 1913, when the liberal kindergarten ideas developed by Hall, Dewey, Hill and others came to dominate the field.

In the 1870s, claiming the 'necessity of kindergarten culture', Elizabeth Peabody (in Barnard, 1890) suggested that play was the critical element missing from earlier (primary school) pedagogy and from the home environments particularly of poor children. The effects of deficiencies in play were clear to her:

> We must play with the child. If we do not, he ceases to play. Charles Lamb has given a most affecting picture of the effects of this in his pathetic paper on the neglected children of the poor; and the statistics of public cribs and foundling hospitals prove, that when children are deprived of the instinctive

maternal nursery play, almost all of them die, and the survivors become feeble-minded ... And what produces idiocy in these extreme cases produces chronic dullness, discouragement, and destruction of all elasticity of mind, in the majority of children ... Not to be attaining habits of order is even for the body unhealthy, and leaves children to become disorderly and perverse.

Susan Blow, at the time when she was still trying to attract attention to, rather than defend, the Froebelian kindergarten, suggested the kindergarten would have the following effects on children:

... an increase in health, development of grace, habits of cleanliness, courtesy, neatness, order, and industry; power to develop ideas of form, to give mastery of material through technical training, to impress fundamental perceptions sharply on the mind, to lead to nice discrimination and choice use of words, and to hint the truths which are the forms in which all creation is cast. (Blow, in Barnard, 1890, pp. 605–6).

William Harris, initiator of the first public school kindergarten in St. Louis in 1873, was an advocate for widespread inclusion of the kindergarten into the American public school system. He treated several practical questions in his attempt to show the worth of the program to public administrators and educators. In 'Kindergarten in the public school system' (in Barnard, 1890), a paper presented in 1879, Harris made a series of fascinating arguments, only a sample of which can be included here. Harris claimed the Froebelian gifts were good for teaching elementary geometry and number, art, crafts, imagination, self-activity, etc. But to convince others of the value of the program as an addition to the public school, he focused on two particular aspects of childhood education that the kindergarten is 'uniquely' suited for:

Kindergartens Prepare for the Trades: Here it becomes evident that, if the school is to prepare especially for the arts and trades, it is the kindergarten which is to accomplish the object: for the training of the muscles — if it is to be a training for special skill in manipulation — must be begun in early youth. As age advances, it becomes more difficult to acquire new phases of manual dexterity ... The child trained for one year on Froebel's gifts and occupations will acquire a skillful use of his hands and a habit of accurate measurement of the eye which will be his possession for life ... I have in this protracted discussion of the significance of Froebels' gifts as a preparation for industrial life, indicated my own grounds for believing that the kindergarten is worthy of a place in the common-school system. It should be a sort of sub-primary education, and receive the pupil at the age of four or four and a half years, and hold him until he completes his sixth year. By this means we gain the child for one or two years when he is good for nothing else but education, and not of much value even for the education of the school as it is and has been. The disciplines of reading and writing, geography and arithmetic ... are beyond the powers of the average child not yet entered upon his seventh year. And beyond the seventh year the time of the child is too valuable to use if for other than general disciplines ... He must not take up his school time with learning a handicraft. (Harris, in Barnard, 1890, pps. 631−4)

Besides the industrial phase of the subject ... The fourth, fifth, and sixth years are years of transition not well provided for either by family life or by social life in the United States. In families of great poverty, the child forms evil associations on the street, and is initiated into crime. By the time he is ready to enter the school he is hardened in vicious habits, beyond the power of the school to eradicate. In families of wealth, the custom is to intrust the care of the child in this period of his life to some servant without pedagogical skill, and generally without strength of will-power. The child of wealthy parents usually inherits the superior directive power of the parents, who have by their energy acquired and preserved the wealth. Its manifestation in the child is not reasonable, considerate will-power, but arbitrariness and self-will — with such a degree of stubbornness that it quite overcomes the much feebler native will of the servant who has charge of the children. It is difficult to tell which class (poor or rich) the kindergarten benefits most. Society is benefited by the substitution of a rational training of the child's will during his transition period. If he is a child of poverty, he is saved by the good associations and the industrial and intellectual training that he gets. If he is a child of wealth, he is saved by the kindergarten from ruin through self-indulgence and the corruption ensuring on weak management in the family. (*ibid.*, p. 634)

Finally, Felix Adler, one of the more interesting, and extreme, representatives of the charity kindergarten movement, provided the following insights into his own perceptions of the aims and effects of the kindergarten program in his Workingman's School:

> A pauper class is beginning to grow up among us, incapable of permanently lifting themselves to better conditions by their own exertions, incapable of obtaining the satisfaction of their most natural desires, and only rendered the more dangerous and furious by the sense of equality with all others, with which our political institutions have inspired them ... And, of all these possible measures of prevention, a suitable, a sensible system of education is assuredly the most promising. Let us use what influence we have to correct the false idea of equality which is everywhere current around us ... Let us impress upon the minds of the children that the business of life will always be carried on in a hierarchy of services, and that there is no shame in doing a lesser service in this hierarchy ... to enable the working people of the future to take pride and find dignity in the work of their hands, is the object of the work education which we are seeking to introduce into our school. (Excerpts from an early speech in Adler, 'Free Kindergarten and Workingman's School', in Barnard, 1890, p. 691)

> ... The results already achieved by our kindergarten work are satisfactory. Children came to us who could not smile; some of them remained for weeks in the kindergarten before they were seen to smile ... The children were taught how to play; they learned how to be joyous. The children came to us unclean in every way; in the kindergarten they are made clean, and a neat appearance and habits of tidiness are insisted upon. The children's minds were awakened; their faculties — physical and intellectual were developed ... Best of all a powerful moral influence has been brought to bear on the children of the kindergarten ... the faults of each child are studied; obstinancy is checked, selfishness is put to the blush, and, by a firm, yet mild treatment, the character is improved. (*ibid.*, p. 688).

As these examples show, by the turn of the century in urban America, charity kindergartens predominantly for 4 to 6 year olds, settlement house day nurseries (for the children of working mothers as young as 2 weeks and as old as 6 years), and Workingman's Schools such as Adler's (for children 4 and older) had become an integral part of the social welfare movement directed at 'helping' poor immigrant children and their families. The majority of these institutions were supported by philanthropic donations from wealthy families and private charitable organizations. The motivations of the supporters of the program were mixed; they mingled concern for the health of poor urban immigrants and their children (predominantly in day nurseries) with their fears that unemployed and uneducated poor immigrant families and their children were the foundation of an immoral and vice-filled society. In addition to providing instruction in moral education for these children, schools were charged with an additional social task. With a growing recognition that the new industrialization taking place required manual workers trained for a particular type and station of work, urban schools for the poor began to emphasize conformity to an organization, obedience to authority, and manual training.

### Dominant Assumptions and Aims of the Nineteenth Century Programs

Throughout the late eighteenth and the nineteenth centuries, moral education seemed to be the dominant educational aim of programs for young children. Educators and philanthropists who financed the majority of the programs favored 'catching children early' in order to teach them what they considered to be appropriate American moral conduct, values, and their 'station in life'. Fostering other forms of knowledge (for example, reading in the earlier period, knowledge of universal truths during the later period) as well as concerns for children's health in dense urban settlement areas also dominated discussions of the purposes of early programs.

In summary, the growth in the number, type, and location of programs for young children, critical for the development of early education in the United States, were based on three assumptions. First, educators and financiers assumed that early out-of-home experiences could be used to rectify perceived deficiencies in the education poor and immigrant children received at home. Second, with the exception of overly indulgent mothers (for example, Harris, in Barnard, 1890), 'adequate' mothers were defined as those who happily centered their life on the home, husband, and children and who had the background to teach children correct values and behavior (for example, see the discussion in Rothman, 1980, pp. 98–132). This assumption led to a lack of out-of-home early education programs for children from wealthier families during this period. Third, although infant schools and settlement house day nurseries took care of the children of working-parents, care for such children was considered to be a last resort and stop gap measure; then, as today, little attention was paid to the long-term needs of working families with children.

## Becoming Professional and Scientific: Early Education in the Early Twentieth Century

In the first third of the twentieth century, the growth and form of the kindergarten and day nursery movements continued to be strongly related to class and cultural assumptions. In addition, the development of the American nursery school in the early 1920s was also grounded in class-based assumptions about the needs of middle-class children for socio-emotional experiences thought to be missing in children's homes. But other philosophical, scientific, and economic movements also influenced attitudes towards early education in the United States. Three of these movements — efforts toward professionalization, to become 'scientific', and to institutionalize — will be discussed in this section.

### *Scientific and Professional Movements in the Kindergarten*

By the late nineteenth century, early childhood education began to emerge as an autonomous field, consisting of the growing number of educators, teacher trainers, and psychologists that worked with Froebelian kindergartens. Several national organizations and kindergarten magazines had been founded by 1900 (Weber, 1969), special training programs had been initiated, and debates about methodology had become increasingly technical and specialized. Kindergarten teaching was more and more frequently provided by certified and trained teachers, and innovations in kindergarten curriculum development began to be discussed by 'experts'. Those working in programs concerned with the education of young children, and particularly the leaders in the field, wanted to be and, in many cases, were beginning to be considered 'professionals'. Yet, while the burgeoning group of people identifying themselves with the kindergarten and 'early education' were convinced of the importance of education for the young, they were still trying to convince others that this was a critical and professional field of endeavor.

In an effort to gain professional status for themselves and for their field, kindergarten professionals (particularly the leaders) attempted to affiliate themselves with new curriculum, theories, and research ideas and with institutions that would add to their own and to their field's professional status. In these efforts, they left behind other organizations, people, and systems of thought that seemed less professional or of questionable status. Specifically, the kindergarten leaders looked toward affiliations with the primary school and away from those with the social welfare day nursery movement. Many in this field also affiliated themselves with new 'scientific' ideas about children, child study research techniques, and education emerging from laboratory schools and university-based psychology and education programs.

G. Stanley Hall, a psychologist at Clark University, initiated the child study research movement in the United States at the turn of the century. While Hall's recapitulation theory of child development was questionable (see the discussion in Sears, 1975), his research ideas were widely influential and he encouraged a number of young kindergarten leaders to do child study research and to build curricula based on their observations of children. In the first 'scientific' research report on the effects of kindergarten attendance on children, Hall emphasized the value of kindergarten education to children by describing test results and teacher ratings of observable behavior and he ignored the unobservable growth in children's knowledge and spirituality that had been emphasized by earlier theorists. The following example of Hall's report, based upon tests of children's knowledge by Boston primary school teachers indicates the shifting assumptions of the effects of early education that were beginning to occur.

> Column 6 shows in a striking way the advantage of the kindergarten children, without regard to nationality, over all others. Most of the latter [children] tested were from the [Froebelian] charity kindergarten, so that superior intelligence of home surroundings can hardly be assumed. Many of them had attended kindergarten but a short time. ... We seem to have here an illustration of the law that we really see not what is near or impresses the retina, but what the attention is called and held to, and what interests are

awakened and words found for. Of nearly thirty primary teachers questioned as to the difference between children from kindergartens and others, four saw no difference, and all the rest thought them better fitted for school work, instancing superior use of language, skill with the hand and slate, quickness, power of observation, singing, number, love of work, neatness, politeness, freedom from the benumbing school bashfulness, or power to draw from dictation. Many thought them at first more restless and talkative. (*Contents of Children's Minds*, 1883, pp. 20–1).

The various changes in society at the end of the nineteenth century in education, psychology, and research led to criticisms of the urban, relatively rigid Froebelian kindergartens. The Froebelians, headed by Susan Blow, defended the value of the Froebelian method against criticisms made by leaders in the fields of educational pedagogy (for example, Dewey, 1900; Hill, 1913), child study (for example, Hall, 1883, 1911), and psychology (for example, Thorndike, 1913). Criticisms centered on the rigid, ritualistic, and mystical ways in which the recent urban charity kindergartens had interpreted and practiced Froebel's original method. The critiques emphasized the need for a new kindergarten curriculum based upon current psychological knowledge about children (gained through child study) and the real rather than articial experiences and interests of children, particularly in urban areas.

Thorndike (1903) summarized the new ideas on curriculum initiated by Hall, Dewey, Anna Bryan (1897) and her protegee Patty Smith Hill, in his article 'Notes on psychology for kindergartners':

I shall now mention briefly some of the tendencies in kindergarten work which seem especially hopeful in the light of the psychological facts so far presented and of the more general knowledge of human nature which we all possess. They are:
    The increase of out-door play even at great sacrifice.
    The arrangement of the room, seating and daily program to suit the body of a child, not the mind of a mystic.
    The increase of large movements and of free play.
    Systematic efforts to remedy bodily and mental defects.
    ... Discarding all efforts to teach abstractions which can be realized only with the help of the maturity and knowledge reached at or near adolescence.
    Limiting the amount of information taught to concrete

characteristics of real things, especially to the simpler activities of the children's natural and social environment, such as the brook, the sea shore, the growth of plants, the house being built, the grocery store, and the railroad station. (p. 399)

Thorndike also pushed the kindergartners to be more scientific and seemed to suggest that, if they were, they might gain a somewhat higher status:

Psychology is passing, and education will soon pass, from the condition of a descriptive to that of a quantitative science. The human mind is being given the quantitative study by exact measurements which has long characterized astronomy, physics, and chemistry. The education of the human child will sometime be treated with the respect and care that we now give to recording eclipses or measuring the brightness of stars. The best service to be done by early education, for instance by that of the kindergarten, will then probably be considered the accurate measurement of the mental powers and tendencies of children, and the accurate recording of their progress. At present this is possible in the case of the sense powers, motor ability, the perceptive and associative processes, and some of the more definite and mechanical of the other mental traits. Needless to say, however, such measurements are quite beyond the capacity of kindergarten teachers. (*ibid.*, p. 65)

Thorndike's comments reflect the new push toward being scientific and the enhanced status thereby given to experimental psychology. Similar views were expressed in the arguments presented during the kindergarten curriculum debate of 1913 (The Committee of Nineteen, 1913). This debate culminated nearly two decades of growing dissatisfaction with the rigidity of the Froebelian method and recent experimentation with new methods based on the new psychological and educational theories. In the 1913 debate, the Froebelian kindergarten perspective was put forward by Susan Blow and other supporters, while the liberal kindergarten group was headed by Patty Smith Hill. No new evidence for the effectiveness of either kindergarten program was cited in the debate report; however, the Hill report argued for the liberal approach by citing its relationship to modern psychological and educational theory. The relations between Thorndike's stimulus and response theory (1913) and his earlier emphasis on instincts were clear. In addition, Hill used phrases that showed the long-term influence of Dewey's educational theories and the more recent influence of educators who pushed for an efficient and organized curriculum.

Hill described the liberal curriculum as follows:

> Three fundamental problems are given as of prime impor-tance in the planning of a kindergarten program. I. The selection of the native tendencies of childhood which make for the development of the individual and the advancement of civilization. II. The selection of the best subject-matter or materials for the creative impulses to act upon and react toward. III. The organization, arrangement, or correlation of subject-matter or materials in such a unity as makes for economy and simplicity ... (p. 276).

In her examples of ways to organize such a curriculum, Hill outlined the most important *native tendencies, impulses*, and *social needs* of children that should be met by the course of study. These included the need to: 'make, construct', 'nurture, protect, or control', 'investi-gate, explore, and find out', 'tell or communicate', 'transmit, record, interpret ...', 'adorn, decorate, arrange, or beautify', 'transmit, record, interpret ...', 'cooperate and compete with ourselves', 'measure, calculate, compute ...', 'wonder ...', and 'cooperate, formulate, and preserve social experience'. These needs were then met, in the sample program she described in the 1913 report, by activities that came from modern life and from children's interests. At this time, these included a version of Froebel's gifts and occupations (for construction); however, they emphasized: care of plants, anim-als, dolls, and home (for nurture); nature study, science, etc. (for exploration); and, for various other needs, art, song, literature, dramatic games and dances, mathematics, religion, and the study of laws and institutions (Hill, 1913, p. 277).

Hill's scientific rationale won the 1913 debate among kindergar-ten theorists and practitioners. Experimental curricula were tried at Columbia, where Hill was the head of the kindergarten program, as well as at several other universities and training schools (Davis, 1925). These experiments and the need to prove the scientific rationale for the kindergarten were also evidenced in Hill's 1923 'Introduction' to *The Conduct Curriculum* (Burke, 1923), which she and others developed at the Columbia University laboratory school. In the following passage, Hill reveals the progress they had made by 1915 toward understanding the effects of the kindergarten as well as the changes made by kindergartners in adapting their ideas to the new definition of good scientific research.

> In this way the school served as a laboratory of democracy, in which the technique of democratic citizenship could be gradually acquired ... Even in 1915, however, this form of social organization impressed the more conservative pedagogical minds as radical and wasteful. In order therefore to justify the results of such training through some more convincing evidence than the mere enthusiasm of those who were conducting the experiment, it was realized that some method of recording daily work must be devised. Up to this time few systematic efforts had been made to record the progress of young children. With no precedent at our disposal, we decided to appoint special observers to make records of what they considered typical outcomes in the individual and social behavior of the group. These were listed as carefully as the scientific training of teachers at that time permitted, and the results were tabulated. The observers, disagreeing in minor details, unanimously agreed that this freer organization offered conditions in which the children learned initiative, independence, perseverance, concentration, and social cooperation such as the old order had never provided. (p. xii).

After World War I, 'scientifically sound curriculum' became synonomous with 'legitimate' education. Scientifically sound curricula were those founded on the latest psychological theory and research and that were legitimated through experimental research and objective measurement and assessment procedures. Primary school curriculum experts also described their curriculum in terms of goals and objectives for the standard child or classroom. Kindergarten curriculum theorists, in their continuing efforts to professionalize their field, linked the curriculum with the scientific movements in primary education.

The conduct curriculum (Burke, 1923) developed by Hill and her colleagues at Columbia best represented this movement during the early 1920s. In *The Conduct Curriculum*, the curricular activities and materials were similar to those described in Hill's liberal 1913 report (Hill, 1913, see above). In the 1923 document, however, the curriculum was discussed in the terminology of learning theory and stressed individual and social habit formation, as well as connections between stimuli (activities and materials) and responses (children's habits and conduct). The prior emphasis on curriculum centered on children's needs, impulses, and interests was replaced by one that focused on helping children to learn teacher-defined desirable habits and conduct.

The conduct curriculum represented an affiliation of kindergarten theory and practice with primary school theory and practices; it signaled a move away from some of the past orientations of the kindergarten and a move toward the narrower academic emphases of the primary school. It was also linked to the movement of the past few decades to institutionalize kindergarten programs within public primary schools. This position was motivated, in part, by the cost of private and charitable kindergartens to its philanthropist supporters (Lazerson, 1973). It was also related to the needs of primary school educators, who, faced with a flood of children from diverse linguistic and cultural backgrounds, had become interested in the kindergarten as a way to ease the children's transition to the first grade primary classroom. During the first quarter of the twentieth century, kindergarten leaders who were anxious to reduce costs and to elevate the professional status of kindergartens through association with the public school system, adopted the move toward affiliation.

Some of the first evidence of the growth in importance of the movement to institutionalize can be found in the first two NSSE yearbooks on early education — *The Kindergarten and its Relation to Elementary Education* (6th Yearbook, 1907) and *The Coordination of the Kindergarten and the Elementary School* (7th Yearbook, 1908). Support *for* affiliation seemed to counter arguments about the cost of publicly financed kindergartens (for example, see Hatch's arguments, quoted in Lazerson, 1973, p. 234).

By 1910, the initial phase of public school affiliation had been achieved. In 1900, of 225,394 kindergarten children, 131,557 were in public schools while 93,737 were in private kindergartens; by 1910 of 346,189 kindergarten children, 293,970 were in the public kindergartens while only 52,219 were in private schools (Spodek, 1980). However, the professional and lay public continued to debate the cost of and need for kindergarten education for *all* children.

In 1922, only 12 per cent of all eligible 5-year-olds were attending kindergartens of any type (Spodek, 1980). Primary educators were still unsure of the virtues of the kindergarten philosophy, especially given its cost (Weber, 1969). The general public was also unclear why kindergarten education was necessary. Kindergarten leaders who wanted the growth to continue responded by trying to convince others with arguments and reports of the superior achievement and progress kindergarten children made in elementary school.

Prominent research articles during the 1920s — including 'The Progress of Kindergarten Pupils in the Elementary Grades' (Peters, 1923); 'The Influence of Kindergarten on Achievement in Reading' (Gard, 1924), 'The Relation Between Kindergarten Training and Success in the Elementary School' (Risser and Elder, 1927); and 'Attendance at Kindergarten and Progress in the Primary Grades' (MacLatchey, 1928) — supported more general arguments that focused on the kindergarten as an economical, efficient, and scientifically sound program. Two specific examples from this period illustrate the nature of the arguments presented:

> There are those that worship at the shrine of Froebel and others who ardently insist that the kindergarten (in its present form) is but a stumbling block to the educational progress of the pupils who attend it. But neither of these factions attempt to show the effect of kindergarten training in terms of educational accomplishments. (Peters, 1923, p. 117) ... [And, after a description of his study]: As stated above, the average difference between the chronological ages of the two (kindergarten and non-kindergarten) groups at the time of entering the first grade was 3.4 months. That is, on the average each non-kindergarten pupil was more than three months older than his corresponding kindergarten pupil. Since both groups completed the work of the first five grades in the same length of time, obviously the kindergarten group completed the work at a younger age ... The one group had received kindergarten training, the other was older and hence possessed the experience resulting therefrom. The two groups, thus different, did the same task, in the same time. The kindergarten group did the work with less irregularity, with similar credit and at a younger age. Obviously, the experience of the kindergarten training matched the greater experience, due to age possessed by the non-kindergarten group ... The kindergarten group saved or gained about 53 years of human life (187 times 3.4 months). The investigation shows that ... kindergarten expedites school life. (*ibid.*, pp. 124–126)
>
> From MacLatchey (1928): In conclusion, when judged by the teachers, the children who have attended kindergarten are

rated higher in social traits, industry, initiative, and oral language, than are the children who have not, and the longer they have attended the higher they are rated. (p. 41) ... The range of mental ages, the character of the distribution, the average mental ages, and the intelligent quotients roughly computed, all indicate that the pupils of the kindergarten group were on the average brighter than the pupils who had not attended kindergarten (p. 65).

By 1930, these arguments had proved convincing: in this year there were 777,899 children going to kindergarten, most of whom (723,443) were in public school programs (Goodykountz, Davis, and Gabard, 1947, p. 46). Thus, by this time the kindergarten had effectively been 'institutionalized' in the public school system.

### Costs and Benefits of Kindergarten Professionalization and Affiliation with the Primary School

The affiliation of the kindergarten with primary education brought a variety of benefits to kindergarten leaders. They had gained a measure of the professional status they desired through their association with primary education and their separation from the lower-status day nursery movement. They had also made kindergarten education more widespread by reducing the need for private funds to support the cost of rooms, equipment, and personnel.

Costs to the kindergarten, and to the field of early education, however, were generally high. Initially, the complete separation of kindergartens from day nurseries divided the field of early education and reinforced the idea that day care was unimportant as an educational institution. Affiliation with the primary school led to a written curriculum focused more on fostering progress in school than on the broad social and moral reforms (and control) that were the goals of the charity kindergartens. To appear scientific, efficient, and standard, the kindergarten program was objectified, and relations between its goals and the social context of kindergarten programs were de-emphasized or made part of the informal or hidden curriculum. The methods and effects of the kindergarten were increasingly justified in terms of tests and measurements that were sometimes inappropriate to the aims of the kindergarten (see Hill's 1934 statement below). By the 1930s, the age-graded nature of the kindergarten also resulted in a narrowing of the group of children served by the kindergarten. In part, the kindergarten move toward the age-graded primary school system also resulted in the beginning of an autonomous and quite different nursery school movement in the 1920s.


## New Divisions in the Field of Early Education

By the early part of the twentieth century, it was clear that kindergartens were moving toward primary schools and trying to distance themselves from the day nurseries. It was not until the 1920s, however, that nursery schools emerged as the third branch of what is now considered the American early childhood system of programs.

Nursery schools had been started by Margaret and Rachel MacMillan in England in 1909. In the early British nursery schools, the curriculum focused on the health and welfare of young poor children (Deasey, 1978); however, by the post-war era, new psychoanalytic ideas based on children's instincts and needs had begun to influence the curriculum. Nursery schools soon began to attract attention in the United States (in 1919, for example, there were three; Goodykounz *et al.*, 1947), and their promoters came from social welfare organizations as well as from the newly-emerging group of professionals interested in child development and in psychoanalysis. Nursery schools in the 1920s combined welfare and health objectives with psychoanalytic theories, resulting in a renewed emphasis on play and the socio-emotional development of young children. At the same time the kindergarten was affiliating with the learning theories popular in the primary education research establishment, the nursery school in the United States began to grow (in 1924, there were twenty-five nursery schools; in 1928, eighty-nine; and in 1930, 203).

Until the advent of WPA-supported nursery schools in the 1930s, the majority of these schools were in private settings and were geared toward largely middle-class children. They were aimed at promoting children's 'adaptability to the group', 'social skills and attitudes', 'social poise', 'ability to live and cooperate with others', and 'freedom as an individual in the group' (Jersild and Fite, 1939, p. 2). In short, programs focused on the socio-emotional needs of the child, his or her freedom of expression, and the development of well-adjusted and 'integrated' (middle-class) children.

The majority of nursery schools were funded either by the Laura

Spellmen Rockefeller Fund, as part of university-based child development research laboratories, or as resources for parent education
efforts in high schools and at universities (Forest, 1937; Schlossman,
1981; Sears, 1975). Middle-class mothers, in particular, were convinced through magazine reports and books that they needed expert
advice in child rearing (see, for example, Rothman, 1980, pp.
209–18). University laboratory and parent cooperative nursery
schools were developed in the 1920s to provide such a base of expert
information (Forest, 1937; Jersild and Fite, 1939; Schlossman, 1981;
Sears, 1975).

Clearly, by 1930, day nurseries, nursery schools, and kindergartens had emerged as different types of 'schools' with different
philosophies and aims, somewhat different populations, and different
professional alliances. Day nurseries were clearly separated from
discussions of nursery school and kindergarten curriculum; and
differences in nursery and kindergarten affiliations seemed to be
resulting in different curriculum priorities. Research on the nursery
school showed that children's social relations with peers and parents
were well adjusted and that children had 'well-integrated' personalities (Forest, 1937; Jersild and Fite, 1939). When the effect of nursery
school attendance on IQ was assessed, for example, it fed into the
nature-nurture debates about intellectual development, not into the
question of progress in kindergarten or primary school (for example,
Goodenough, 1928; Hildreth, 1928; and Wellman, 1933).

In the early 1930s, some kindergarten leaders worried about the
divisions in the orientations of those educating young pre-primary-
age children. They also noticed the costs of affiliation with the
primary school on curriculum for young children. The following
passage from a 1934 article entitled 'The practical value of early
education' by Patty Smith Hill, then Director of the 'nursery-
kindergarten-primary' unit at Columbia University, summarizes the
research on kindergarten attendance that had been done in 1920. It
also shows Hill's attempts to regain unity within the field of early
education and to link the kindergarten with child development
theories. It also shows her own continuing uneasiness with the
theories, priorities, and research methods imposed on the kindergarten by its affiliation with the primary school:

> There are not yet available many adequate research studies
> dealing with the effect of kindergarten education on progress
> in the elementary school. In general, conclusions in favor of
> the kindergarten training may be summarized as follows

[numbers in parentheses refer to the bibliography in Hill's article]:

1  Kindergarten children progress faster in the grades. (3) (8).
2  Kindergarten children make higher scores on certain mental and achievement tests than do non-kindergarten children. (7) (8).
3  Kindergarten children show a lower percentage of failures in the grades. (7) (8).
4  Kindergarten children receive a better rating on social traits. (8) (11).

[However ...] Since the philosophy and objectives of nursery school and kindergarten education, as set forth in the first section of this pamphlet, have to do with the development of a healthy, well-integrated child, data concerning rate of progress through the elementary schools are inadequate materials on which to judge the success or failure of the educational program outlined. Studies of social-trait ratings have more direct bearing on the problem of what the nursery school and kindergarten are able to do in actually fostering the development of young children. Unfortunately, few such studies have been reported.

## Summary: Sociohistorical Perspectives on the Aims and Effects of Early Education

This section presents a summary of the aims, effects and contextual factors which have influenced the development of early education in the United States. It is based on an analysis of the professional reports in the field from 1800 to 1930. The final section examines relationships between past and present practice in early education and care programs and debates which have affected these practices.

### *Persistent Aims of Early Education and Child Care*

The preceding historical review has shown that certain aims have been important in many early education and care programs throughout the period, while others have varied in priority depending upon the program (for example, kindergarten, day care, nursery school) or on specific factors present during a given sociohistorical period.

Upon reviewing the various reports made, six broad domains were identified in which specific aims consistently appeared in each historical period. These included aims of the following types: (i) intellectual and academic; (ii) moral or character development; (iii) socio-emotional; (iv) imaginative and artistic; (v) motoric; and (vi) health-related. These six domains, broken into specific aims found in reports of different educators, are listed in table 1. Those that seemed most important in different programs or periods are highlighted (signaled by a plus ⟨+⟩).

Several general domains were consistently cited as important aims throughout the period under review. The most persistent of these seemed to be in the area of socio-emotional development, while those stressing moral or character development and intellectual/ academic goals appeared to vary in importance over the time span under study. Motor and health aims and artistic/imaginative aims were cited as important in different programs and at different periods; however, these aims seemed to be of secondary importance relative to others in all but the custodially oriented day nursery/day care movement.

The review showed that the specific aims of a period, even within a given domain (for example, socio-emotional development) might be quite different from those of another period. The specific emphasis placed on the various aims therefore, must be taken into account.

In some programs and in certain historical periods, for example, socio-emotional aims were oriented toward conformity, obedience, industry, and responsibility (for example, in the turn-of-the-century Froebelian kindergarten programs), while in other programs or periods, socio-emotional aims were directed toward independence, exploration, and peer cooperation (for example, in the nursery school). In some programs 'motoric aims' were focused entirely on fine motor aspects, while in others gross motor aims were considered to be most important. Some of the shifting focus on these aims and some of the factors affecting the differences in perceptions, meanings, and assignments of value will be discussed next.

In the past, reports that focused on socio-emotional and moral or character aims such as conformity, obedience, and proper moral behavior and conduct seemed to be focused on education for children from poor, working-class, and frequently, newly-immigrant families. When health aims were important, they also seemed to be associated with programs serving children from poor backgrounds. Programs with these specific aims seemed to have two more general goals: (i) to teach children normative 'American' moral behavior and conduct;

# Marianne N. Bloch

Table 1

| Aims of Early Education | Infants schools (18 months–6 years) | Primary schools (3–7 years) | Froebelian Kindergartens 1856–1870s (3–7 years) | 1870–1913 Charity School | Liberal kindergarten (4–6 years) | Day nurseries (2–6 years) | Public school kindergartens (5–6 years) | Nursery schools (2– ) | Day nurseries (18 months–5 years) | Kindergarten (5 years) [NOT REVIEWED] | Nursery schools [NOT REVIEWED] | Day care [NOT REVIEWED] | Kindergarten (5 years) | Pre-school | Head Start (3–4 years) | Day care (2–5 years) |
|---|---|---|---|---|---|---|---|---|---|---|---|---|---|---|---|---|
| | 1800–1870 | 1800–1870 | 1856–1913 | 1856–1913 | 1893–1919 | 1893–1919 | 1920–1934 | 1920–1934 | 1920–1934 | 1935–1960 | 1935–1960 | 1935–1960 | 1961–1983 | 1961–1983 | 1961–1983 | 1961–1983 |
| 1 Intellectual and academic | + | + | + | + | | | + | | | | | | + | + | + | + |
| A Reading (readiness) | + | + | | | | | | | | | | | + | + | + | |
| B Number-related concepts | + | + | + | + | + | | + | | | | | | + | + | | |
| C Progress in school, retardation | + | + | | + | + | | + | | | | | | + | + | + | |
| D Conceptual development | | | + | | + | | | | | | | | + | + | + | |
| E Language: oral-standard English | | | | + | + | + | + | + | | | | | + | + | | |
| 2 Moral or character | + | + | + | + | + | + | + | | + | | | | | | + | |
| A Spiritual | | | + | + | + | | | | | | | | | | | |
| B 'Prevention' of vice, crime | + | + | | + | | + | | | + | | | | | | + | |
| C Normative values and American behavior | + | + | | + | | + | | | | | | | | | | |
| D Knowledge of occupation or station | | | | + | | | | | | | | | | | | |
| 3 Socio-emotional (concepts, behavior, habits and traits) | + | + | + | + | + | + | + | + | | | | | + | + | + | + |
| A Self-concept | | | | | | | | | | | | | + | + | + | + |
| B Industry, responsibility | | + | | + | + | | + | | | | | | + | | | |
| C Initiative, exploration | | | | | + | | + | + | | | | | + | + | + | + |
| D Independence | | | | | + | | + | + | | | | | | + | + | + |
| E Cooperation (peers), adjustment | + | + | + | + | + | | + | + | | | | | + | + | + | + |
| F Obedience to authority | | + | | | + | | | | | | | | + | + | | |
| G Punctuality, attentiveness | | | | + | + | | + | | | | | | + | | | |
| H Social knowledge | | | | | + | | | | | | | | + | + | | + |
| 4 Imaginative, artistic | | | + | + | + | | + | + | | | | | + | + | + | |
| A Imagination | | | + | + | + | | + | + | | | | | | + | + | + |
| B Art, music, dance | | | + | | + | | + | + | | | | | | + | | + |
| 5 Motor | | | + | + | + | | + | + | | | | | | + | | |
| A Fine, manual, self-help | | | + | + | | | | | | | | | | | | |
| B Gross motor, activity | | | | | + | | + · | + | | | | | + | + | | + |
| 6 Health | + | | | + | + | + | | | + | | | | | + | | + |
| A Cleanliness, tidiness | + | + | + | + | + | + | | | + | | | | | + | | + |
| B Less illness | + | | + | + | | + | | | | | | | | | | + |
| C Growth patterns | | | | + | + | | + | + | + | | | | | + | | + |

54

and (ii) to aid society by preventing disease, vice, or future crime. Liberal kindergarten programs of the 1920s and the nursery schools of the 1930s that focused on curriculum for non-poor populations (and, in the nursery school, on children from middle-class families) assumed proper behavior and values were being taught in children's homes; these programs seemed to be aimed more toward creative social and aesthetic behavior, independence, and curiosity.

While intellectual and academic aims were important throughout the late eighteenth and the nineteenth centuries, these aims were less important during the first half of the twentieth century. In this case, pedagogical theories concerned with the inappropriateness of reading instruction for young children, the fixed nature of intelligence, and the importance of social and emotional behavior began to dominate the kindergarten and nursery school movement. The current renewed attention toward academic language and intellectual aims in early childhood programs is related, in part, to new changes in conceptions about children and to pedagogical theories in these areas.

### *Persistent Effects Attributed to Early Education Programs*

The most consistent effects of early education on child development reported seem to be in the general areas of social and moral behavior and in the academic areas concerned with progress in school. According to a number of reports, children who were in pre-first-grade programs learned to be attentive, generally cooperative, punctual, and conforming; in other reports, usually associated with the liberal kindergarten and nursery school movement, the focus was on children's industry, initiative, and cooperation with peers. Across periods, the reports seemed to be consistent in maintaining that programs helped to teach social behavior needed for primary school (attentiveness, cooperation with peers, and punctuality), but they were inconsistent in whether pre-primary programs taught children to be obedient or disobedient to adults, quiet or restless.

Through the first third of the twentieth century, it was reported that children learned appropriate 'American' moral behavior and conduct, to be tidy and clean, and to use healthy habits. It was believed that these 'habits' learned in infant, primary, kindergarten, and day nursery programs would eventually result in a reduction of disease, vice, and crime. Although no evidence was ever given to support the long-term effects, Hall's (1883) and Hill's (1923) claims supported the earlier arguments for short-term benefits. Steinfels

(1973) also reported lower disease rates in day nurseries in the early 1900s.

Finally, claims that pre-primary programs were cost-effective and were related to progress and achievement in school and the prevention of retardation were fairly consistent across the different periods reviewed. The one notable exception to this was at the end of the infant school movement, when detractors claimed that even one hour of school might result in imbecility.

### Relating the Past to the Present: Persistent Aims and Effects

The aims and effects reported during earlier periods are surprisingly similar to those reported today (see page 26). We still claim, for example, that pre-school (for children from low-income families, in particular) is related to achievement and progress in school. Because we now have longitudinal studies, we also claim, with supporting evidence, that children with pre-school education are more likely to graduate from high school and gain employment than those without such an education. Although no current report explicitly maintains that pre-school attendance prevents 'vice', the estimates in savings in welfare payments, etc. that are made in some reports (for example, Berrueta-Clement, *et al.*, 1984) might be used to suggest this effect. Finally, some current reports claim that the most important effect of pre-first-grade programs for young children is to socialize them for the primary grades — to make them quiet, obedient, and attentive (for example, Gracey, 1975); and when some programs do not seem to do this, there is cause for concern. The achievement of appropriate school conduct (obedience and attentiveness vs. restlessness and disobedience) was also of concern in the earlier reports on program effects.

### Consistent Influences and Persistent Issues in the Field of Early Childhood Education and Child Care

Certain factors and assumptions seem to have consistently influenced the way in which aims and attributed effects have been reported, in the past as well as in the present. These factors have been, and continue to be, important for the growth, form, and content of early childhood education and child care programs; they also represent crucial issues in current debates. Based upon the preceding historical

review, the following factors seem to have been consistently important and therefore should be recognized as such in current debates:

1   *Conceptions concerning the significance of early childhood
    education and changing philosophies concerning children's
    nature, abilities, and need for different types of education
    affected and continue to affect curricular aims and attributed
    effects*
        Current American debates about the importance of
    reading for young children, for example, reflect these issues
    in present practice. Increased recognition of the historical
    shifts in opinion about children's capabilities and recognition
    of the historical basis for current curricular aims is critical for
    the field.

2   *Definitions of 'good' science and research affected and con-
    tinue to affect the legitimacy, value, and expression of 'knowl-
    edge' and the perceived importance of different aims and
    effects*
        Many early childhood programs are still evaluated on
    the basis of quantitative IQ and achievement test results,
    whether or not these are the most appropriate indicators of
    program effectiveness. Early educators continue to look to
    psychological theory and research to form appropriate
    theoretical models and to serve as standards for valuable,
    good and important research. The fact that there are varying
    definitions of 'legitimate' education, 'value and effectiveness',
    'knowledge', and 'good scientific research' should be recog-
    nized by those in early education and used to formulate
    broader more flexible, and, at times, more appropriate stan-
    dards for the field.

3   *Social assumptions and beliefs about the educational capabil-
    ities and needs of children from different socio-economic and
    ethnic backgrounds affected and continue to affect the quanti-
    ty, quality, and aims of programs that are available for
    different children*
        More pre-school programs are available for middle-class
    children than for lower-class children; day-care centers, most
    needed by working-class families, continue to be under-
    funded and of relatively low status in the United States;
    many curricular model programs continue to be grounded in
    class- and ethnic-based assumptions about the different
    learning opportunities available in different family environ-

ments. To the extent that assumptions that have guided past developments and, in some cases, present development are incorrect, or serve certain groups at the expense of others, they need to be reexamined and adjusted accordingly.

4  *Social assumptions about whether the family, in particular the mother, could/should provide 'adequate' education or child care for young children has affected and continues to afffect the availability, quality, and status of out-of-home child care in the United States*

    Assumptions that young children should ideally be reared at home by mothers still guide much private and public opinion, funding, and policy development. Again, implicit assumptions underlying a policy that serves some groups, while ignoring others, need to be recognized and reexamined, and efforts to change them need to be made.

5  *The status, funding, and affiliation of people and organizations in early education and child care affected and continue to affect stated aims and reports of effects, aspirations of program leaders, and funding of programs*

    Current debates about whether pre-school/day-care programs for 3–4 year olds should receive public support, perhaps as part of the public school system, as well as debates concerning the need for increased professional status in the field, have many points in common with the debates and movements regarding the kindergarten in the early part of this century. The costs as well as the benefits of increased professional status, as well as possible affiliation with and support from public schools, need to be assessed in light of similar costs and benefits experienced by programs in the past.

## Notes

1  This chapter was made possible, in part, by a grant to the author from the Spencer Foundation, administered through the School of Education, the University of Wisconsin-Madison. The author would also like to acknowledge the research assistance of Nwobiara Kalu.

2  The principal sources for this project are published papers by influential educators and professionals. In addition, secondary sources which focused on similar issues and provided useful insights were also consulted. Primary and secondary source materials were selected when they contained detailed information about the educators' perceptions of aims or

goals for early education and child care for the period and any perceived effects of the programs on children. Reports were used if they appeared to represent a common point of view during the period and if they had been widely cited in the secondary literature in recent reviews of the history of early education and child care (for example, BRAUN and EDWARDS, 1972; DEASEY, 1978; FOWLER, 1983; ROSS, 1976; STEINFELS, 1973; WEBER, 1969). Finally, various yearbooks published by the National Society for the Study of Education (NSSE) that concentrated on early education (kindergarten, nursery school) or child care were used as primary and secondary reference sources.

## References

ADLER, F. 'Free kindergarten and workingman's school', in BARNARD, H. (Ed.). *Kindergarten and Child Culture Papers: The American Journal of Education*. Hartford, CT, 1890.

BANE, M.I., LEIN, L., O'DONNELL, L., STEUVE, C.A. and WELLS, B. 'Child-care arrangements of working parents', *Monthly Labor Review*, 102, 1980, pp. 50–6.

BARNARD, H. (Ed.) *Kindergarten and Child Culture Papers: The American Journal of Education*. Hartford, CT, 1890.

BELSKY, J., and STEINBERG, L.D. 'The effects of day care: A critical review', *Child Development*, 49, 1978, pp. 929–49.

BLOW, S. 'Some aspects of the kindergarten', in BARNARD, H. (Ed.) *Kindergarten and Child Culture Papers: The American Journal of Education*, Hartford, CT, 1890, pp. 605–6.

BRAUN, S., and EDWARDS, E. *History and Theory of Early Childhood Education*. Worthington, OH: C.A. Jones, 1972.

BRYAN, A. 'Report of the child study committee', *Report of the Second Annual Meeting of the International Kindergarten Union*, 1897, pp. 36–42.

BURKE, A. *The Conduct Curriculum*. New York: Teachers' College Press, 1923.

CLARKE-STEWART, A.K. *Day Care*, Cambridge, MA: Harvard University Press, 1982.

CLARKE-STEWART, A., and FEIN, G. 'Early childhood education and child care', in MUSSEN P.H. (Ed.), *Handbook of Child Psychology* (Vol. 2). 4th ed, New York: Wiley, 1983.

COMMITTEE OF NINETEEN, *The Kindergarten*. Boston, MA: Houghton Mifflin, 1913.

DAVIS, M.D. *General Practice in Kindergarten Education in the United States*, Washington, D.C.: National Education Association, 1925.

DARWIN, C. *On the Origin of Species by Means of Natural Selection*, London: John Murray, 1859.

*Marianne N. Bloch*

DEASEY, D. *Education under Six*, London: Croom Helm, 1978.

DEMOS, J. *A Little Commonwealth: Family Life in Plymouth Colony*, New York: Oxford University Press, 1970.

DEWEY, J. 'Froebel's educational principles', *The School and Society*. Chicago: University of Chicago Press, 1900.

FINKELSTEIN, B. 'Reading, writing, and the acquisition of identity in the United States: 1790–1860', in FINKELSTEIN, B. (Ed.). *Regulated Children/Liberated Children*, New York: Psychohistory Press, 1979.

FOREST, I. *Preschool Education: A Historical and Critical Survey*, New York: MacMillan & Co., 1937.

FOWLER, W. *Potentials of Childhood: Volume 1: A Historical View of Early Experience*. Lexington, MA: Lexington Books, 1983.

GARD, W. 'Influence of the kindergarten on achievement in reading', *Educational Research Bulletin of Ohio State University*', 1924, pp. 136–8.

GOODENOUGH, F.L. 'A preliminary report on the effect of nursery school training upon the intelligence test scores of young children', in *The Twenty-Seventh Yearbook of the National Society for the Study of Education. Nature and Nurture: Part I: Their Influence upon Intelligence*, Public School Publishing Co., 1928, pp. 361–69.

GOODYKOUNTZ, B., DAVIS, M. D., and GABBARD, H.F. 'Recent history and present status of education for young children', in HENRY, N.B. (Ed.). *Early Childhood Education; The National Society for the Study of Education: 46th Yearbook*, Chicago: University of Chicago Press, 1947.

GRACEY, H. 'Learning the student role: Kindergarten as academic boot-camp', in STUB, H.R. (Ed.). *The Sociology of Education: A Sourcebook*, Philadelphia, PA: Temple University Press, 1975.

HALL, G.S. 'Aspects of child life and education: The contents of children's minds on entering school', *Princeton Review*, II., 1883, pp. 249–72.

HALL, G.S. 'The pedagogy of the kindergarten', *Educational Problems*, I. New York: D. Appleton, 1911, pp. 11–41.

HARRIS, W. 'The kindergarten in the public schools', in BARNARD, H. (Ed.). *Kindergarten and Child Culture Papers: The American Journal of Education*, Hartford, CT, 1890.

HILDRETH, G. 'The effect of school environment on Stanford Binet Tests of Young Children' in the *Twenty-seventh Yearbook of the National Society for the Study of Education. Nature and Nurture. Part I. Their Influence Upon Intelligence*, Chicago: Public School Publishing Company, 1928, pp. 354–9.

HILL, P.S. Second Report. Committee of Nineteen. *The Kindergarten*, Boston: Houghton Mifflin, 1913.

HILL, P.S. 'Introduction', in BURKE, A. *The Conduct Curriculum*, New York: Teachers' College Press, 1923.

HILL, P.S. *The Practical Value of Early Childhood Education*, Washington, DC.: Bulletin of the Association of Childhood Education, 1934.

JERSILD, A.T. and FITE, M.D. 'The influence of nursery school experience on children's social adjustments'. *Child Development Monographs*, 25, New York: Teachers' College, Columbia University, 1939.

KAESTLE, C.F. *Pillars of the Republic*, New York: Hill and Wang, 1983.

KAESTLE, C. and VINOVSKIS, M. 'From apron strings to ABCs: school entry in nineteenth-century Massachusetts', in KAESTLE, C. and VINOVSKIS, M. *Educational and Social Change in Nineteenth Century Massachusetts*. Cambridge, MA: Cambridge University Press, 1980.

LAZAR, I., DARLINGTON, R., MURRAY, H., ROYCE, J., and SNIPPER, A. 'Lasting effects of early education', *Monograph of the Society for Research in Child Development*. Serial No. 194. Vol. 47 (1–2), 1982.

LAZERSON, M. 'Urban reform and the schools: Kindergartens in Massachusetts, 1870–1915', in KATZ, M. *Education in American History*, New York: Praeger Press, 1973.

MACLATCHEY, J.H. 'Attendance at kindergarten and progress in the primary grades', *Bureau of Educational Research Monographs*, Ohio State University, OH, No. 8, 1928.

MAY and VINOVSKIS, M. 'A ray of millennial light: Early education and social reform in the infant school movement in Massachusetts, 1826–1840', in HAREVEN, T. (Ed.). *Family and Kin in American Urban Communities, 1700–1940*, New York: Watts, 1977.

NATIONAL SOCIETY FOR THE STUDY OF EDUCATION. *The Kindergarten and its Relation to Elementary Education: Sixth Yearbook*, Bloomington, IL: Public School Publishing Society, 1907.

PEABODY. 'The necessity of kindergarten culture', in BARNARD, H. (Ed.). *Kindergarten and Culture Papers: The American Journal of Education*, Hartford, CT, 1890.

PETERS, W.J. 'The progress of kindergarten pupils in the elementary grades', *Journal of Educational Research*, 7, 1923, pp. 117–26.

RISSER, F. and ELDER, H.E. 'The relation between kindergarten training and success in the elementary school'. *Elementary School Journal*, 28, 1927, pp. 286–9.

ROSS, C.J. 'Early skirmishes with poverty: The historical roots of Head Start', in ZIGLER, E. and VALENTINE, J. (Eds) *Project Head Start*, New York: Free Press, 1979.

ROSS, E.D. *The Kindergarten Crusade*, 1976.

ROTHMAN, S.M. *Women's Proper Place: A History of Changing Ideals and Practices, 1870 to the Present*, N.Y.: Basic Books, 1980.

SCHLOSSMAN, S. 'Philanthropy and the gospel of child development', *History of Education Quarterly*, Fall, 1981, pp. 275–99.

SCHWEINHART, L. and WEIKART, D. *Changed Lives*, Ypsilanti, MI: High Scope Press, 1984.

SEARS, R.R. 'Your ancients revisited: A history of child development', in

HETHERINGTON, E.M. (Ed.) *Review of Child Development Research*, Volume 5, 1975, pp. 1–73.

SPODEK, B. 'The kindergarten: A retrospective and contemporary view', in KATZ, L. (Ed.) *Current Topics in Early Education*, Vol. III. New York: Ablex, 1980.

STEINFELS, M.O. *Who is Minding the Children*, New York: Simon and Schuster, 1973.

TAKANISHI, R. 'Federal involvement in early education (1933–1973): The need for historical perspectives'. in KATZ, L. (Ed.). *Current Topics in Early Education*, Volume 1, New York: Ablex, 1979.

THORNDIKE, E.L. 'Notes on psychology for kindergarters', *Teachers' College Record*, IX, 1903, pp. 45–76.

THORNDIKE, E.L. *The Psychology of Learning*, II. New York: Columbia University Press, 1913.

*Time*. 'Pricklies' vs. 'Gooeys', 9 November, 1981, p. 107.

VANDEWALKER, N.C. *The Kindergarten*, New York: The MacMillan Co., 1908.

WEBER, E. *The Kindergarten*, New York: Teachers' College Press, 1969.

WELLMAN, B.L. 'The effect of preschool attendance upon the IQ, *Journal of Experimental Education*, 1, 1933, pp. 48–69.

ZIGLER, E., and GORDON, E.W. *Daycare: Scientific and Social Policy Issues*, Boston, MA: Auburn House, 1982.

ZIGLER, E. and VALENTINE, J. *Project Head Start*, New York: Free Press, 1979.

## 3 Art Education as Social Production: Culture, Society, and Politics in the Formation of Curriculum

*Kerry Freedman*

### Abstract

Art education emerged in relation to a number of cultural influences. The influences framed school art in terms of a least four strands of purpose. The first strand is the use of art education for developing skills for a labor market. The second strand views the purpose of public access to art as cultural education and a leisure time activity for the middle class. The third strand concerns art as an illustration of moral character and aesthetic taste for the social person. The fourth strand conceives of art has healthful and creative self-expression. The strands have historically interacted and their conflicts have involved deeper issues of an American society involving conceptions of work and play, democracy and individuality, and what constitutes scientific and social reality.

Art emerged in American public schools in relation to a number of cultural influences. The influences included the social effects of industry, middle class life and thought, and social science in the decades near the turn of the century. Art education grew out of tensions between a desire for practical versus intellectual returns from public schooling, and the support or denial of a class-bound social system.

It is within the context of the social purposes of art education that we may understand the development of the school subject. Art was to meet the perceived needs of social groups who defined the functions and practices of schooling. The definitions gave direction to a shift in urban education from a mechanism for industrialist control of laborers to a vehicle through which the middle class supported its own values and beliefs.

The purposes of art in schooling may be considered strands that historically interweave; in different contexts, at different times, different priorities have emerged. The present discussion will consider four strands in art education in relation to American life and the functions of public schooling. The first strand is the use of art education for developing skills for a labor market. The second strand involves a conception of public access to art as cultural education and a leisure time activity for the middle class. The third strand concerns art as an illustration of moral character and aesthetic taste for the social person. The fourth strand conceives of art has healthful and creative self-expression. While the strands continually interweave and impinge up on each other, their conflicts involve deeper issues of American society: conceptions of work and play, democracy and individuality, and what constitutes scientific and social reality.

## Skills for the Labor Market

Art became a state requirement in American public schools for industrial purposes. It began as a mandate for industrial drawing passed by the Massachusetts government in 1870. The law resulted from pressure by Boston industrialists for public education in industrial design. The legislative action was initiated by a petition signed by a number of influential businessmen, primarily involved in the newly developing textile trade.

The petition stated:

> Our manufacturers ... compete under disadvantages with the manufacturers of Europe ... At this time, almost all the best draughtsmen in our shops are men thus trained abroad ... In England, within the past ten years, very large additions have been made to the provisions, which were before very generous, for free public instruction of work men in drawing ... boys and girls, by the time they are 16 years of age, acquire great proficiency in mechanical drawing and in other

arts of design ... men and women who have been long
engaged in the processes of manufacture, learn readily and
with pleasure, enough of the arts of design to assist them
materially in their work. (*Thirty-fourth Annual Report of the
Board of Education*, 1871, pp. 163–4.)

The industrialists requested that drawing be required of all urban
public school children, largely from immigrant and working class
families, as well as being the subject of night classes for adults and
teacher education.[1]

Although drawing education had been carried on in American
public schools for over fifty years, there was a belief that the
particular type of program needed by industry demanded metho-
dological changes. Drawing had been handled by teachers who
had little or no experience or training, was taught on an irregular
schedule, and varied in procedure, philosophy and quality. However,
there were a number of drawing teachers, locally and nationally,
who could have been asked to coordinate the Massachusetts program. But, American art educators were not sought.

Massachusetts officials looked to England when they put the
new law into practice. Boston's nineteenth century controlling classes
had a reverence for English values and practices; English culture and
fashion were in great demand in urban America. More fundamentally, England had little competition in areas of industrial production.
The political and economic power that English production brought
was sought by American industrialists.

The design education program at South Kensington in London
was considered particularly successful by Massachusetts industrialists. Students graduated from South Kensington with skills
in the design of textiles and other trade manufacturing. Traditional
design patterns were taught in a procedurally defined manner that
was to train students efficiently. Designers were to reconstruct
popular forms and decorations that could be effectively applied to
mass produced objects. Design, which had once been integral to
production by a craftsperson, was taught in school independently of
production. The student learned that the designer's task was not one
related to the various parts of production on the assembly line.

Walter Smith, an English art teacher and headmaster who had
been trained at South Kensington, was brought to the United States
to oversee school drawing program development and teacher education in Massachusetts. Smith's knowledge of the English system of
industrial design and his administrative capabilities fit the "needs" of

the school system. Smith had the management skills and sympathies necessary for the position which was politically tied to the aims of industry. The Massachusetts program soon became a model for a number of developing industrial states.

Industrial design education was to support the labor market in at least two ways. The first was through management. The design instruction followed a model of labor drawn from a managerial factory system. Industrial management broke the day of the worker into periods of time that had particular activities associated with them. Certain tasks were done at certain times and other periods were set aside for non-work activities. Students were to learn that their time and production were managed in school in ways similar to that of adult work in industrial society: time in school was relegated to particular subjects and tasks. In a similar way the procedures for drawing were timed and done step-by-step. Drawing in school was to train the eye, the hand, and the mind (making the parts of the body as separate as the parts of drawing) for the rigors of industrial work.

A second support of industry was the preparation of students for work. There was a concentration on training students in particular manual skills. Isolated skills were taught that were conceptualized and organized in ways to suit occupations defined by the market place. Students were also systematically deskilled. The priorities of design education only selectively allowed for the possibilities of competence and ingenuity. The training prepared students to accept what was considered productive by industrial standards.

Vocational skill training in design became integral to the emergence of art education. Public school drawing was based on the precise copying of illustrations drawn by adults. Children were taught the parts of shapes first. Drawings of individual shapes, and then objects, followed. The criteria for evaluation, that is, the accuracy of the copy, was measured with a ruler. Initially, children did outlines. Sometimes the teacher would copy a leaf outline, for example, in front of the class from a textbook, while the students followed her as she drew. Eventually drawings of great sculptures were studied so that children could copy form and shading. Finally, older children were allowed to do a whole composition of a pastoral scene. The use of color was not often allowed until the last year due to a belief that color would feed a student's desire for fanciful experimentation.

By the turn of the century, the notion that all public school children should be prepared for the work force through art diminished as manual training schools emerged. Schools specifically for manual training, in art and design media, became popular during the strong promotion of vocational education between 1905 and 1915 (Krug, 1969). The manual training schools were largely public and attended by the labor class in urban areas (Bailey, 1909). It was believed that manual training could aid in assimilating urban immigrants through the use of crafts materials thought to be familiar to them, such as clay, wood and metal. The materials, once part of rural culture, had become the media of industrial production.

Manual training became an issue of shifting class differentiation after the turn of the century. Although students gained proficiency in the technical skills of particular jobs, a concern developed about the exclusion of aesthetic issues in manual training, and a lack of technical training for the middle class immersed in a developing aesthetic awareness. In the journal *Handicraft*, Ross (1903), stated,

> . . . we have all the fine impulses where there are no abilities to follow them, and all the ability where there are no fine impulses . . . the people of education, of judgment, and the people who have merely technical training and ability form two distinct classes . . . and these classes have almost nothing in common, have, indeed, very little to do with one another. (p. 232)

The emphasis on the artistic possibilities of manual training had a dual social purpose. In a 1909 edition of *Craftsman*, Sercomb indicated that art was to relieve class tensions through enhancement of the vocational preparation of industrial laborers and aid in the understanding of manual activities for the middle class. Manual training in arts and crafts media was to acquaint well-to-do boys with activities done with the hands.

## The Quest of Culture and Leisure Time

Near the turn of the century, the purposes of public art education changed in a number of ways in relation to new interests defined by the middle class. As well as easing tensions between the middle and lower classes, public school art was to neutralize differences between the middle and upper classes. The quest for middle class enrichment was seen in the movement toward a public liberal education. Previously, the liberal education of the private schools and colleges had been for a privileged few. Middle class parents wanted public preparation for their children who would then be sent to institutions of higher learning.

Kerry Freedman

### The Aquisition of Culture

A vision of the good life developed as part of middle class consciousness in nineteenth-century America. Middle class life became more secularized. To live well became not so much for the sake of redemption in a life hereafter. Rather, worldly knowledge and the appreciation of natural and human creations became the symbols of a quality life.

Good living was to involve the acquisition of culture. Nineteenth-century America 'contained a particular idea of culture as a privileged domain of refinement, aesthetic sensibility, and higher learning' (Trachtenberg, 1982, p. 143). A new middle class hoped to achieve reputations as people of culture through the study and collection of art objects. Culture represented the financial and social success of higher living, and higher living was an indication of progress (Krug, 1969). Public education had the responsibility of preparing the laborer and the housewife for social life in industrial society by stressing the aquisition and appreciation of a higher standard of living (Kingsley, 1914). The rich were not only to be respected for their wealth, they were also the caretakers of culture and higher learning.

As the desire for the transmission of high culture emerged, there developed a belief that great works of art should be easily accessible and appreciated by all. The foundations of the public institutions of culture were laid in pursuit of this goal. In a mere decade, beginning in 1870, the Metropolitan Museum of Art in New York, the Boston Museum of Fine Arts, the Philadelphia Museum of Art, and the Art Institute of Chicago were established. Although the museums were public institutions, the organization and administration of the museums were handled by the wealthy.

A shift in the belief that fine art was a concern of the upper class was illustrated by the introduction of art appreciation in public schools. Studies in art appreciation had previously been held at the college level, initiated in 1874 at Harvard. The original courses were to aid wealthy young men with their choices of art investments. When art appreciation became part of public schooling, it was to support the acculturation of the middle class. Fine art could not be presented in public school as a subject for the elite.

By the 1920s, educational reformers promoting scientific programs were to take issue with the idea that school should include cultural education. According to the reformers, schooling was to include only those subject areas which would ultimately result in efficient social functioning. Snedden (1927) saw culture as 'intellectuality, aesthetic superiority, refinement, and non-practicality . . . there appear to be no conscious and concrete demands for cultural education' (pp. 240–241). It was Snedden's belief that workers were to 'seek out' (p. 247) culture in their free time.

### Art as a Leisure Time Activity

The emergence of art as an independent subject in American education did not originate in public schools. It began as private instruction. One early example of art training for children was the needlework classes in private girls' schools (Winkelman, 1985). Young ladies, with well-to-do parents, were given instruction in designing and producing decorative flourishes with the needle. The courses concentrated on ornate surface decoration unrelated to the function of the object. Instruction in needlework was to prepare girls for the practical duties of womanhood. Part of those duties was to make the home pleasant and attractive. Decorative needlework beautified the well-to-do home.

Private instruction represented art as not tied to work duties. Although needlework design and production were considered pleasurable and an indication of a girl's quality, they were unnecessary activities suited for ladies who had time on their hands. The courses in needlework supported attitudes concerning the role of a lady and provided parents with an identification of their status.

Art moved toward democratization as the concept of leisure changed after the turn of the century. The preparation of students for activities not associated with labor emerged in public school art. With the development of middle class consciousness, and due to technical changes such as a shortened work day, came the conception of time away from work as leisure time. American individualism offered the possibility that anyone, who would work hard and with ingenuity, had hope of financial security. After putting in a day of restricted work activity, an individual was alotted time for pleasure. Leisure time was to be a release from the tensions of work.

The productive use of leisure time became a social concern. The Kingsley Report of 1918 specified that school was responsible for preparing the individual for meritous leisure. In *The Shaping of the American High School*, Krug (1969) quoted the report of the Commission on the Reorganization of Secondary Education (the Kingsley Report) in stating: 'Leisure, "if worthily used," would enable the individual to "recreate his powers and enlarge and enrich life, thereby making him better able to meet his responsibilities". Contrawise, "unworthy" use of leisure would impair health, disrupt home life, lessen vocational efficiency, and destroy civic mindedness' (pp. 387–8).

The concern about leisure time reflected shifting interests in schooling in at least three ways. In one way, leisure time was for the achievement of high culture which, as discussed, had become a vital interest of the middle class. Art as leisure was to prepare students with an appreciation of what should be valued as culture.

Second, art had a particular place in the new conception of fragmented time and self. The efficient use of time became a social priority. It was argued that science was replacing art in the vital issues of life, but that art could be reserved for recreation (Snedden, 1917). As an adult, the socially efficient citizen would budget time for culture (Krug, 1969). Instruction in art was to aid cultural scheduling.

Third, there was a concern for a working class with free time on its hands. It was believed that the development of an appreciation for beauty would 'take the place of less wholesome pleasures' (Course of Study for the Elementary Schools of Oregon, 1911, p. 50, from Kern, 1985). The suggestion was that art would make productive use of otherwise unproductive free time.

## Molding the Good Citizen

The moral education of children was taken over by a secularized mass schooling during the industrial revolution. American urban public schools were conceived of as having a responsibility for the moral development of immigrant children which were to adopt the new values of industrial labor (Handlin, 1974). In the late eighteenth century, immigrants, largely from rural Europe, settled in American cities. The development of the new urban population of industrial laborers saw changing social relations. The school became responsible for conveying conventions of civility previously passed on through family, community, and religion. The particular values supported in public schools were carefully chosen, not to support learning as we currently define it, but rather to prepare the child for moral citizenship and industriousness.

*Picture Study: Art as an Illustration of Morality*

Picture study programs emerged during the 1890s and lasted through the 1920s to support the didactic objectives of public schooling. The art education was to raise the morality of public school students by illustrating good and moral character. Picture study focused up on the depiction of moral activities or stories in artists' work.

There was an explicit religious flavor to the art education. Religious pictures were shown as cannons of morality and beauty. In the North Dakota state curriculum of 1927, for example, art was to instill a 'love of truth and beauty developed through study of God's handiwork in nature and achievements of men', (p. 14, from Kern, 1985).

The particular conception of moral values in school art was shaped by the assumed responsibility of the individual. Children of American workers were schooled in the moral trappings of polite society, for which they had a personal obligation to strive. Art illustrated lofty values such as loyalty, thrift, and family responsibility. The values were considered important for social behavior in home and work life. The good citizen and laborer would learn the virtues of obedience, punctuality, and efficiency through picture study.

Picture study was made possible through the development of new technologies that reproduced pictures cheaply and in color. The printing processes were developed largely to fulfill advertising needs and then used to produce inexpensive reproductions for people who could not afford original art. The pictures used in school were often made for commercial purposes and were overly sentimental, such as, pictures of a 'perfect' child with his mother or wild animals tamed by human influence.

There was debate as to whether the low quality of the reproductions would somehow diminish the perception of a good original, or whether even poor reproductions could carry the essence of the art, to students (Stankiewicz, 1985). The pictures continued to be shown in school because the quality of the picture was not as important as its moral message. Further, most art teachers had never seen the original works of art that were reproduced, so they were unaware of how different the copies were from the original.

*Kerry Freedman*

## *Good Taste and A Community Art Education*

To some extent, an objective of art in the public schools was, from the beginning, to train the masses in a particular notion of good taste. In 1879, Walter Smith wrote, '. . . good taste in design, which sound instruction in drawing imparts to the creators of industrial products, is of general interest and pecuniary value in manufactures . . .' (from Wygant, 1983, p. 226). Thirty years later, the first sentence of the initial report on Instruction in The Fine and Manual Arts in the United States made to the National Bureau of Education stated: 'Art instruction aims to raise the standard of taste' (Bailey, 1909, p. 7). It was assumed that the taste of American public school children was bad and that education would improve the quality of art production and taste in consumption.

Change in art education was tied to shifts in American conceptions of good taste. The presentation of aesthetic values in school changed in relation to adult tastes. Taste, in turn, reflected various positions in society, as from an indicator of popular culture, to a form of elitism. Further, taste represented numerous implications in the social life of the individual. How far and how fast the future adult would go not only relied on competency and morality, but on social appearances as well.

Near the turn of the century, Social Darwinism was incorporated into discussions of changing aesthetic values. Fine quality art was judged to be so 'naturally'. In 1903, Walker wrote of the 'natural selection to a high standard of excellence and to the choice of fine art' (p. 30). He was concerned about the lack of taste of his contemporaries due to new reproduction technologies and 'the consequent supply along the lines of least resistance, that is with the rapid, inferior, cheap work of many, rather than the comparatively occasional masterpieces of the few' (p. 31). Art became commodified as there was a concentration on the mass produced object rather than on the unique creation of the artist.

The training of students in the visual elements of taste and prestige focused on the study of masterpieces near the turn of the century, but was illustrated in art curriculum by a concentration on furniture arrangement, clothing, and landscaping by the 1930s (see for example, Kern, 1985). During the 1930s, an urban elite notion of art was rejected in favor of a social realism concerned with rural community and mass popular culture. For example, much of the art funded by the Federal Art Project portrayed the life and work of the laborer.

In Owatonna, Minnesota, education in good taste took the form of a project funded by the Carnegie Foundation that sought community involvement. The project began in 1933 and was initiated by the Dean of the College of Education at the University of Minnesota, Melvin Haggerty. Haggerty (n.d.) conceived of the project as a unification of school and community efforts to upgrade the aesthetic sensibilities of Owatonna citizens and to enhance the local environment. The project involved various opportunities for study and production. Funding paid for curriculum development, for guest speakers to come into the community, and for adult night classes that were free to the public.

Owatonna became a primary example of a philosophy of art in everyday life that emerged in the 1930s. During the depression, art education became centered on the beautification of the working family's surroundings. There was a use of inexpensive materials to make the home more aesthetically pleasing at a time of great economic hardship. The Owatonna elementary school art curriculum included instruction in making decorative objects for the home, such as, a cleanser can cover and paper holiday ornaments.

Part of Owatonna's educational horizon was the industry of the community. Children in school were to develop an appreciation for, and technical skills in commercial art and industrial design. Art lessons were based on consumer and industrial interests such as making posters that would 'create a desire for a product' (Owatonna Art Education Project, *Second Annual Report*, 1934, n.p.). *The Fourth Annual Report* of the Project (1937) included a high school unit involving commercial architecture which taught students of the 'poor conditions of commercial design' in America, that the 'possibility of renting store and office space makes it profitable to build structures of considerable height and size in restricted commercial areas', and· that important technological advances could be seen in that 'intensifed research has developed and elaborated methods of display, advertising and publicity' (pp. 405–6). There were also studies of local landscaping, gardening and interior design.

Although the original premise of the project was to focus on the art interests of a community, and for the art teachers involved with the project to be 'guides, rather than masters' (*Owatonna Journal Chronical*, 1933), conflicting messages came from the experts. A particular notion of good taste was embedded in the art curriculum and in the adult classes and lectures. For example, the objectives for a lesson on making a decorative map of Owatonna were to 'give experience in selecting good architectural design ... and to increase appreciation of architecture' (Owatonna Art Education Project, *Second Annual Report*, 1934, n.p.). The lesson included copying simplistic, stereotyped patterns of tree shapes. Continual references were made to efficient, well-balanced, inexcessive design in everything from gardening to the free expression of young children.

Art education as learning good taste had at least three messages. Two of the messages were that the conception of taste presented in school was class-bound and that experts defined and managed good taste. A third message was that the form of good taste had become a commodity.

To this point, three themes have been discussed. The themes have conceived art education as labor skill training, as culture and a leisure time activity, and as an aid in shaping the moral and tasteful citizen. The fourth, and final, theme is the presentation of art in school as a necessary form of self-expression.

## The Healthy Individual and the Scientific Study of the Child

By the end of the nineteenth century, a struggle had developed between a believed need for individual autonomy and a perceived threat of anonymity due to mechanistic production (see, for example, Lears, 1981). A sense of mass industrial conformity and political consensus confronted, and often conflicted with, a belief in American rugged individualism which depended on a supporting interest in independent democratic values. The confrontation was seen, in part, in the emergence of new middle class notions of career, professionalism, and a social science (Bledstein, 1976).

Public schooling reflected the changing consciousness, in part, through a focus on the individual. Individualism responded to a belief about life advancement defined by the middle class. The concerns were for the perceived rights, needs, and powers of the individual. The rights of the individual included public schooling to the fullest capacity of each student. The needs of the individual involved free self-expression. The powers of the individual were to include the functional use of education and innate abilities for a career.

After the turn of the century, the conception of the individual became an organizing principle for art education. Individuality was to be realized in the form of objects. Technical skill plus self-expression equaled art. The student had a responsibility to learn selected aspects of art and to perform them in the decided manners.

A child was believed to contain unique qualities when the performance was considered an indication of talent.

## The Idea of Art Talent in School Children

The belief that children could freely produce artifacts of aesthetic value emerged near the turn of the century. School was to develop talent in the child. Although some public documents held that public art education was to 'consider the needs of the masses rather than the advancement of the talented few' (Course of Study for the Elementary Schools of Pennsylvania, 1918, p. 119, from Kern, 1985), there was also a call for special consideration of the gifted. The goal was 'to discover and develop exceptional talent, so that the gifted students may develop to their best potential' (Idaho State Course of Study, 1915, p. 17, from Kern, 1985).

The movement of public school curriculum toward a discovering and nurturing of art talent developed in relation to middle class values. From the early decades of this century, the notion of giftedness in schooling sought to support that which was valued by the middle class. The public school was to enable children to develop their unique identity through the development of their latent abilities. The development of art talent was for personal pleasure, and economic and social status.

The conception of talent in art education had particular social definitions. American entrepreneurial thought supported the notion of genius and individual achievement. However, talent in art was not discussed as a social construction tied to the aesthetic taste of the time. Talent was viewed as inherent in the individual and without social context. It was believed that those people who created objects of beauty and culture had innate capabilities that were beyond normative definitions. Success in developing technical expertise in art or an awareness of art through family access to high culture were conceived of something special in the child.

An appreciation of the work of the individual was also seen in the study of pictures in school. The artist was conceived as personally struggling to produce an object of greatness. The artist created a masterpiece through a combination of talent and diligence.

Kerry Freedman

## The Science of Artistic Development

Conceptions of the individual were closely related to the emergence of social science. Social science became a way of viewing dynamic qualities of social life as stable and concrete. As will be discussed, changes in the individual were to be understood in terms of discrete and predictable properties. The predictability became a prescription for action in social life.

One of the early research programs in social science to have an impact on art education was the child study movement. Through the work of G. Stanley Hall and others, child study began to affect art education near the turn of the century and has continued to be influential. The 'help from psychology and psychiatry on the problems of the primary and kindergarten years' that child study provided was considered vital to art education (Wiecking, 1928, p. 261).

Child study required the adoption of 'the scientific mood' (Drummond, 1907, p. 9). The scientific mood included conceptions of psychology and biology which reflected the influence of a Darwinian conception of evolution. In adopting the scientific mood, 'it matters not what branch of biology is chosen for study ... the greatest thing is that the student learn to see things for himself; to learn to make sure what he really sees and what he does not see' (p. 15). What became important was the crystallization of possibilities into facts.

A consequence of child study was the scientific analysis of child art. Much of the child study research was based on samples of children's drawings which were collected and interpreted as data. From those studies and from later research, psychologists and art educators constructed theories of artistic development.

Child study understood children in terms of psychological constructs of development. There was an assumption that children grew universally in relation to a normative progression. The drawings of children were decontextualized to be interpreted as illustrating stages of growth not related to sociohistorical location (see, for example, Lowenfeld, 1947; Schaefer-Simmern, 1948). Contained within the framework of artistic development stage theories was the assumption that child art unfolds naturally.

Child study research in artistic development was to change methods of teaching (see, for example, Drummond, 1907). Interpretations of the developmental stages were to be the foundations of art curricula. Developmentally based arguments were raised against technical, segmented drill. Art education was to allow children to 'begin with the human form, animals and other interesting things' (Drummond, 1907, p. 280) that exploited children's 'natural' interests and desire to draw. Teachers facilitated art by providing materials 'and by showing them how to improve their work' (p. 280) which still largely meant representation based on adult standards.

## Creative Self-Expression and Therapy

The idea that children could make expressive art, and the notion of expression itself did not become an issue in public art education until after the turn of the century. Until that time, expression in art referred the potency of a work of art in representing a particular aspect of the world (Wygant, 1983). The 'projection of the self' (p. 134) was not yet within the realm of artistic expression.

In the decades following the turn of the century, school art was to build the self-esteem of the child. 'We have begun to realize that handwork is valuable not only for its product in things made, but also for the effect upon the maker' (Dobbs, 1917, p. 2). Self-esteem became tied to the notion that school art was therapeutic; art was to make children develop a sense of self-worth. It became important for school to provide the individual with opportunities for artistic success.

> From any point of view it seems but a statement of a self-evident truth to assume that the school should employ such a variety of mediums of expression that each pupil could do at least one of them with fair success ... (p. 7).

By the 1920s, success became tied to conceptions of the creative process. The quality of the artistic experience, rather than the quality of the child's art product, was supposed to become the primary focus. Evaluation of the creative process was determined by what was believed to be the free expression of the child.

However, expression was to be indicated by presence of ideal formal and representational characteristics of the product. During the 1920s and 1930s, expression in child art could be viewed as a map or an imagined pastoral landscape. For example, a child could 'build up a ... Greek Landscape ... imaginatively and artistically. He will easily then eliminate non-essentials because he has no object present with which to compare, whereas if he tries to paint the Brooklyn Bridge he may be dashed by his inability to have the cables absolutely right' (Steele, 1939, p. 53).

An influential philosophy of expressive child art was that of Franz Cizek, an Austrian art teacher. Cizek's influence was brought to the United States through traveling exhibitions of his students' work. The exhibitions began in 1919 and continued through the 1920s.

Cizek's believed that art education should involve as little instruction as possible (Viola, 1936). He proclaimed that children should be free of adult imposition. Adult influence would inhibit a child's natural ability and desire to be expressive.

Although Cizek professed a belief in uninhibited expression as art education, his methods were not as free as he claimed (Duncum, 1982). He taught in an explicitly demanding, even domineering, manner. Cizek did not allow adult art to be present in his classroom for fear that the children would be influenced. However, the students invoked familiar cultural images in their work. The art of Cizek's students had a particular stylized look that closely resembled the adult popular aesthetic in Austria at the time.

Cizek's methods were transformed when they became immersed in American Progressive Education in the 1920s. During the decade before the 1920s, an influx of contemporary European works of art and publicity about a new order in avant-garde imagery was seen in the United States. Expression in art took on a new meaning that included highly abstracted forms of representation. The art community was no longer to define art solely in terms of skills in representation. 'By 1920, alert art teachers were aware that nothing short of an artistic revolution had occured in Europe, and they could see its growing influence on American artists' (Chapman, 1978, p. 11). The bold use of form, color and painterly brushwork of twentieth-century Western European painters influenced art in school.

The social function of school art toward creativity and self-expression became a central concern of the Progressive Education movement. Artistic activities were to allow children to express themselves freely and children's natural expression would result in aesthetic objects. Like Cizek's discourse, the language of Progressive Education stated that children were to be free of adult inhibition, in order to achieve the results of natural expression. The book *Creative Expression* (Hartman and Schumaker, 1939), written for the Progressive Education Association, stated:

> With very young children practically all the teacher has to do is to give them art materials and plenty of time to paint. They are fearless with color. They need no technique. They have much to express pictorially and, above all, they have perfect unself-consciousness, since no adult standards have as yet interfered with their ideas. (Steele, 1939, p. 51)

The same book began with a chapter titled 'The Creative Spirit and its Significance for Education' The author stated:

> That is the title suggested by the editor. My own preference was 'All God's Chillun Got Wings' until I remembered that all God's chillun are not permitted to use them . . . the wings of God's children are gradually and painlessly removed. (Mearns, 1939, p. 13)

Victor Lowenfeld, who became perhaps the most influential art educator in America, supported self-expression in art education. Lowenfeld came to the United States in 1938, escaping from the German invasion of Austria. He was 35 years old and already a prominent educator. In the United States, Lowenfeld taught at the Pennsylvania State University and developed the first research doctoral program in art education in the country. Through the university program, as well as numerous publications and presentations, Lowenfeld defined the theoretical foundations for much of the research still current in art education.

Lowenfeld was greatly influenced by his European child study training and his colleagues in art and science. A number of respected researchers and teachers, including Cizck, have been credited for the foundations of his work (Michael and Morris, 1985). Among the influences were psychologists James Sully, one of the first scientists to study child art (publishing possibly the earliest book on the subject in 1898) and Karl Buhler, who introduced experimental method to child study. Other influences included the work of George Luquet, who studied the differences in styles of child art done in school, and that done spontaneously.

Lowenfeld established a particular psychological framework for teaching and research in art education that more completely crystallized the conception of art as what was natural and necessary in children. Child study directed his interpretation of the imagery of children as a stage model of artistic development. Lowenfeld viewed the mission of art education as meeting particular needs of children. He stated:

(Children's) needs must be discovered from the very beginning. Without imposing upon our children adult standards,
we should be able to promote their own efforts, their own
potential abilities that are slumbering in them (Brittain, n.d.,
pp. 21–2).

Lowenfeld's conceptualization assumed that art would be valuable in
awaken something dormant in the child. The value was in the positive
feeling the child would have through the form of production termed
creative. Art education was to function as a release from the pressures
of contemporary society and the necessary impositions of schooling.
Self-expression through the artistic process was to be included in
school to develop healthy individuals in a psychotherapeutic sense.

## Conclusions

The strands of school art have developed in relation to the purposes
of various public interests. The argument has been made that art
emerged in urban public schools of this country largely to promote
lower class labor to satisfy industrialists' needs. The interests of art
education shifted as it became a vehicle through which the middle
class supported its values and beliefs.

Social goals conceived of as natural for all who came to school.
A fundamental issue in the development of art education was the
transition from the aquisition of cultural skills and appreciation as
ways of elevating one's social status to a conception of personal
growth and healthy development of the productive individual.

The interiorization of the social priorities were directed by
developments in social science and the notion of individual. Moral
education through art was transformed into moral development
considered independent of schooling. Moral training in school was
replaced by an emphasis on a growing autonomy of the individual.
The individual became personally responsible for her or his beliefs
and activities. The possibilities and responsibilities of child art
in school were defined by social science. Psychology modified
traditional conceptions of moral schooling by treating values as if
they were objective realities.

With the conception of socially disconnected qualities of the
individual, the child became the 'owner' of talent and expression. Not
all children had talent, but it was conceived that all had the potential

for expression. Concern was raised if the child did not indicate through production of an object, that she was expressing herself. The child was responsible for expressing values and beliefs.

These conceptions responded to ideologies emerging in larger society. What were considered 'natural', uninhibited qualities and rights possessed by the individual, became purposes of school art.

Art education involved a number of conflicts related to the notion of scientific schooling. There was an inherent contradiction in social science applied to art education; the science appeared to be neutral and yet addressed questions that were value-laden. The struggle was not only in relation to the content of curriculum, but also to questions of efficiency in learning. At the same time that art educators continued to perceive a therapeutic purpose to instruction, curriculum became more systematic. Part of the struggle emerged as art educators looked more to the art community for resolutions of curriculum issues. The art community did not often seek efficiency.

The history of school art may aid in the understanding of contemporary developments in art education. The trends of history are the foundations on which the present is built. Aspects of the early strands of school art have resurfaced in more recent program and curriculum discussions.

Art curriculum has continued to be defined as something naturally ordered in relation to the development of the child and conceived of as information ordered in a rational way. Theories of artistic development placed the drawing behaviors of children in a rational framework. The rational structuring of often non-rational behavior for non-rational ends, such as the free expression of children, has been a continual conflict in contemporary art education. Art curricula have commonly been framed in terms of isolated media, subject matters, or what have been conceived of as objective art elements, such as line, shape, and color.

The emergence of the scientific in public art schooling has resulted in a number of contemporary developments. Two further examples must suffice. First, during the 1960s, professionals in the arts disciplines were asked to define the art concepts that should be included in public school art education (Chapman, 1978). A movement toward the professional art community as a resource for curriculum design occurred during the decade before.[2] Seeking curriculum answers from the content area professional community had a dual quality. The involvement of artists was to include the social life of the non-scientific subject area, but the formulation of the request implied a reductionist research method and a reverence for professional knowledge that has been closely tied to the development of social science (Bledstein, 1976).

Second, the first national examinations to assess art knowledge and skills were given in the 1970s. The examinations were based on stringently defined concepts and values, such as whether or not an aritst had the right to experiment in a particular way and whether or not a particular composition was more creative than another, and were in a standarized testing format. The success or failure of the students at a given location were to indicate changes needed in curriculum.

Although the history of American art education has been relatively brief, it has involved transitions relating to some complex issues. Early public school art curriculum content and methodology were selected in relation to particular social priorities. The more contemporary shifts in art education have been no less culturally located.

## Notes

1 The students most affected by the Massachusetts Drawing Act were public school children and working class adults. The public schools in Boston were to educate lower class, immigrant children. Only about one in five children born in Boston between 1863 and 1865 was not a child of immigrant parents (see, for example, HANDLIN, 1974).
2 The 1950s included the popularization of abstract expressionism, the first international avant-garde art movement to develop in the United States. Since that time, American rather than European culture has been in vogue.

## References

BAILEY, H.T. *Instruction in the Fine and Manual Arts in the United States*, U.S. Bureau of Education, Bulletin No. 6, Washington, D.C.: 1909.
BLEDSTEIN, B.J. *The Cultures of Professionalism: The Middle Class and the Development of Higher Education in America*, New York: W.W. Norton, 1976.
BRITTAIN, W.L. (Ed.). *Viktor Lowenfeld Speaks on Art and Creativity*, Reston, VA: National Art Education Association, n.d.
CHAPMAN, L. *Approaches to Art in Education*, New York: Harcourt Brace Jovanovich, 1978.
COMMISSION ON THE REORGANIZATION OF SECONDARY EDUCATION. *Car-*

*dinal Principles of Secondary Education*, U.S. Bureau of Education, Bulletin No. 35, Washington, D.C.: 1918.

DOBBS, E.V. *Illustrative Handwork for Elementary School Subjects*, New York: MacMillan, 1917.

DRUMMOND, W.B. *An Introduction to Child-study*, London: Edward Arnold, 1907.

DUNCUM, P. 'The origins of self-expression: A case of self deception', *Art Education*, 35, 5, 1982, pp. 32–5.

HAGGERTY, M. *The Owatonna and Education Project*, pamphlet, n.d.

HANDLIN, O. *Boston's Immigrants: A Study of Acculturation* (rev. ed), New York: Atheneum, 1974.

HARTMAN, E. and SCHUMAKER, A. *Creative Expression: The Development of Children in Art, Music, Literature and Dramatics*, Milwaukee: Hale, E.M., 1939.

KERN, E.J. 'The purposes of art education in the United States from 1870 to 1980', paper presented at the History of Art Education Symposium, State College, PA, 3–5 November, 1985.

KINGSLEY C. 'The relation of the high school to higher educational institutions', in JOHNSON, C.H. (Ed.). *The Modern High School*, New York: Charles Schriner & Sons, 1914.

KRUG, E.A. *The Shaping of the American High School: 1880–1920*, Madison, WI: University of Wisconsin, 1969.

LEARS, T.J.J. *No Place of Grace: Anti-modernism and Transformation of American Culture 1880–1920*, New York: Pantheon, 1981.

LOWENFELD, V. *Creative and Mental Growth*, New York: Macmillian, 1947.

MEARNS, H. 'The creative spirit and its significance for education', in HARTMAN, G. and SCHUMAKER, A. (Eds.) *Creative Expression: The Development of Children in Art, Music, Literature and Dramatics*, Milwaukee: Hale, E.M., 1939.

MICHAEL, J.A. and MORRIS, J.W. 'European influences on the theory and philosophy of Viktor Lowenfeld', *Studies in Art Education*, 26, 2, 1985, pp. 103–12.

OWATONNA ART EDUCATION PROJECT SECOND ANNUAL REPORT, unpublished curriculum, 1934.

OWATONNA ART EDUCATION FOURTH ANNUAL REPORT, unpublished curriculum, 1937.

OWATONNA JOURNAL CHRONICAL, 6 October, 1933, n.p.

ROSS, D.W. 'The arts and crafts: A discipline', *Handicraft*, 1, 10, 1903, pp. 229–35.

SCHEAFFER-SIMMERN, H. *The Unfolding of Artistic Acitivity: Its Basis, Processes and Implications*, Berkeley, CA: University of California, 1948.

SERCOMB, P.H. 'The evils of American school systems', *Craftsman*, 16, 1909, pp. 603–11.

SNEDDEN, D. 'The waning power of art', *American Journal of Sociology*, May, 1917.

SNEDDEN, D. *What's Wrong with American Education*, Philadelphia PA: LIPPINCOTT, J.B., 1927.

STANKIEWICZ, M.A. 'A picture age: Reproductions and picture study', *Studies in Art Education*, 26, 2, 1985, pp. 86–92.

STEELE, E.W. 'Freeing the child through art', in HARTMAN, G. and SCHUMAKER, A. (Eds.) *Creative Expression: The Development of Children in Art, Music, Literature and Dramatics*, Milwaukee: Hale, E.M., 1939.

SULLY, J. *Studies of Childhood*, New York: APPLETON, 1898.

THIRTY-FOURTH ANNUAL REPORT OF THE BOARD OF EDUCATION, Boston, MA: Wright and Potter, 1871.

TRACHTENBERG, A. *The Incorporation of America: Culture and Society in the Guilded Age*, New York: Hill and Wang, 1982.

VIOLA, W. *Child Art and Franz Cizek*, New York: Reynal and Hitchcock, 1936.

WALKER, C.H. 'The museum and school', *Handicraft*, 2, 2, 1903, pp. 290–342.

WIECKING, A.M. *Education Through Manual Activities*, Boston: Ginn and Co, 1928.

WINKELMAN, R. 'Art education in the non-public schools of Pennsylvania: 1720–1870', paper presented at the History of Art Education symposium, State College, PA. 3–5 November, 1985.

WYGANT, F. *Art in American Schools in the Nineteenth Century*, Cincinnati, OH: Interwood, 1983.

# 4 The Reader, The Scribe, The Thinker: A Critical Look at the History of American Reading and Writing Instruction

*E. Jennifer Monaghan and E. Wendy Saul*

## Abstract

Historical examples are used to explore the disparity in attention given to these two important subjects. Definitions of reading and writing, the relationship of theory and practice, the marketing of curricular materials, and the impact of social and political forces are all seen as factors in understanding change in these fields. These categories are then used to explain the inordinate attention given to reading to the late 1960s as well as the unprecedented current concern with the teaching of composition.

In a history of American school subject matter, one might expect separate chapters on reading and writing instruction. Traditionally, these have been taught as distinct areas of the curriculum, and an expert in one field, to date, has had to know little about the other. But we assume here that reading and writing are two sides of the same literacy coin, and ask first, how the two fields have come to be viewed as separate, and second, why reading instruction has, in every time period and at every grade level (with one very recent exception which we discuss later), been favored over writing instruction.

The answers to these questions are neither tidy nor simple. This lopsided language curriculum must be explained in terms of various influences: assumptions about the nature of language learning and the purposes of instruction, the history of the professions and their professional organizations, the business interests of publishers, and the political realities to which all educational institutions react. To document this argument we loop back through the historical record several times; in this sense the account provided is not strictly chronological.

## The Weight of Tradition

In determining curricula, one necessarily orders the information to be presented to the child, both in terms of its significance and its assumptions about how children learn. Practices based on once valid assumptions have a way of perpetuating themselves long after the original raison d'être has vanished.

In colonial times, and until perhaps as late as the third decade of the nineteenth century, children were taught to read prior to, and independently of, being taught to write. New England Puritans felt morally and spiritually obliged to teach their children to read the Bible, so that their young would have access to the means of salvation. Reading was also important for 'social control' reasons. In fact, a law passed by the Massachusetts Bay Colony in 1642 actually empowered the selectmen to remove from their parents any children who had not been taught 'to read and understand the principles of religion and the capital laws of this country' and apprentice them to some one else (quoted, in modernized spelling, in Cremin, 1970, p. 124). Though infrequently carried out, the law codified the right the government felt it had to require parents to provide reading instruction.

When, five years later, the Massachusetts colony passed a law requiring a schoolmaster for every fifty families, the curriculum was identified as both writing and reading (*ibid*, p. 181). Girls, however, for the most part did not attend the town schools and generally had to obtain writing instruction privately, for while writing was a career skill for boys with ministerial or commercial ambitions, it was more important for girls to know how to sew than to write. Writing was a mark of social status for girls rather than a survival skill. Literacy teaching itself was divided along the lines of gender: particularly in the seventeenth century, women were considered capable of teaching reading, but it took a man to teach the more difficult art of penmanship (Monaghan, 1984, pp. 8–14 and pp. 29–42).

Technical difficulties also contributed to delaying writing instruction in the colonial period and beyond. The quill pen, virtually the only writing tool in use from the time of the Middle Ages, was a difficult instrument to manage. The feather's tip had to be repeatedly sharpened. Schoolmasters, no doubt reluctant to entrust a knife to inexpert fingers, usually performed this task for their pupils. To judge from the age at which boys first began to attend writing school, children were not considered to have adequate motor dexterity for manipulating the quill pen until the age of 7 (Nash, 1959, p. 10). Ink, too, was a messy business. While pencil was used in colonial writing schools to sketch out a piece before penning it, arithmetic and writing copybooks surviving from the eighteenth and early nineteenth centuries show that ink continued to be the preferred medium ('Miscellaneous American Calligraphy'). Wholesale manufacture of pencils did not begin in the United States until 1827. Manufacture of metal slip-on pen nibs began at about the same time as pencil manufacture; these would eliminate the quill pen by perhaps the mid-nineteenth century.

By the beginning of the twentieth century, religious, technological and developmental reasons for delaying the teaching of writing — in the sense of penmanship — were no longer compelling. Nonetheless, it was widely held that it was not appropriate to begin composition instruction until the third grade. This, at least, was the conclusion reached in 1894 in an influential report on English by the so-called Committee of Ten (Eliot, 1894, p. 87). (This report is discussed in more detail below.) In most contemporary classrooms, composition instruction is still deferred until reading instruction is well under way. The force of long habit may be making a contribution to our present practice, but we must look further for an explanation of the continued domination of reading over writing instruction.

## Definitions of Reading and Writing

How a curricular subject is defined naturally has important consequences for how it is to be taught. It will be seen that, even though definitions of literacy skills have not been constant over time, reading has been defined more clearly than writing. Writing has been interpreted in a variety of ways from the start. This is all the more remarkable when one considers that the reading process is intangible (for children are encouraged to read silently), while writing generates a physical product.

Reading and writing clearly stand, in relation to the written language, as do listening and speaking in relation to the spoken. Reading is a receptive skill — though not a passive — like listening; writing is a productive skill, as is speaking. Historical definitions of reading and writing, however, belie this straightforward dichotomy.

Until the end of the nineteenth century, reading was to a large extent defined as oral production of the written word. The major focus of the higher level reading textbooks was on elocution: fifth readers were studded with instructions on articulation, inflection, on using accent for emphasis, and so forth (Venezky, 1986). This emphasis on reading as oral rendition is clearly seen in nineteenth century assessments of minimal reading competence. For instance, from 1866 on, the admission requirements for a candidate for the State Normal School of Maryland included to 'read accurately and intelligibly from a newspaper'. The requirement was altered in 1873, but only by dropping the clause 'from a newspaper' (*Annual Catalogue of the State Normal School of Maryland*, 1866, 1873, p. 8). Similarly, part of the entrance requirement for Harvard, in 1865 and thereafter, was 'reading English aloud' (Applebee, 1974, p. 30).

Comprehension was not, of course, ignored completely; rather, early authors linked oral reading neatly to understanding. As one late eighteenth-century expert on elocution put it, 'For *reading* is nothing but *speaking* what one sees in a book, as if he were expressing his *own* sentiments, as they rise in his mind ... And hence it is, that no one can *read* properly what he does not *understand*' (Burgh, 1775, p. 10). Emphasis on meaning was spotty, however, in reading textbooks throughout the nineteenth century. The contemporary interest in reading as comprehension has been largely a feature of the twentieth century. The late nineteenth- and early twentieth-century change in pedagogy in favor of silent reading has obviously aided the definition of reading as comprehension. Teachers now test for 'good' reading by evaluating how well a child has understood a text, not by how well he or she has read it aloud.

Writing has undergone many more changes in definition than reading. Early in the history of education, writing was on occasion considered equivalent to spelling. (One schoolboy, asked by another — in a dialogue in a 1596 spelling book — to write the word 'people', replies that he cannot write. 'I meane not so, but when I say write, I meane spell; for in my meaning they are both one,' is the response [Coote, 1596, p. 32]).

In colonial America writing was often defined, at least for instructional purposes, as penmanship. Given the utilitarian purposes of the eighteenth-century writing schools, there may have been no formal teaching of composition as such. For instance, in a collection of 188 penmanship pieces produced by boys at Boston Writing schools between 1748 and 1782, only one manuscript is clearly an original composition. All the others are copied from some model — copying being, of course, the standard pedagogical mode for penmanship instruction ('Miscellaneous American Calligraphy').

In the nineteenth century, writing was 'an integral part of the study of grammar', and the medium for expressing previously memorized language rules (Donsky, 1984, p. 795). The pedagogical emphasis was prescriptive: 'good' writing was taken to mean a mastery of capitalization, punctuation and syntax as well as correct spelling and pleasing handwriting. English grammar was being offered in most American schools by 1810, and was an admission requirement for many colleges by 1860 (Applebee, 1974, pp. 7–8).

By the middle of the nineteenth century, a shift in educational thinking allowed writing to emerge in the form of composition (Donsky, 1984, p. 795). Textbooks that discuss the teaching of composition, often in association with rhetoric, are available by the 1870s (Carpenter, 1963, p. 114). Nonetheless, unless teachers and students alike failed to recall their composing efforts, the emphasis on composition in the average small town or rural school was not strong: in a study of more than 1000 sources describing nineteenth-century education, only two instances were found of composition writing and speech preparation (Finkelstein, 1974, pp. 81 and 88).

By the end of the nineteenth century, the role of English as a school subject was clarified in a manner that still holds good today. The 1894 Report of the Committee of Ten, mentioned earlier, for the first time in the history of American education presented a unified view of English teaching from the earliest grades through high school. As the Committee put it (Eliot, 1894, p. 86):

> The main direct objects of the teaching of English in schools seem to be two: (1) to enable the pupil to understand the expressed thoughts of others and to give expression to thoughts of his own; and (2) to cultivate a taste for reading, to give the pupil some acquaintance with good literature, and to furnish him with the means of extending that acquaintance.

Writing at the higher grades was, in effect, defined as a pupil's written response to the great works of English literature. In this sense, writing was subordinated to, and necessarily followed, reading. In the lower grades, the Committee identified three strands of instruction: '(*a*) "language" and composition, (*b*) formal or systematic grammar, (*c*) reading, or lessons in literature' (Eliot, 1894, p. 87). As discussed earlier, children would not begin composition writing until the third grade.

Even when writing is defined as composition, there appear to be more than one kind of composing. As would be expected, changes in pedagogical assumptions gave rise to different emphases on the purposes of composition.

The most pervasive meaning for composition in the high school was expository writing. From the 1870s to the 1930s, eligibility for admission to colleges was evaluated by written examinations — at least by the eastern colleges — on works from the English literary canon (Applebee, 1974, pp. 30–2, 49 and 94–6; Sizer, 1964, p. 58). The need, therefore, for students to perform well on college entrance examinations exerted a pressure on high schools to spend time on exposition as well as on the prescribed literary texts.

A second important interpretation of writing was as a utilitarian tool. In the 1930s, Wilbur Hatfield headed a team of educators to respond to the call of the progressive education movement that schooling ought to be a preparation for life. The result of the team's efforts was a major publication of the National Council of Teachers of English, *An Experience Curriculum in English* (1935). The authors identified a series of curricular 'experiences'. The objectives of the 'writing experiences' in the elementary school were practical activities such as writing thank-you letters, filling out forms, and making signs (Hatfield, 1935, pp. 185–207).

A third aspect of elementary writing was purely personal. In the *Experience Curriculum*, this sort of writing was contrasted sharply with functional writing. It fell under the rubric of what was termed 'creative expression experiences', which emphasized storytelling, pantomime and dramatization — validated as ends in themselves, though serving no practical function. Composition in this context was essentially autobiographical and biographical. One objective, for instance, was to write a paragraph on 'a short and definite unit of experience in which emotion, either one's own or another's is the center of interest'. A suggested activity for this was a description of 'How My Dog Acts When I Have Hurt His Feelings' (*ibid*, p. 120).

What we are more likely to think of as 'creative' writing — imaginative writing — was conspicuously absent from any portion of the *Experience Curriculum*. When imaginative writing was eventually welcomed into the elementary grades, as it was by the 1950s, it was labeled 'creative writing' and regarded as something of a frill. There were debates over whether all children should be allowed to engage in it, or if it were a subject only for the gifted ('Creative Writing', 1971).

The point here is that reading has been and continues to be clearly defined and therefore better able to define itself and its assumptions to the pedagogical community at large. Moreover, reading as a field has embraced those who identify themselves as interested in the teaching of reading, whereas writing is the servant of many masters. Because writing — once it was defined more broadly than physical letter formation — has been viewed largely as the handmaiden of English, its interpretations are as various as the reasons for which it is used. This is evident, for instance, from a quick browse through the *Encyclopedia of Education* of 1971. 'Reading' is a heading with numerous sub-categories ranging from *reading: reading readiness* to *reading instruction: training of teachers*. 'Writing', however, has no entry of its own; instead, one has to look up 'writing' in the index to be referred to topics as diverse as *broadcast training; creative writing, teaching of; punctuation, American; rhetoric; composition, teaching of;* and *handwriting, teaching of* (Deighton, 1971).

## Issues of Control

Nonetheless, however variously reading and writing have been defined, it still remains the case that reading, even when oral, is the receptive skill (for reading aloud is only pronouncing what someone else has written), while writing is the productive skill. This distinction is relevant when the issue of control is considered. The curriculum is, at least in part, the formal statement of what society believes it is important for students to know. Society has focused on children as readers because, historically, it has been much more interested in children as receptors than as producers of the written word.

Education, in the great experiment in democracy that was created by the American Revolution, was seen by all who pondered it to be the bulwark of the state. Only an educated citizenry could be relied upon to preserve the Republic. In pursuing that goal, however, the emphasis was not on creative individuality, but on obedience to the law. Reading and listening were the desired modes. There was nothing new in this, of course. In 1642, the Massachusetts Bay Colony had required that all children be taught to read, so that they could understand the Bible and the law. It is by requiring children to read the writings of adults that society has consistently attempted to transmit its values.

In colonial times it was texts such as the *New England Primer* that served to introduce children to the religious belief system of their time, as they learned to read. Those whose religious views differed from the prevailing Congregationalism of New England took care to provide schoolchildren with other texts for reading instruction. The Quaker George Fox, for example, composed a spelling book himself. (It was printed in Philadelphia and elsewhere from 1702 on [Fox, 1769].) In the nineteenth century, textbooks of all kinds, from readers to geographies, promoted such a remarkably uniform — and conservative — value system that they have rightly been dubbed 'the guardians of tradition' (Elson, 1964).

In our own century, the materials composed for teaching adult illiterates to read are as good a yardstick as any of the continuing use of reading materials to promulgate values. The readers prepared for American-born illiterates who had enlisted in World War I gave a capsule lesson on the American mission (Cook, 1977, p. 18):

Why are we at war?
To keep our country free.
To keep other people free.
To make the world safe to live in.

Nor is this approach merely a relic of earlier years. Until all too recently, basal reading series suggested that the only families sanctioned by schools were white, suburban, and male-dominated. The fact that today our basal series offer a little ethnic variety and a few females in leadership roles simply shows that values have changed. It certainly does not show that society has abandoned the need to represent its beliefs in textbooks for reading instruction. Reading texts have been, and must ever be, value-laden.

In contrast, writing, which comes from the child, is significantly less subject to societal control. Writing also allows children to preserve their integrity and individuality amid a bombardment of adult messages emanating from every source, from the basal reader to television (Burrows, 1951; Haley-James, 1981, pp. 4–5).

## The Teachers' Control of Literacy Instruction

Only a few — language experience devotees, for instance — have suggested that children might learn how to read without a textbook of some kind. In today's schools, as has been the case ever since the graded series of readers entered the school system, the reading series adopted by the school *is* the language curriculum. This series of books is a very powerful tool — powerful not only in the influence it exerts upon children, but also upon teachers. To a large extent, the selected series defines not only the content to be read, but the reading methodology to be used. If, for instance, a teacher wishes to use a sounding and blending approach, but the assigned textbook is based on a sight vocabulary, his or her choice of instructional approach will be hampered, if not stymied. The concept of 'teacher-proof' materials springs directly from the notion that textbooks can dictate method as well as content.

Moreover, the basal reading series is seldom selected by the teachers who are to use them. The choice of text may rest in the hands of the local school, the district, an entire school system, or even, under the state adoption system, an entire state. Even once the textbook is in the teacher's hands, the teacher is, in the American classroom today, systematically deprived of control. As one observer has put it, one of the great ironies of American education is that as we have given more and more training to our teachers, the authors of textbooks have assumed that they knew less and less, and expanded the length of their teachers manuals correspondingly (Venezky, 1986).

A study of the teachers guides put out by two publishing companies between 1920 and 1980 documents a decline in trusting the teacher as a professional. By the 1970s, the teachers manuals no longer included discussions of philosophies of education or of research; instead, implementing the basal program as written was — and still is — assumed to be all that was necessary to teach reading. Answers were provided for the most literal questions on the stories. The teacher often had words put in her mouth: 'Say such and such'. The overdesigned manual, according to the study, is a 'metaphor of the decline in trust and confidence in teachers and a concomitant increase in confidence in the efficacy of the technology of the textbook' (Woodward, 1985, p. 2).

Writing instruction, in contrast, is at least theoretically under the teacher's control. All that is needed to set the stage for a child to be able to write is a pencil, paper, and enough time. Teachers and children alike are safe from the domination of textbooks, because textbooks on composition are rarely assigned in elementary school. For even if such a textbook is assigned in the later grades (and it is almost invariably considered a necessity at the college level), there is only one book involved, not an entire series.

The fact that either no money, or only a modest amount of money, is needed for a teacher to be able to teach writing, has had important consequences for the classroom. The publishing industry is well aware that there is little money to be made from textbooks for writers. Even textbooks on the mechanics of writing — including spelling and handwriting — do not garner much of a market. The basal reading series, however, is a bonanza.

Reading textbooks have always been the prop and stay of their publishers. The *New England Primer* is said to have had a lifetime sale, over dozens of publishers, of 3 million copies (Ford, 1897, p. 45). The sales of Noah Webster's blue-back speller in its various versions have been conservatively estimated at 70 million (Monaghan, 1983, p. 219). The *McGuffey Readers* had sold some 122 million copies by 1920 (Smith, 1963, p. 21). The evolution of the graded series has increased, to a dramatic extent, the sheer number of books that any publisher now presents as part of its basal series. Whereas editions of the *McGuffey* series between 1836 and 1901 never included more than six readers, a couple of primers, a speller and a high school reader (Minnich, 1936, pp. 39–40), the modern basal reading series can reach a total of some fifteen separate books. In addition, there are supplementary texts, workbooks, kits, and so on that add to the bulk of the package.

More books cost more money. The chart below illustrates vividly the disparity in the expenditures on textbooks for reading instruction as compared with those for writing instruction.[1]

Table 1: *Sales of Elementary Language-Related Textbooks by Category in Thousands of Dollars*

|  | 1982 | 1983 | 1984 |
|---|---|---|---|
| *Books sold* |  |  |  |
| Reading | 202,390 | 234,649 | 241,766 |
| Literature | 3,607 | 5,825 | 5,842 |
| English | 47,063 | 46,666 | 69,687 |
| Spelling | 33,866 | 30,137 | 32,424 |
| Handwriting | 4,078 | 4,715 | 847 |
| Total language-related | 291,004 | 321,992 | 350,566 |

While textbooks for reading instruction, by virtue of their numbers, have been costing more, the materials associated with writing have generally become less expensive over time. The cost of an exercise book today is modest. The advent in 1930 of a new process for manufacturing pencils with points that had more resistance to breaking has made this lowly instrument, formerly a symbol of impermanence, the mainstay of schoolwork in the elementary school. The price of the ballpoint pen (which, while patented in 1937, was not in widespread use in the schools until the 1960s) has declined greatly since its introduction. In sum, with the notable exception of the word processor, there has been a continuous move in writing toward cheaper and more manageable equipment. In contrast, the material associated with reading instruction (a basal reading series) has systematically increased in bulk, and quite possibly (relative to a school's income) in price.

It is, in short, much easier for a teacher to demand that her pupils buy a new pencil than that the school purchase a new basal reading series. Our point here is obvious: because of the disparity in the cost of equipment, it is very much easier for a teacher to change writing instruction than reading instruction.

## The Power of Theory

At a time when some publishers no longer feel a need to refer teachers to the theories that underpin their pronouncements on classroom practice, it is all the more important for us to examine theory. Theories are very powerful, for they generate pedagogy. Reading and writing instruction involve theories, whether these are explicitly formulated or not. They involve, at the least, theories about what the written language is (the definitions of reading and writing that we have touched on, above); about the nature of the child; and about how the child learns. We focus here on the educational theories in colonial times and in the first half of the twentieth century.

In colonial New England, educational ideology was based largely on Calvinist doctrine. Children, like adults, were held to to be heirs to original sin. They were naturally 'bad'. Learning, therefore, had to be drummed into them, and the appropriate method of instruction was repetition. In addition, literacy learning was held to proceed incrementally, from small units (the letters of the alphabet) to large ones (sentences). Successful reading was the faithful reproduction, orally, of what the author had written. As most of the texts were religious, they were not open to debate. Moreover, reading was thought of as hard work. The function of the teacher was to drill the child to make his way through the long columns of words in spelling books (Monaghan, 1983, pp. 31–3). Writing, at least in the sense of penmanship, was similarly hard work in colonial America. Mastery of the pen was to be achieved by constant repetition — namely, copying.

Our second example of the power of theory relates to the first half of the twentieth century. The prevailing notion of the child could hardly have been more different from the pessimism of colonial times. Since about 1880, there had been growing optimism about the 'eternal promise' of childhood (Wishy, 1968, p. 114). In education, two very different theories were competing against each other for professional acceptance. One, of course, was the philosophy associated with the name of John Dewey, progressive education. The other was the 'scientific' approach to education with its attendant measurement movement.

Around the turn of the century, progressive education was best represented by the program at the Cook County Normal School in Chicago, where Colonel Francis Parker was principal. Literacy instruction in this context proceeded from the students' interests. Children created their own stories, which were then printed up as 'Reading Leaflets' and used instead of textbooks for reading instruction (Cremin, 1964, p. 132; cf. Huey, 1968, pp. 339–41; Tippet, 1927, pp. 274–82).

As a method, the sight approach was much in favor with progressives. As one commentator put it in 1908, 'The word method ... was very little used in America until 1870, when progressive teachers began using it in various parts of the country' (Huey, 1968, p. 272). Given the right environment, it was believed that reading acquisition would largely occur by itself (*ibid*, pp. 311–2, and pp. 336–9; cf. Balmuth, 1982, pp. 196–7).

The second, and competing, theory was the behaviorally-based scientific movement. Under the name of 'connectionism', its greatest proponent in educational circles was of course Edward Lee Thorndike. Learning, in Thorndike's view, was habit formation; habits tended to be stamped in by a 'satisfyer' and weakened by an 'annoyer'. He believed in the possibility of establishing education as a science, and was convinced that quantitative measurement was the most powerful tool at his disposal (Cremin, 1964, p. 114; Thorndike, 1949).

As the 'father' of educational measurement, Thorndike had a

direct influence on reading instruction through his word lists (Clifford, 1978). With his customary appetite for counting, he tabulated the frequency of words in children's speaking vocabularies. Progressivism provided the motive: it appeared important to know which words children most often used, so that these could be the ones they first learned to read. The measurement movement provided the means: a meticulous tabulation based on sophisticated sampling techniques. Thorndike's influential *The Teacher's Word Book*, based on this research, was first published in 1921; and he produced a dictionary for young people in 1935 which, with its companion dictionaries in the 1940s, would prove immensely popular (Clifford, 1978, pp. 122–7).

Thorndike's second contribution to the field of reading was his definition of reading. His classic 1917 study, *Reading as Reasoning: A Study of Mistakes in Paragraph Reading* (Thorndike, 1971) has been credited with being the starting point for the twentieth-century emphasis on reading as thinking (Otto, 1971; Clifford, 1978, p. 121).

Nonetheless, Thorndike's young colleague, Arthur I. Gates, was of even more importance to the reading field than Thorndike himself. The two men worked closely together. Thorndike had been a member of the doctoral committee for Gates' dissertation in psychology at Columbia University in 1917, and almost immediately thereafter had offered Gates a position at Teachers College. Gates revised Thorndike's college textbook on educational psychology, and the revision appeared under their joint authorship in 1929 (Thorndike and Gates, 1929). Three years earlier he, like Thorndike, had published a vocabulary — *A Reading Vocabulary for the Primary Grades* (Gates, 1935). A prodigious researcher, Gates wrote a succession of books on reading and reading disability (Gates, 1922, 1927, 1928 and 1930; Vance, 1985). Successful teaching of reading was, he believed, a function of arranging situations in such a way that learning became inevitable (Gates, 1930, pp. 193–5).

It is instructive to look at Gates' own view of his relationship to progressive theory. In his old age, he remarked that for the first quarter century of his professional life (that is, roughly 1917 to 1942) he was often criticized for being unresponsive or hostile to Dewey's ideas. (He went on to add that for the last quarter of a century he had been criticized for being a naive victim of Dewey's progressive notions!) (Gates, 1971, p. 211; cf. Gates, 1926).

The other great figure on the reading horizon was William S. Gray. By 1914, Gray had received what his biographer calls a 'double dose of the scientific approach to education'. His training at the

University of Chicago had been in psychology, under Charles Judd, a strong proponent of the cause of education as a science. When Gray spent the academic year 1913–1914 at Teachers College, he took one course with Dewey, but two-and-a-half courses with Thorndike, who was also in charge of his master's thesis (Mavrogenes, 1985, p. 15; Mavrogenes, 1986, pp. 106–7). In short, Gates and Gray, who would become perhaps the two most respected figures in reading education and research, derived their theoretical views much more from the scientific measurement movement than from progressivism.

In terms of reading, then, there were two possible, and very different, roads to follow. As Nila Banton Smith put it, speaking of the period between 1925 and 1935, 'One group believed that children should be given practice on sequential skills carefully planned by an adult. The other group was convinced that learning best took place when the child was permitted to carry out his own purposes ... solving attendant problems within the context of his own experiences ...' (Smith, 1965, p. 197).

Those who believed in sequential skills — the adherents of the scientific measurement movement — used basal readers as the vehicles for reading instruction. One of the readers' most prominent features was that the vocabulary selected for the primers and first readers were high-frequency words derived from lists such as those published by Thorndike or Gates (*ibid*, p. 216). Both Gates and Gray put their theories into practice by becoming authors of basal reading series. Gates was one of the authors of *The Work-Play Books* (1932); Gray's first authorship of a basal reader was in 1930, when he became a co-author of the *Elson Basic Readers*, a Scott Foresman publication. (The title of the first pre-primer was *Dick and Jane.*) Gray's contribution was even more important to the 1936–1938 revision, which was now called the *Elson-Gray Basic Readers*. He became senior author for the series in the revisions of 1940–1948 and 1951–1957 (Stevenson, 1985, p. 71).

Those who favored progressive education continued to advocate the approach to literacy instruction so well exemplified at the turn of the century by the Cook County Normal School. Laura Zirbes was an outstanding example of a reading educator with such views. Her doctoral dissertation, which she completed in 1928 while a lecturer at Teachers College, compared progressive reading practices with traditional ones. That same year she joined the Faculty of Ohio State University — like Teachers College, an acknowledged center for progressive education. She was a member of the writing team for *An Experience Curriculum in English* in 1935. In some 200 publications over a long career, Zirbes continued to espouse a child-centered view of reading instruction, calling for student-set purposes for reading and an integrated language arts curriculum (Moore, 1986).

The fact that the names of Gates and Gray are so much more familiar to students of education today than that of Zirbes speaks for itself. In the custody battle for curriculum the winner was clear: 'practice in sequential skills' became the watchword of educational practice. The basal reader, now fortified by a 'scientifically controlled vocabulary' remained the preeminent text for reading instruction. Moreover, basal series after 1930 or so embodied a broad measure of agreement as to how reading should be taught. (Jeanne Chall later dubbed it the 'conventional wisdom' [Chall, 1967, pp. 14–15]). Its major focus was on comprehension. The basic unit for instruction was not the letter, as in colonial times, but the whole word. Children were to read for meaning and interpretation from the start. They were to learn a certain number of words by sight before proceeding to master a series of 'word attack skills'. 'Phonic analysis' — the use of a knowledge of the 'sounds' of letters to identify a word — was usually placed last on this list.

Progressivism had an impact on writing instruction that would eventually surface in similar forms today. Much of the contemporary interest in the 'process' of writing over the 'product' has its analogs in the discussions of composition included in textbooks published between 1900 and 1950. The possibility of teaching reading through writing, and the importance of students' revising their compositions, were discussed in a 1912 textbook; peer teaching and group conferencing were advocated in the *American Language Series* (one of whose authors was James Hosic) in 1932. Social revision — in which children discuss the merits and shortcomings of their compositions with one another — was a standard feature in textbooks published in the 1930s (Donsky, 1984, pp. 801–2). We have already noted the consequences for writing instruction of the progressive emphasis on schooling as a preparation for life, as exemplified in Wilbur Hatfield's *Experience Curriculum* (1935).

The effect of the scientific measurement movement on writing instruction was less direct: composition simply does not lend itself easily to behavioristic description. It is hardly surprising that the measurers turned their attention toward those aspects of writing that were more amenable to objective measurement. Handwriting, historically one of the earliest of the ways in which writing had been viewed, was also the earliest aspect of writing to be measured: in fact, Thorndike's Handwriting Scale of 1910, the first testing instrument

to be nationally standardized, marked the beginning of the educational measurement movement.

What is perhaps more surprising is that there were any efforts
to measure composition. In spite of the difficulties of both sample
and scoring reliability, several researchers from 1911 on, including
Thorndike himself, attempted to evaluate essays by means of rating
scales. However, the use of these was generally abandoned by the
1940s (Haley-James, 1981, pp. 14–15).

The difficulty of measuring composition objectively is evident
from the struggles of the College Entrance Examination Board
(known more familiarly today as the College Board) to assess composition. When the Board was created in 1900, all school subjects
were evaluated by essay examination. In 1937, in the interests of
reliability, the Board's achievement tests were for the first time
administered — as, with only a few exceptions, they still are today —
in the multiple-choice format. (The Scholastic Aptitude Tests had
been introduced as multiple-choice tests in 1926.[2]) During the 1940s,
some forms of the achievement test in English composition did
include essays, but such were the problems of rater reliability that
these were abandoned. Throughout the 1950s the typical College
Board test of English composition consisted of either three multiple-
choice sections (which tested aspects of writing such as grammar and
punctuation) or two multiple-choice tests and an interlinear exercise.
(This asked students to edit a piece of text to identify specific writing
errors.) An experimental reintroduction of essay testing in 1954 was
judged a failure after three years (Donlon, 1984, pp. 89–90). In the
1950s and later, therefore, students could perform well on the
College Board English Composition Tests without having to
demonstrate any competence whatever in writing connected prose.

Not only was composition difficult to measure, but it also
suffered from an absence of theory. While theories of rhetoric
abounded in the field of English, theories on composing processes
were conspicuously lacking. In fact, researchers who investigated
composition in the 1950s and 1960s took it for granted that the important questions for research were pedagogical ones, and operated
— mistakenly — on the assumption that they in fact knew what
composition actually was (Cooper and Odell, 1978, p. xi).

One major consequence of all this was a dramatic difference in
the attention professionals paid to the two aspects of literacy. That
the effects have been longlasting can be seen by looking at the
descriptors used in the databank of the Educational Research Information Center (ERIC). Even in the 1984 *Thesaurus*, there are

many more descriptors for reading than for writing: thirty-two major descriptors include the word 'reading' (for example, *reading improvement*), compared with thirteen for writing (for example, *writing improvement*). Nor are the categories parallel. There are, for instance, descriptors named *reading diagnosis, reading difficulties,* and *reading failure,* but, while there are indeed *writing difficulties,* there is no such descriptor as *writing diagnosis* or *writing failure.* There are *reading specialists (consultants),* but not *writing specialists, reading centers* but not *writing centers. Reading processes* and *research* both date as descriptors from 1966 (the date of ERIC's inception); *writing processes* and *research* only from 1980. Significantly, the descriptors *reading skills* and *writing skills* both date from 1966 (Houston, 1984, pp. 213–14 and pp. 288–9). (Some of the reasons for this will emerge in our next section.)

It is the actual volume of studies, however, that speaks louder than words. Table 2 below shows the number of studies stored in ERIC to which either 'reading' or 'writing' was assigned as a descriptor, at each of five-year intervals.[3] 'Reading' and 'writing' are the general categories, while headings such as 'reading research' represent sub-divisions of these. It should be noted that the figures on 'writing' have been generated by using that descriptor up to 1979, and then the new descriptor 'writing (composition)' introduced in 1980.

Even allowing for the fact that many more studies are now being submitted to ERIC than in its earliest years, the preponderance of reading studies over writing, up to 1980, is striking. Reading, when conceptualized as skill acquisition, clearly lent itself better to being studied: it was perceived as falling within the domain of educational

*Table 2: Number of Studies Added to ERIC, in Five-Year Periods, Categorized by Descriptor*

| Descriptor | 66–70 | 71–75 | 76–80 | 81–85 | 86 | (Total) |
|---|---|---|---|---|---|---|
| Reading | 4,087 | 10,112 | 11,434 | 9,261 | 728 | (35,622) |
| Writing | 1,281 | 2,852 | 5,462 | 6,288 | 614 | (16,497) |
| { Reading Research | 599 | 1,907 | 2,795 | 2,394 | 169 | (7,864) |
| { Writing Research | — | 2 | 147 | 882 | 85 | (1,116) |
| { Reading Processes | 1,729 | 450 | 896 | 605 | 69 | (3,749) |
| { Writing Processes | — | 5 | 154 | 1,073 | 131 | (1,363) |
| { Reading Instruction | 1,001 | 3,234 | 3,508 | 3,446 | 269 | (11,458) |
| { Writing Instruction | 16 | 28 | 697 | 3,163 | 294 | (4,198) |

psychology. But writing was still seen as rhetoric, and within the province of the humanists in college English departments, who did not submit their papers to ERIC. This has recently changed. Writing has become a major research focus. We shall account for the startling increase, from 1981 on, in the number of studies on writing processes, in our final section.

The legacy of Thorndike and those he inspired is nowhere more apparent than in such a table. The measurers, as rulers of the educational domain, continued to pronounce upon the field of reading, while leaving composition relatively undisturbed. Not until the reemergence of cognitive psychology and the birth of psycholinguistics in the 1960s, with their concomitant interest in qualitative research, would quantitative research find any challengers, and research into both reading and writing processes become viable.

## The Professionalization of Reading and Writing

Once a field has been defined, its subscribers seek a professional identity and recognize certain activities as being within or outside their own professional interests. An examination of the development of reading and writing as professions once again reveals how the curriculum has been shaped by non-neutral forces.

Reading and writing part professionally at several points. Until very recently, writing has been viewed overwhelmingly as the province of the high school, while reading has always been considered the purview of the elementary school. Moreover, teachers of writing in search of a professional organization would in all likelihood turn to the National Council of Teachers of English (NCTE), while teachers of reading automatically look to the International Reading Association (IRA).

The NCTE is by far the elder of the two professional societies. To understand the genesis of the National Council of Teachers of English, it is necessary to understand the difficulty with which English was accepted as part of the school and college curriculum. The acceptance of English as a legitimate subject for study was only achieved in the last decades of the nineteenth century. The pressure then exerted by college requirements in English upon the high school curriculum was considerable: high schools in the 1880s and 1890s felt compelled to teach the narrow selection of English classics which would serve as subjects for examination by the colleges, at a time when college entrance was still, as we have seen, being controlled by written examinations (Applebee, 1974, pp. 29–32). The 1892 Committee of Ten had been formed in this context.

The resentment engendered by these restrictive college requirements ultimately served as the catalyst for the creation, in 1911, of a national, permanent body for teachers of English — the National Council of Teachers of English (*ibid*, pp. 49–53; Hook, 1979, pp. 7–17). As the name suggests, it was an organization devoted to English teachers in general, not merely to teachers of writing. As NCTE's constitution put it, its object was to 'increase the effectiveness of school and college work in English' (*ibid*, p. 286).

Because the organizers of NCTE were interested in the college-high school relationship, there were no elementary school teachers among the founding members. Their numbers increased only slowly, in spite of the creation of an elementary section in 1912. On its own admission, NCTE was consistently unsuccessful in attracting elementary school teachers to its ranks. In the early years, the editor of NCTE's *English Journal* appealed in vain for the submission of articles on teaching English in the primary grades. Even NCTE's elementary journal, introduced in 1924, was all too often devoted to 'dull recitals of sometimes inconsequential research' of interest only to theoreticians (*ibid*, pp. 5, 51 and 86–8).

Given the emphasis in English courses upon literature, the NCTE could easily have also included elementary reading within its purview. The Council did, in fact, have a few publications on reading: its *Reading for Fun*, a reading list put out in the 1930s for the elementary grades, was popular, and it had published a monograph on reading edited by William S. Gray in 1946. But, as NCTE's historian has phrased it, this gesture toward reading in the elementary school came 'too little, too late' (*ibid*, pp. 122 and 150). By that time, those interested in reading, particularly at the elementary level, were more than ready to go their own way.

The International Reading Association was a union of two organizations, both concerned with reading failure. The aims of the International Council for the Improvement of Reading Instruction (ICIRI), the first of IRA's parent bodies, were defined in its first constitution in 1947 as follows:

1   To stimulate and encourage research in
    (a)   developmental, corrective, and remedial instruction in reading;
    (b)   the diagnosis of disabilities in reading;
    (c)   readability; and

(d) the improvement of textbook construction and publication from the point of view of the reading problems therein . . .

Its second major aim was to publish the results of experimental research in reading, in order to improve reading instruction generally (Jerrolds, 1977, p. 2).

The second parent of the International Reading Association was even more attuned to reading disability. Named the National Association of Remedial Teachers (NART) at its first official meeting in October 1947 (held a few months after the creation of ICIRI), the Association was in theory designed for all professionals interested in preventing and correcting 'difficulties in learning' in general (*ibid*, pp. 20–1). In practice, its focus was often on reading disability in particular. When the two organizations combined in 1956 under the name International Reading Association, the emphasis on reading disability continued to be an important aspect of the new organization's interests.

The creation and subsequent rapid growth of the IRA could never have occurred if the field of reading had not already been well defined. The research generated by those interested in reading, such as Gates and Gray, was one of the factors that promoted the definition of the field as an academic specialty.

Also important to professional identity is the national recognition of leaders in the field. Two of the prominent names in the NCTE were those of James F. Hosic and W. Wilbur Hatfield. Both men edited the organization's first professional journal, the *English Journal*: Hosic from 1912 to 1921 and Hatfield from 1922 to 1955 (Hook, 1979, p. 290). (As we have seen, Hatfield chaired the NCTE Curriculum Commission which produced the 1935 report *An Experience Curriculum in English*, while Hosic's publications included an English textbook.) By 1947, when ICIRI and NART were organizing independently, there was similarly a number of acknowledged experts in the fields of both reading instruction and reading disability. William S. Gray was pre-eminent in both areas.

By 1947, Gray had 370 professional publications to his credit; all but a few score of so of them were on reading. His remarkable breadth of interests spanned the range from remedial to adult reading; and he had been producing annual summaries of research related to reading since 1925 (Stevenson, 1985, pp. 37–60). He was also already the senior author of what would prove to be the most successful basal reading series of its day. When, in 1955, ICIRI and NART looked for a candidate to head their combined organizations, Gray, the newly-elected President of ICIRI, was the natural choice. He became IRA's first President in January 1956. Arthur Gates was named the chair of IRA's Research Committee (Jerrolds, 1977, pp. 19, 251).

The origins of NCTE and IRA, therefore, were strikingly different. The former focused on the teaching of English in general, particularly literature, and its members were largely drawn from the ranks of high school teachers of English. The latter was organized by those who were concerned not only to improve reading instruction generally, but specifically to address the question of reading disabilities. Moreover, from the first, the IRA directed itself to elementary teachers, whereas the NCTE failed to attract them. To a great extent, this distinction in membership affiliation holds true today. For the years 1984 through to January 1986, NCTE membership figures reveal that its elementary membership was just under 15 per cent (as compared with a 63 per cent high school membership). The IRA, however, reports that over 60 per cent of its members currently identify themselves as working in grades 9 or below.[4]

The metaphor of disablement (if not of disease) that was inherent in the organization of the parent bodies of the International Reading Association is one that is crucial to an understanding of the profession. It was based on genuine concern: studies in the 1920s had revealed that low reading skill was a major cause of school failure (Smith, 1965, pp. 189–93; Clifford, 1978, pp. 118–9). Between 1935 and 1950 the growing interest in reading disability could be seen from the number of studies undertaken on the topic, from the spate of articles in professional journals, and from a battery of new books with titles like *Why Pupils Fail in Reading* and *The Prevention and Correction of Reading Difficulties* (Smith, 1965, pp. 301–4; Robinson, 1946; Betts, 1936). The position of 'reading specialist' was developing as a new field of expertise. By 1956 there were reading specialists in both schools and colleges, but perhaps only a fourth of them had been specifically trained in reading. Increasingly thereafter states began to sanction the certification of the reading specialist as a specific profession. Seven states had such certification in 1960; by 1964, the total had reached twenty-one (Smith, 1965, pp. 416–7 and 419).

E. Jennifer Monaghan and E. Wendy Saul

## The Impact of the World at Large

Given the discussion up to this point, it should be easy to predict which of the two literacy skills would generate more public excitement. Sure enough, it was citizen concern over reading instruction that provoked the profession into responding to public complaints. It is not surprising that educational institutions respond to societal pressures. What is surprising, from the perspective of those who believe in the power of educational institutions to control educational concerns, are those moments when public opinion flies in the face of educational practice.

Rudolf Flesch's *Why Johnny Can't Read and What You Can Do About It*, appeared in 1955, at a time when the cold war competition was chilling the American climate. It was on the bestseller list for over thirty weeks, and sold 99,000 hardcover copies when it first appeared. The first mass market version sold 144,000 copies, while the trade paper version as late as 1966 produced a sales volume of yet another 124,000. Its publishers claim that over half a million copies have been purchased overall.[5] These are remarkable sales figures for a book on so seemingly mundane a subject.

Flesch's book is not only a tirade against the whole word method of teaching reading, but also an indictment of the American school system in general. The point Flesch made, vehemently, is that the sight approach ignored man's greatest invention, the alphabet. He charged that teachers, if they had their way, would never tell children that letters represent sounds. Furthermore, Flesch accused the reading profession of having ignored the results of its own research. One after another, the doyens of the reading profession were identified on his pages as believers in the sight approach. Flesch also made much of the fact that so many of the best known reading experts were involved as senior authors of leading basal reading series. Finally, he presented a 'how-to' section — with word lists that remind one of the old colonial spelling books — that his converts were to use as they taught their children to read (Flesch, 1955, pp. 4–21, 60–8 and 135–222).

The point here is not the justice or otherwise of Flesch's charges, but the powerful effect of his book on American reading instruction. Parents apparently saw *Why Johnny Can't Read* as a way of rallying against the experts and reasserting control. The desire on the part of parents to control the education of their offspring is deep-rooted in American society. Farmers in the midwest, to offer just one example, had put up a tough fight to keep control over their little rural schoolhouses at the turn of the twentieth century (Fuller, 1982). With his how-to approach, Flesch offered parents a way of wresting control back from the professionals.

Those reviews that praised Flesch's book support this interpretation. 'Parents . . . will not be put off with "teacher knows best",' said one. 'There has been enough dissatisfaction with the failure of schools to teach the basic skills to ensure an audience reaction at home for this', said another. Yet another claimed that parents, previously 'inarticulate in the face of the pompous and condescending "explanations" of the educators', had finally found a spokesman. Not surprisingly, reviews of *Why Johnny Can't Read* in the professional journals were damning. They claimed that Flesch's method would produce 'word callers' — that is, children who would read without understanding (James and Brown, 1956, p. 305).

There is nothing in the official history of the International Reading Association that suggests that it was created in any way as a response to *Why Johnny Can't Read*. In fact, the plans for a merger of the ICIRI and NART were well in hand before Flesch's book appeared. It is also true, however, that those in both organizations who had been hesitating about a merger put aside their differences. *Why Johnny Can't Read* appeared early in 1955. In November of the same year the bylaws and ballot for the new organization were mailed out to NART and ICIRI members. The merger was overwhelmingly approved with only 7 per cent voting in opposition. In December 1955, the *Reading Teacher*, in its last issue under ICIRI sponsorship, published a group of articles which the editor hoped would help clarify 'the proper place of phonics in reading instruction and how it should be taught'. On 1 January 1956 the International Reading Association was born (Jerrolds, 1977, pp. 18–19 and 29).

Flesch's book appears to have influenced the reading curriculum in several ways. Not only did the reading profession close its ranks, but the experts further dug in their heels against the kind of phonics that Flesch had recommended — 'synthetic' phonics ('sounding out' the letters and 'blending' the sounds into a word) — while they continued to support the sight approach and 'analytic' phonics, which banned treating letters as sounds in isolation. (It should be noted that the history of American reading instruction from the 1880s up to the 1910s is replete with examples of synthetic phonics instruction [for example, Smith, 1965, pp. 131–41]; and in England and Scotland it is still standard practice for teachers to identify letters not by their alphabetic names but by their 'sounds'.)

Second, Flesch's book had an effect in the political arena. It was received enthusiastically by conservatives who had already become convinced that the country, thanks to the influence of progressive education, had gone soft. Their suspicions were confirmed when Sputnik was launched in 1957. Admiral Rickover was only one of those who called for a return to the basics (Rickover, 1959). 'Johnny' became a household word, a rallying cry for those who thought education had moved in the wrong direction. Books such as *What Ivan Knows That Johnny Doesn't* expressed the anxiety of the nation; and titles like *Why Johnny Can't Add* (an attack on the New Math), not to mention Flesch's own *Why Johnny Still Can't Read* (which, unlike its predecessor, was not a commercial success) would appear decades after the publication of the original *Johnny* (Trace, 1961; Kline, 1973; Flesch, 1981).

Third, the climate that *Why Johnny Can't Read* fostered unquestionably had an impact on the publishing industry. As so many of the persons attacked by Flesch were, indeed, senior authors of reading programs, it is hardly surprising that their textbooks remained committed to the 'conventional wisdom', as Chall called it when she examined the issue in 1967 (Chall, 1967). (Her own book, titled *Learning to Read: The Great Debate*, would have more influence on the traditional basal reading series than Flesch's [Chall, 1983, p. 3], as she was a highly respected member of the reading profession). Several publishers, however, were willing to look outside the reading profession for their authors. The early 1960s saw the introduction of several basal series whose senior authors were not only independent of the reading profession but critical of it (for example, McCracken and Walcutt, 1963; cf. Terman and Walcutt, 1958). As the years passed, the pace of innovation in beginning reading programs accelerated rapidly (Vilscek, 1968; Wittick, 1968). Some of the flurry would, as we shall see, be the result of government money provided by the passage of the Elementary and Secondary Education Act of 1965.

## Summary

This chapter has pointed to a series of factors that contributed markedly to the formation of the English language curriculum as it existed up through the 1950s: (i) it was taken for granted that reading instruction must precede writing instruction; (ii) there is strength that comes to a field whose mission is clearly defined; (iii) reading instruction is a better vehicle than writing for transmitting societal values, and has therefore attracted more attention; (iv) the interests of the publishing industry are better served by reading than by writing instruction; (v) teachers can control writing instruction more readily than reading instruction; (vi) theories of learning and language are powerful in terms of both classroom practice and research. A behaviorally-based theory promotes an emphasis on reading instruction, because reading lends itself better than writing to behavioral description and evaluation. (That which is not tested may not be taught.); (vii) reading teachers could more readily find professional specialization and identity in their professional organization than writing teachers could in theirs; (viii) Public opinion is an important influence on publishers (and so curricula) and on professional organizations.

If these categories are indeed useful, they should serve well as heuristics for explaining two recent and important moments in the history of literacy instruction — the enormous resources directed toward reading in Lyndon B. Johnson's Great Society, and the current increased emphasis on writing instruction.

## Reading Instruction and the Great Society

Lyndon B. Johnson's vision of a better tomorrow was translated into major expenditures on education. The passage of the Elementary and Secondary Education Act in 1965 provided over a billion dollars to improve the educational experience of underprivileged and minority children. No school subject matter was considered as important as reading. The Title I portion of the Act financed extensive remedial programs in reading and in mathematics instruction, in both public and parochial disadvantaged schools. There was no comparable Title I program for remedial writing instruction.

The reasons relate to the factors that we have just identified as influential. Not only did the notion still prevail that the acquisition of reading should precede that of writing, but, as discussed, the very nature of reading encouraged the public conviction that reading mattered more than writing. The content of children's readers had always been considered important; more recently, thanks to the furor over *Why Johnny Can't Read*, methods of reading instruction had received high visibility as well. Writing in the elementary schools, on the other hand, had been treated more or less as a frill.

At least as important was the definition of the problem: society had an illness and needed specialists to make it well again. NCTE members had never claimed, of course, to be specialists in disability;

their interest had been primarily in literature and expression. The reading professionals, on the other hand, were ready for the challenge. They could point to a substantial body of research on reading failure. For decades now they had used the vocabulary of testing, diagnosis and remediation; recently they had begun to acquire specific qualifications as reading specialists. Alert schools of education added Masters' degrees in reading to their graduate programs to meet the need. Armed with their powerful orthopedic metaphor, the reading specialists were well-equipped to enter the schools of America and bring their expertise to the disabled reader.

The way the money was dispensed also worked to the advantage of the reading profession. Federal money, in education, cannot be used to pay for services the states already finance. It could not, therefore, be used simply to purchase more teachers for the elementary classroom, but could be used to hire specialists. The reading professionals had a cadre of specialists already trained and many more coming through the graduate school pipeline. There was, in truth, no such creature as a writing specialist for the elementary school. When teachers of writing were funded by the government (and a few were), they were not likely to be NCTE members, but poets and writers with no formal professional affiliations.

In addition, the need to spend quantities of money on materials worked to the advantage of reading rather than writing. Federal money had to be spent before each deadline or it was simply lost. Book publishers were for the first time in the position of barely being able to keep up with the demand. Textbook houses created one new program after another. Schools bought a newspaper for every child. There was an orgy of book, newspaper and program purchasing.

When the government looked for ways to spend money on research, and asked to see the theories underlying instruction, the writing professionals were still at a disadvantage. The NCTE itself would later deplore the absence of convincing, or even generally accepted, theories of composition. The reading profession, in contrast, was still happy with its focus on skill acquisition, which it explored through studies that adhered to the experimental paradigm. Behaviorism itself had even been invigorated by a recent shot in the arm: in the 1960s, it was adopted by a new set of young reading experts, who, inspired by the work of B.F. Skinner, were creating behaviorally-based programs, kits and even whole reading systems (cf. Bereiter and Engelmann, 1966; Glaser, 1978). 'Programmed instruction' could be found in the form of the 'individualized reading labs' that were adopted by a large number of junior high schools, or the programs evolved for the early grades and even kindergartens (for example, Sullivan Associates, 1963–66; Engelmann, Osborn and Engelmann, 1969).

In addition, the research agenda for reading seemed clearer: questions on which reading methods were superior had yet to be solved. The US Office of Education funded an extensive research effort to investigate the reading performance of 25,000 children in twenty-seven first-grade reading programs (Bond and Dykstra, 1967).

All the factors we have identified, then, were indeed operating in favor of an emphasis on reading, in the government expenditures of Johnson's Great Society. These same factors are also present, though in many cases in a reversed form, in a new development in American literacy instruction: the recent interest in writing in general, and a particular involvement with the writing of children in the earliest grades of the elementary school.

## The Current Emphasis on Writing

Over the past decade or so, there has been a major shift in literacy instruction towards emphasizing writing at all levels of the educational enterprise. The pressure began at the college level, and seems to be coming both from the world within and outside college. From the 1970s on, there has been talk of a 'writing crisis'. Corporations have wearied of employing college graduates who can barely rub two sentences together, and colleges themselves are trying to reintroduce to their own curricula a renewed emphasis on essay writing, long threatened by the seductive ease of scoring multiple-choice tests.

The realization of how appallingly some high school graduates write was in part a consequence of more liberal admission policies in some college systems in the late 1960s. The influx of underprepared students on certain campuses, such as those of The City University of New York (CUNY), created a need for extensive remedial programs in all areas. There have been some unanticipated benefits from this. In writing instruction, programs have profited from their attraction to teachers genuinely interested in remediation. The remedial writing programs are likely to be staffed not by those who would much prefer to be teaching Chaucer, but by teachers who believe that their students are academically salvageable, and who are able to see method in the apparent madness of their students' writing (Shaughnessy, 1977).

In addition, even if only to a certain extent, the pressure that colleges exert on high schools to produce essay-writers is being restored. The fate of the essay test of the College Board is a case in point — and it also indicates how powerful pressures for change can be when they are sponsored jointly by groups both inside and outside the educational community. In the 1950s, the Board's English Composition Test was administered entirely in the multiple-choice format. In 1963, one form of the test a year included an essay, but this was abandoned in 1971, on the grounds of expense. For the next several years, English teachers 'pressed for the reinstatement of the writing component. As the "writing crisis" became a major concern in American education, the College Board responded by introducing the 20-minute essay once again in December 1977, in order to signal the importance of writing in the secondary curriculum' (Donlon, 1984, p. 90). (Advances in techniques of holistic scoring were key to this successful reintroduction.)

It is doubtful that this new interest in writing could have produced so much fruit if it had not also been accompanied by a change in theory. One such theoretical change has occurred among the writing professionals, but has been to the advantage of reading rather than writing. It has taken place at the highest echelons of English as a field of study, and has served to redirect the attention of English specialists toward the importance of the reader of a text: 'new criticism' has been largely displaced by 'reader-response' theory. Where, under the former approach, a piece of literature was to be viewed as a self-contained work of art, the latter views the reader's response to a text as a potentially crucial ingredient of the literary experience. This has had a trickle-down effect on the English profession at all levels.

Much more important to writing itself, however, has been the reemergence of cognitive psychology in the 1960s — after decades in the doldrums — together with the growth of the new field of psycholinguistics. These have been instrumental, at least in part, in changing the face of research. Table 2 above reveals the striking recent increase in research into writing in general, and into writing processes in particular. (We noted earlier that ERIC only introduced the categories 'writing research/writing processes' in 1980.) Between 1981 and 1985, there were nearly 1100 new studies on writing processes, actually outstripping those on reading processes. (This was the first time in ERIC that studies in a writing category outnumbered those in the corresponding reading category). Moreover, while ERIC entries on reading instruction hovered, for any given five-year period since 1971, between 3200 and 3500, entries on writing instruction soared up to the 3000 mark in the 1981–1985 period. Writing research, as 1986 figures confirm, is an area in its ascendancy.

Qualitative, longtitudinal case-studies of the processes of both reading and writing acquisition have been increasing in popularity since the 1970s. For writing, this new research focus — new in both content and method — is generally dated from Janet Emig's dissertation on the composing processes of twelfth-graders, in 1969, and Donald Graves' study for his dissertation in 1973 of how 7-year-olds composed (Emig, 1971; Graves, 1981, pp. 93–6; Burrows, 1977, pp. 37–41). A key aspect of this ethnographic research is its focus on the development of literacy acquisition over time. The young child's acquisition of the written language is compared to that of the spoken: a gradual approximation to adult forms.

One notable feature of this research is that those who undertake it have made it readily accessible to teachers. In a manner reminiscent of William S. Gray, Donald Graves and others have drawn the implications of their research for classroom practice, in a series of lectures and books (for example, Graves, 1983; Calkins, 1986). It is, of course, no mere coincidence that they have have succeeded at this, where former researchers into writing (such as there were) failed: research into classroom processes translates easily into advice on classroom procedures.

Children's ability to control the writing implement has long been, as we have seen, technically possible, thanks to the pencil (or wax crayon and magic marker, in the kindergarten). The profession's realization that children are able to compose at grades lower than the third grade has been materially assisted by studies that show that children who learn to read while very young actually prefer to start on the road of literacy by writing, not by reading (Durkin, 1970), and that young children's invented spellings reveal that they enter school already able to detect subtle phonetic relationships (Read, 1975). The long-cherished assumption that reading instruction must precede writing instruction has been shattered. The resultant movement is often known as the 'whole language' approach. Its unifying feature is its stress on literacy acquisition as a language-driven, not a skill-driven, process. (cf. Haley-James, 1981)[6]

Once the advice to elementary-school teachers to focus more on writing instruction has been proffered, it has proven relatively easy to put into practice. The greater control that teachers have over writing instruction works to the advantage of reform: teachers who wish their pupils to spend more time on writing in their first-grade or even kindergarten classes are in a much better position to do so than if they wanted to change the reading program. Further, we believe that teachers welcome the change because they regain the control over their own pedagogy — 'empowerment' would be a better term — that so many basal reading programs seek to deny them. Equally important, young children, too, are empowered by being allowed to write about what interests them, without being scolded for mis-spellings.

One last, and welcome, aspect of all this is that there has been somewhat of a professional rapprochement between the reading and the writing professions. Those who were involved with research into children's writing quickly saw the artificiality of the division between the two literacy skills: children who wrote invariably read not only what they had written but what other children wrote. Donald Graves and his co-workers began to attend conventions of the International Reading Association. In addition, in an important move, the IRA has, since 1977, broadened its focus to include literacy, not reading alone. The result of this shift is now visible in the boom in sessions that include writing at the IRA's annual conventions. (In 1981, the word 'writing' appeared in the titles of twenty IRA sessions; in 1986 there were forty-six instances. As a proportion of all the sessions, this was an increase from 6 to 12 per cent.) There has been a similar shift at the NCTE, resulting in, for example, an increased number of articles on reading in NCTE's elementary journal, *Language Arts*.

The new emphasis on writing has the very real advantage of transferring some of the thinking back from the reading process to the writing. Throughout the last fifty or so years, reading has had to bear the weight — from the child's earliest reading experiences, as we have seen — of the need for educators to include interpretation and criticism in the elementary curriculum. Thinking was loaded onto the back of reading instruction, we suggest, by default: children were doing so little writing that if thinking had been postponed until they could write, they would never have come to it at all. We are not, we hasten to add, recommending that children not be asked to think as they read; rather, we agree with those who claim that the new view reinstates writing as a form of thinking (for example, Emig, 1977; Fulwiler, 1982). No longer does all the thought have to precede the writing; it is now accepted that thought develops along with the writing. The new perception of writing has shifted from 'knowing how to write' to 'writing in order to know'. This also has applications for the reading arena: the conceptual push today in both reading and writing is toward strategies for making meaning. The emphasis on process over product potentially reconnects the thinker to both the scribe and the reader.

This has implications for teachers as well as schoolchildren. Elementary school teachers have not, we believe, traditionally thought of themselves as writers, although they probably consider themselves to be readers. Texts like Graves' *Writing: Teachers and Children at Work* (1983) value the teacher as creator as well as the child.

We would be remiss, however, if we left our audience with the feeling that all was now rosy in the literacy garden, and that those who care about the literacy acquisition of the young can sit back and relax. In the first place, these innovations in writing are no more standard practice at the elementary school level than progressive education ever was. For another, even if they were to become so, they echo many features of the progressive education movement of the early decades of this century (Donsky, 1984, pp. 801–2; cf. Myers, 1986, who invokes Leonard, 1917). None of us needs to be reminded of the fate of the progressive movement (Cremin, 1964; Zilversmit, 1976), which sank, in part, under its presumed permissiveness. Today's writing approach may differ from its progressive predecessor in its attitude toward self-discipline. After all, there are those who argue that control and discipline are basic even to composing poetry (Livingston, 1984, p. 309). If not, and if children who have been encouraged to express themselves naturalistically in the first grades fail to develop ability at, say, expository writing in the higher grades, as well as a mastery of adult writing forms, then the contemporary back-to-basics movement (itself an expression of genuine parental concern) may well insist on reintroducing some of the more conventional features of prior conventional wisdoms.

Nor should it be thought that the literacy curricula of the future will be any less susceptible to the influences we have identified than have those of the past. Our tale has, after all, been in essence one of a struggle among various groups — professionals, textbook publishers, parents, teachers — for control.

We predict, for instance, that it will continue to be reading instruction that will bear the brunt of public and political pressures. There are tremendous political interests involved in the allocations of the 3.8 billion dollars now made available for education under Chapter I funds. (It is not irrelevant to note, in this connection, that the IRA has just increased its lobbyist from a quarter to a half-time position; the NCTE has no salaried lobbyist at all.) Reading instruction will also, we believe, remain the prime attraction for commercial interests: reading textbooks will always outnumber writing textbooks.

There is, however, one notable qualification to this last stricture. For almost the first time in the history of literacy instruction — the typewriter being a prior instance — it has become possible to spend money, big money, on writing instruction, thanks to the invention of the word processor. This has turned out to be a highly desirable tool for writing, as it makes textual revision and the production of a fair copy so easy. Of course, the personal computer, which the word processor presupposes, can equally well be used to run computer reading programs. It will be interesting to see whether teachers and children will choose — or be permitted to choose — the personal computer as an aid to writing, or whether computer applications to reading instruction (which would suit big business better) will prevail.

We have one final prediction, and it presents a nice historical irony. The computer, that most modern of tools, is likely to promote an ancient pedagogical emphasis. Both the computer keyboard and monitor present text letter by letter in a linear fashion. This, we suggest, will be a powerful force for reinstating the most basic element of colonial instruction, the letter, in place of the whole word which has undergirded so much of twentieth-century literacy instruction.

## Afterword

Lewis Mumford, in *The Myth of the Machine*, discusses the generalist's need to forfeit detail so that overall patterns can be seen (Mumford, 1967, pp. 16–17). Forfeiting detail means taking academic risks and inviting criticism from specialists. It also means sacrificing some of the control one has when exploring the terrain on foot. We have taken this risk, however, because we believe that the pattern that emerges in the aerial view is important. It is hoped that this chapter will be read as the beginning of a conversation; we wait for pieces to be fitted into the map only tentatively outlined here.

## Acknowledgements

We would like to express our appreciation to Richard L. Venezky (without necessarily invoking his endorsement of our chapter) for his valuable criticisms of an earlier draft of this chapter, and for bibliographical suggestions.

## Notes

1 Figures provided courtesy of Don Ecklund, American Publishers Association.
2 We extend our thanks to Anne Grosso of the College Board for information on the Board's English composition test.
3 We are most grateful to Howard Curnoles, Robin Klein, and Simmona Simmons, University of Maryland-Baltimore County Library, for obtaining the ERIC figures.
4 We thank Kent Williamson of National Council of Teachers of English and James Sawyer of the International Reading Association for providing us with membership figures. NCTE reports, for 1984, figures as follows: elementary: 6068; high school: 25,627; university: 9268 (total: 40,963). Figures as of January 1986 are: elementary: 7457; high school: 32,397; university: 10,810 (total: 50,664).

  IRA membership numbers are not broken down into categories by affiliation, but the figure of 60 per cent was obtained from responses to the question: 'Where were your major responsibilities?' IRA membership totaled 57,686 in 1984; 65,481 as of the end of February 1986.
5 Figures provided courtesy of Harper and Row.

## References

*Annual Catalogue of the State Normal School of Maryland, 1866.* n.p.: State Normal School of Maryland, 1866.

*Annual Catalogue of the State Normal School of Maryland, 1873.* n.p.: State Normal School of Maryland, 1873.

APPLEBEE, A.N. *Tradition and Reform in the Teaching of English: A History,* Urbana, IL: National Council of Teachers of English, 1974.

BEREITER, C., and ENGLEMANN, S. *Teaching Disadvantaged Children in the Preschool.* Englewood Cliffs, NJ: Prentice-Hall, 1966.

BETTS, E.A. *Prevention and Correction of Reading Difficulties.* Evanston, IL: Row, Peterson, 1936.

BOND, G.L. and DYKSTRA, R. 'The cooperative research program in first-grade reading instruction', *Reading Research Quarterly,* 2, 1967, pp. 5–142.

BRADDOCK, R., LLOYD-JONES, R. and SCHOER, L. *Research in Written Composition.* Urbana, IL: National Council of Teachers of English, 1963.

E. *Jennifer Monaghan and E. Wendy Saul*

BURGH, J. *The Art of Speaking* ..., 4th edn Philadelphia: Aitken, 1775.

BURROWS, A.T. 'Children's writing and children's growth', *Elementary English*, 28, 1951, pp. 205–7.

BURROWS, A.T. 'Composition: Prospect and retrospect', in ROBINSON, H.A. (Ed.), *Reading and Writing Instruction in the United States: Historical Trends*. Urbana, IL: International Reading Association and ERIC, 1977.

CARPENTER, C. *History of American Schoolbooks*. Philadelphia, PA: University of Pennsylvania Press, 1963.

CHALL, J.S. *Learning To Read: The Great Debate*. New York: McGraw-Hill, 1967.

CHALL, J.S. *Learning to Read: The Great Debate*, updated edn, New York: McGraw-Hill, 1983.

CLIFFORD, G.J. 'Words for schools: The applications in education of the vocabulary researches of Edward L. Thorndike', in SUPPES, P. (Ed.) *Impact of Research on Education: Some Case Studies*, Washington, DC: National Academy of Education, 1978.

COOK, W.D. *Adult Literacy Education in the United States*. Newark, DE: International Reading Association, 1977.

COOPER, C.R. and ODELL, L. (Eds) *Research on Composing: Points of Departure*. Urbana, IL: National Council of Teachers of English, 1978.

COOTE, E. *The English Schoole-Maister* (1596), in HART, W.R. '*The English Schoole-Maister* (1596) by Edmund Coote: An edition of the text with critical notes and introductions', dissertation University of Michigan, 1963.

'Creative Writing, Teaching of', in DEIGHTON, L.C. (Ed.) *Encyclopedia of Education*, New York: Macmillan and Free Press, 2, 1971, pp. 548–52.

CREMIN, L.A. *The Transformation of the School: Progressivism in American Education, 1876–1957*, New York: Vintage Books, 1964.

CREMIN, L.A. *American Education: The Colonial Experience, 1607–1783*. New York: Harper and Row, 1970.

DEIGHTON, L.C. *Encyclopedia of Education*, New York: Macmillan and Free Press, 1971.

DONLON, T.F. (Ed.) *The College Board Technical Handbook for the Scholastic Aptitude Test and Achievement Tests*, New York: College Entrance Examination Board, 1984.

DONSKY, B. VON BRACHT. 'Trends in elementary writing instruction, 1900–1959', *Language Arts*, 61, 1984, pp. 795–803.

DURKIN, D. 'A language arts program for pre-first-grade children: Two-year achievement report', *Reading Research Quarterly*, 5, 1970, pp. 534–65.

ELIOT, C.W., (chair) *Report of the Committee of Ten on Secondary School Studies*. New York: National Education Association, 1894.

ELSON, R.M. *Guardians of Tradition: American Schoolbooks of the Nineteenth Century*. Lincoln, Nebraska: University of Nebraska Press, 1964.

EMIG, J. 'Writing as a mode of learning', *College Composition and Communication*, 28, 1977, pp. 122–8.

EMIG, J. *The Composing Processes of Twelfth Graders*. Urbana, IL: National Council of Teachers of English, 1971.

ENGELMANN, S., OSBORN, J. and ENGELMANN, T. *Distar Language I: An Instructional System*. Chicago: Science Research Associates, 1969.

FINKELSTEIN, B.J. 'The moral dimensions of pedagogy: Teaching behavior in popular primary schools in nineteenth-century America', *American Studies*, 15, 1974, pp. 79–89.

FLESCH, R. *Why Johnny Can't Read And What You Can Do About It*. New York: Harper and Row, 1955.

FLESCH, R. *Why Johnny Still Can't Read: A New Look at the Scandal of Our Schools*. New York: Harper and Row, 1981.

FORD, P.L. *The New-England Primer: A History of Its Origin and Development with a Reprint of the Unique Copy of the Earliest Known Edition*. New York: Dodd, Mead, 1897.

FOX, G. *Instructions for Right Spelling, and Plain Directions for Reading and Writing True Englsih ...* Newport: S. Southwick, 1769.

FULLER, W.E. *The Old Country School: The Story of Rural Education in the Middle West*. Chicago: University of Chicago, 1982.

FULWILER, T. 'Writing: An act of cognition', in GRIFFIN, C.W. (Ed.) *New Directions for Teaching and Learning: Teaching Writing in All Disci plines*, 12, San Francisco: Jossey-Bass, 1982.

GATES, A.I. *The Psychology of Reading and Spelling with Special Reference to Disability*. New York: Teachers College, Columbia University, 1922.

GATES, A.I. 'A modern systematic versus an opportunistic method of teaching. An experimentals study', *Teachers College Record*, 27, 1926, pp. 679–700.

GATES, A.I. *The Improvement of Reading, A Program of Diagnostic and Remedial Methods*. New York: Macmillan, 1927.

GATES, A.I. *New Methods in Primary Reading*. New York: Bureau of Publications, Teachers College, Columbia University, 1928.

GATES, A.I. *Interest and Ability in Reading*. New York: Macmillan, 1930.

GATES, A.I. *A Reading Vocabulary for the Primary Grades*, rev. and enlarged. New York: Teachers College, Columbia University, Bureau of Publications, 1935 (first published in 1926.)

GATES, A.I. 'An autobiography', in HAVIGHURST, R.J. (Ed.) *Leaders in American Education: The Seventieth Yearbook of the National Society for the Study of Education. Part II*, Chicago: National Society for the Study of Education, 1971.

GATES, A.I., HUBER, M.B. and AYER, J.Y. *The Work-Play Books*. New York: Macmillan, 1932.

GLASER, R. 'The contributions of B.F. Skinner to education and some counterinfluences', in SUPPES, P. (Ed.) *Impact of Research on Educa-*

*tion: Some Case Studies*, Washington, DC: National Academy of Education, 1978.

GRAVES, D. *Writing: Teachers and Children at Work*. Exeter, NH: Heinemann, 1983.

GRAVES, D. 'A new look at research on writing', in HALEY-JAMES, S.M. (Ed.) *Perspectives on Writing in Grades 1–8*, Urbana, IL: National Council of Teachers of English, 1981.

HALEY-JAMES, S.M. 'Twentieth-century perspectives on writing in grades one through eight', in HALEY-JAMES, S.M. (Ed.) *Perspectives on Writing in Grades 1–8*, Urbana, IL: National Council of Teachers of English, 1981.

HATFIELD, W.W., (chair) *An Experience Curriculum in English: A Report of the Curriculum Commission of the National Council of Teachers of English*. New York: National Council of Teachers of English, 1935.

HOOK, J.N. *A Long Way Together: A Personal View of NCTE's First Sixty-Seven Years*. Urbana, IL: National Council of Teachers of English, 1979.

HOUSTON, J.E., (Ed.) *Thesaurus of ERIC Descriptors*, 10th edn, Phoenix, AZ: Oryx Press, 1984.

HUEY, E.B. *The Psychology and Pedagogy of Reading*. Cambridge, MA: Massachusetts Institute of Technology, 1968 (first published in 1908)

JAMES, M.M., and BROWN, D. (Eds) *Book Review Digest, 1955*. New York: Wilson, 1956.

JERROLDS, B.W. *Reading Reflections: The History of the International Reading Association*. Newark, DE: International Reading Association, 1977.

KLINE, M. *Why Johnny Can't Add: The Failure of the New Math*. New York: St. Martin's Press, 1973.

LEONARD, S.A. *English Composition as a Social Problem*. Boston, MA: Houghton, 1917.

LIVINGSTON, M.C. *The Child as Poet: Myth or Reality?* Boston, MA: Hornbook, 1984.

McCRACKEN, G. and WALCUTT, C.C. *Lippincott's Basic Reading*. Philadelphia, PA: Lippincott, 1963.

MAVROGENES, N.A. 'William S. Gray: The person', in STEVENSON, J.A. (Ed.) *William S. Gray: Teacher, Scholar, Leader*, Newark, DE: International Reading Association, 1985.

MAVROGENES, N.A. 'More commentary on William S. Gray', *Reading Research Quarterly*, 21, 1986, pp. 106–7.

MINNICH, H.C. *William Holmes McGuffey and His Readers*. New York: American Book Co., 1936.

'Miscellaneous American Calligraphy', MSS., Houghton Library, Harvard University.

MONAGHAN, E.J. *A Common Heritage: Noah Webster's Blue-Back Speller*. Hamden, CT: Archon Books, 1983.

MONAGHAN, E.J. 'The three R's: Notes on the acquisition of literacy and numeracy skills in seventeenth-century New England', paper presented at the annual meeting of the American Educational Research Association, Chicago, April 1984 [ED 257 205].

MOORE, D.W. 'Laura Zirbes and progressive reading instruction', *Elementary School Journal*, 86, 1986, pp. 663–72.

MUMFORD, *The Myth of the Machine: Technics and Human Development.* New York: Harcourt, Brace, Jovanovich, 1967.

MYERS, G. 'Reality, consensus, and reform in the rhetoric of composition teaching', *College English*, 48, 1986, pp. 154–5.

NASH, R. *American Writing Masters and Copybooks: History and Bibliography Through Colonial Times.* Boston, MA: Colonial Society of Massachusetts, 1959.

OTTO, W. 'Thorndike's *Reading as Reasoning*: Influence and impact', *Reading Research Quarterly*, 6, 1971, pp. 534–65.

READ, C. *Children's Categorization of Speech Sounds.* Urbana, IL: National Council of Teachers of English, 1975.

RICKOVER, H.G. *Education and Freedom.* New York: Dutton, 1959.

ROBINSON, H.M. *Why Pupils Fail in Reading.* Chicago: University of Chicago Press, 1946.

SHAUGHNESSY, M.P. *Errors and Expectations: A Guide for the Teaching of Basic Writing.* New York: Oxford University Press, 1977.

SIZER, T.R. *Secondary Schools at the Turn of the Century.* New Haven, CT: Yale University Press, 1964.

SMITH, N.B. *American Reading Instruction.* Newark, DE: International Reading Association, 1965.

SMITH, W.E. *The McGuffeys: William Holmes McGuffey and Alexander H. McGuffey.* Oxford, OH: Cullen Print, 1963.

STEVENSON, J.A., (Ed.) *William S. Gray: Teacher, Scholar, Leader.* Newark, DE: International Reading Association, 1985.

SULLIVAN ASSOCIATES, *Programmed Reading.* Manchester, MO: Webster Division, McGraw-Hill, 1963–66.

TERMAN, S. and WALCUTT, C.C. *Reading: Chaos and Cure.* New York: McGraw-Hill, 1958.

THORNDIKE, E.L. *Selected Writings from a Connectionist's Psychology.* New York: Appleton-Century Crofts, 1949.

THORNDIKE, E.L. 'Reading as reasoning: A study of mistakes in paragraph reading', *Reading Research Quarterly*, 6, 1971, pp. 425–34.

THORNDIKE, E.L. and GATES, A.I. *Elementary Principles of Education.* New York: Macmillan, 1929.

TIPPET, J.S., (chair) *Curriculum Making in an Elementary School.* Boston, MA: Ginn, 1927.

TRACE, A.S., Jr. *What Ivan Knows That Johnny Doesn't.* New York: Random House, 1961.

VENEZKY, R.L. 'Primers, spellers, readers, and speakers: A history of the basal reader', in HOFFMAN, J.V. and ROSER, N. (Eds) *The Basal Reader in American Reading Instruction*, a special issue of the *Elementary School Journal*, 1986.

VILSCEK, E.C., (Ed.) *A Decade of Innovations: Approaches to Beginning Reading. Proceedings of the 12th Annual Convention*, 12, 3. Newark, DE: International Reading Association, 1968.

WISHY, B. *The Child and The Republic: The Dawn of Modern American Child Nurture*. Philadelphia, PA: University of Pennsylvania Press, 1968.

WITTICK, M.L. 'Innovations in reading instruction: For beginners', in ROBINSON, H.M., (Ed.) *Innovation and Change in Reading Instruction: The Sixty-seventh Yearbook of the National Society for the Study of Education, Part II*, Chicago: NSSE, 1968.

WOODWARD, A. 'Taking teaching out of teaching and reading out of learning to read: A historical study of reading textbook teachers guides 1920–1980', paper presented at the annual meeting of the American Educational Research Association, Chicago, April 1985.

ZILVERSMIT, A. 'The failure of progressive education, 1920–1940', in STONE, L. (Ed.) *Schooling and Society: Studies in the History of Education*, Baltimore, MD: John Hopkins University Press, 1976.

# 5 Emergence of the Biology Curriculum: A Science of Life or a Science of Living?

*Dorothy B. Rosenthal and Rodger W. Bybee*

## Abstract

This paper traces the history of biology as it developed from natural history into separate courses in botany, zoology and human physiology during the nineteenth century. In the early years of the twentieth century, these courses were integrated into general biology, following the model developed by Thomas Huxley. Since its inception, biology education has been characterized by changing emphasis among three primary aims: the knowledge aim, the methods aim and the personal/social aim. The degree of relative emphasis among the three aims has varied in response to historical, intellectual and social developments, including industrialization, immigration, religious movements, temperance, compulsory education, educational psychology and scientific advances in biology. A major theme throughout the history of biology education has been the continuing debates about its primary goal: whether it should be a science of life and emphasize knowledge or whether it should be a science of living and emphasize the personal needs of students and the social needs of society.

The history of biology education has been characterized by changing emphasis among three primary aims: the knowledge aim, the methods aim, and the personal/social aim (Bybee, 1977). Conflict among these three basic aims was already apparent in the life science courses that preceded biology and continued throughout the period of emergence and establishment of biology as a standard high school offering. Many of the present day debates about the proper relationship among these three primary aims are echoes of ones that have been heard many times over in science education. Throughout the 100-year history of high school biology, the degree of relative emphasis among the three competing aims has varied in response to historical and social forces.

One of the debates that emerged in the first quarter century of biology education, which happened to coincide with the first quarter of the twentieth century, was that of biology as a science of life or biology for living. The first is a statement of the knowledge aim, that is, the goal of biology education should be the transmission of biological knowledge. The second is a statement that biology education should be concerned with matters of personal or social relevance for students. The question is still unresolved and the two points of view continue to form the extremes of swings of the pendulum in biology education.

High school biology courses emerged around the turn of the century as a way of endowing life science education with greater social relevance for the increasing numbers of non-college bound students attending high school. Before that there were no biology courses *per se*, but only separate courses in botany, zoology, and human physiology. These three courses had developed, under the influence of the German universities (Rosen, 1959), from an early form of general science known as natural history. The historical, intellectual, and social forces that led to the development of high school biology are illustrative of the interactions among science, society, and education that have characterized the history of science education in this country and which are still at work today.

### Biology as Natural History

Natural history, like the game of *Twenty Questions*, divided natural objects into three categories, animal, vegetable, or mineral, and focused primarily on description and study of specimens. Interest in natural history had been stimulated by the discovery of the many new plants and animals found in the New World (Barry, 1965). During the early history of America, naturalists [as they] went forth into the wilderness, facing deprivation and even death were bent on perhaps the great enterprise of all time — the grand attempt to assemble a complete catalogue of information on the world's phenomena. The observations and descriptions that would come from their efforts would eventually establish that first great body of information which would be called science (p. 601).

At first, the naturalists' 'efforts were directed toward making their observations compatible with the philosophic interpretation of nature that prevailed at that time — a world descendent from Genesis and a world without change' (*ibid*, p. 602), i.e. 'to show God's work through living things' (Finley, 1926, p. 3). Courses in natural history, as well as early courses in botany and zoology, reflected the interest in description and classification of living things and the religious interpretation of natural phenomena. The religious aim, which can be thought of as an early formulation of the personal/social aim,

> was perhaps, the dominant aim in early botany . . . . The first years of zoology found a number of texts written by clergymen. Many of them were catechetical in nature. The textbook method then dominant was undoubtedly similar to the catechetical method of teaching church precepts. (Christy, 1936, p. 293).

The first natural history course taught in an American high school was given at the English Classical School in Boston, Massachusetts, beginning in 1821. It was an eclectic course, consisting of studies in metallurgy, navigation, geography, astronomy, chemistry, electricity and galvanism, magnetism, optics, meteorology, mythology, heraldry, literature, and morals and religion as well as botany and zoology. A major theme of the course was 'the wonderful harmony of nature and its relation to moral behavior' (Rosen, 1959, pp. 473–89).

This course evolved into one in the 'Philosophy of natural history' and the school itself became simply the English High School in 1825. Not long after, natural history courses emerged in the curricula of other high schools in the east (*ibid*, p. 474). Apparently such courses were not taken seriously by schools because public examinations in natural history were not offered. This is not surprising since the preface to the most popular textbook of that period (*The Philosophy of Natural History*, by William Smellie, 1824) stated that the knowledge of natural history would 'afford innocent and virtuous amusement, and . . . occupy agreeably the leisure or vacant hours of life' (quoted in Rosen, 1959, p. 475).

## Botany Courses

The first specialized course in the life sciences in high school was botany, which was first offered in 1826 at Girls' High School in Boston. This course adopted a natural history approach to the study of plants, and dealt primarily with description and classification. At first, botany was considered particularly well suited to females and suffered from low enrollments. Later, professional botanists, such as Asa Gray at Harvard, began to exert more influence, and to counteract the stereotype of botany as 'unmanly' (Christy, 1936). By 1857, botany had become a required subject in Massachusetts towns with populations of 5000 or more (Rosen, 1959), evidence that the tide had turned somewhat by then.

Asa Gray was the author of *How Plants Grow* (1858), which became very popular and was itself most influential in popularizing descriptive botany as a course and as an avocation. The evolutionary influence on botany reached the United States somewhat later than Europe because of the distractions of the Civil War. In the colleges and universities, Darwin's 'work centered attention on the structure and growth processes of plants' (Rosen, 1959, p. 426). Gray, although a spokesman for Darwinism, did not follow the evolutionist trend towards an emphasis on morphology, physiology, and laboratory work in his high school texts. Gray's botany was based on Goethe's doctrine of metamorphosis and focused almost exclusively on flowering plants (Coulter, 1911).

After 1860, the idea of teaching science as a means of developing mental discipline in students became popular. It was part of 'a revolt against the old textbook type of teaching . . . [and] the laboratory method was hailed as the perfect instrument for the attainment of the mental discipline aim' (Christy, 1936, p. 174). Mental discipline was an example of an early attempt to make method the primary goal of science education, albeit a method that was to aid in the personal development of students. The 'revolt' shifted emphasis from textbook to laboratory, and from classification to morphology. In the 1880s, Bessey brought more recent German ideas to the United States, ushering in the 'dawn of modern botany in the United States' (Coulter, 1911, p. 816). The more modern approach dealt with the whole plant kingdom and with reproductive organs, as well as roots, stems, and leaves. Soon after, botany replaced physiology as the most frequently offered life science in schools (table 1).

*Table 1: Percentage of Schools Offering the Different Life Sciences 1860–1900*

| Subjects | 1860–65 | 1866–70 | 1871–75 | 1876–80 | 1881–85 | 1886–90 | 1891–95 | 1896–90 |
|---|---|---|---|---|---|---|---|---|
| Physiology | 85 | 75 | 85 | 95 | 92 | 87 | 80 | 70 |
| Botany | 70 | 25 | 85 | 85 | 72 | 97 | 82.5 | 82.5 |
| Zoology | 20 | 20 | 40 | 45 | 40 | 64 | 37.5 | 42.5 |
| Biology | — | — | — | — | — | — | — | 10 |

*Source:* Christy, 1936, p. 176

When the Committee of Ten of the National Education Association published its Report in 1894, it declared that preparation for college was not the primary goal of secondary schools. However, the Report then went on to make recommendations which seemed to describe a curriculum for college preparation (DeYoung and Wynn, 1972, p. 194). This was certainly true in the case of botany for which the Committee recommended replacing half-year botany electives then in the high schools with a full-year botany course with laboratory work. The full-year course accentuated the comparative morphology of plants and the study of microscopic anatomy (Rosen, 1959). In practice, many secondary school teachers presented a version of their college botany courses to their high school students, often even using the same textbooks.

The morphological approach, carried to the extreme, paralleled the taxonomic approach, in that it dealt with non-living specimens and terminology. A call for a more practical and lively plant science was heard, spearheaded by Bailey's *Botany, An Elementary Text for Schools* (1900), in which Bailey stated:

> The ninety and nine cannot and should not be botanists, but everyone can love plants and nature .... Education should train persons to live, rather than to be scientists. (quoted in Christy, 1936, p. 175)

The change in emphasis from knowledge to personal/social goals was largely due to new attitudes accompanying the rise of interest in general biology courses which developed around the turn of the century.

The next twenty-five years have been described as one of confusion for high school botany. While some schools implemented the courses suggested by the Committee of Ten, many more did not. Disagreement about the proper focus for secondary botany courses was rampant. The popularity of botany, as reflected in enrollments, decreased and by 1936 the College Entrance Examination Board removed botany from its list (Rosen, 1959).


## Zoology Courses

Zoology was introduced into the high school curriculum in 1849 at Waltham High School in Waltham, Massachusetts (Downing, 1925). Like the early botany courses, the first zoology courses adopted a 'natural history' approach, however, zoology was presented as less technical. High school zoology had its scientist-champion in the person of Louis Agassiz. Not only did Agassiz write the most popular zoology textbook of his time (Agassiz and Gould, 1851, *Principles of Zoology*), but he taught classes in high schools and brought high school teachers into his laboratory for further education. Under Agassiz's influence, comparative anatomy and classification replaced natural history. Agassiz explicitly stated the religious aim in his textbook. Natural history, he said, reaches its highest fulfillment as it reveals the hand of God in nature (Christy, 1936, p. 293).

While Agassiz took a broad, philosophical approach to zoology in his textbook, another popular textbook, Tenney and Tenney's *Natural History of Animals* (1871) took a more traditional approach and emphasized description and classification. Agassiz's approach received encouragement at the high school level from his pupil, Edward S. Morse, through his textbook *First Book of Zoology* (1875). This was the first textbook written for high school students that departed from prior approaches, namely, compendia of animal life from man to protozoa. The greater emphasis on lower animal forms and collecting and preserving such forms from easily accessible habitats brought zoology within the range of the ordinary student. As laboratory work became more prominent in science education, zoology adopted a more morphological approach, with the emphasis on type-animals promoted by Huxley around the turn of the century. This period of zoology paralleled the morphological period in botany. Both were dominated by the same major aim, mental discipline (Christy, 1936).

Darwin's ideas on evolution, published in his *Origin of Species* in 1859, were slower to receive acceptance from most American scientists (Gray was an exception) than from European scientists. The influence of Agassiz, an outspoken opponent of Darwinism, and then Edward Morse, on high school zoology, added to the lag between the publication of Darwin's theory and the teaching of evolution in American high schools, which did not begin until after 1900. This lag occurred in spite of the fact that Darwin's ideas were embodied in an influential college textbook published in 1876, *A Course of Practical Instruction in Elementary Biology* by Thomas Huxley and Henry Martin, and that many students who used this textbook later incorporated the content, methods, and ideas of the book into their high school teaching. In 1894, the Committee of Ten recommended a full year zoology course for high schools, as it did for botany, with emphasis on microscopic anatomy.

The conflict between the morphological approach and the natural history approach continued in high school zoology through the turn of the century and into the first quarter of the twentieth century. When zoology achieved the status of being accepted for admission to Harvard University in 1898, twenty-two years later than botany, the outline prepared by Charles B. Davenport represented a victory for the idea that natural history should be the central approach of high school biology courses. The College Board Examination in biology was a mixture of nautral history and Huxley's method of anatomy of animal types. Soon other authors of textbooks were emphasizing still other aspects of zoology, such as ecology. In spite of these changes, zoology declined in popularity and the College Board Examination was discontinued in 1936.

## Human Physiology Courses

Human physiology became part of the curriculum of the normal schools in Massachusetts, beginning in 1939. It differed from both botany and zoology in that it was taught in elementary schools as well as secondary schools. The first high school course was taught in Philadelphia Central High School in 1839 and included gross anatomy and body functions. The subject was considered important enough to be legislated as part of the public school curriculum in Massachusetts in 1850. By the end of the nineteenth century, human physiology was taught in virtually every high school in the country (Rosen, 1957, p. 309). Many of the physiology textbooks were written by physicians, who stressed anatomy, with considerably less attention to physiology and hygiene. The two aims expressed by textbook authors, the health aim and the religious aim, can be considered as types of personal/social aims but in practice, these were secondary to the knowledge aim.

After 1865, the emphasis on hygiene in physiology courses increased. Part of the reason for this was that the temperance forces saw physiology courses as a means of instilling 'dread and hatred' toward alcohol and tobacco. The Women's Christian Temperance Union was organized in 1875 and in 1879 it mounted a concerted effort to get temperance into the public school curriculum. By 1886, temperance education was required in eighteen states and the District of Columbia and by 1902 in all states bar Georgia (Christy, 1936).

The WCTU 'spelled out exactly how many pages of a textbook should be devoted to alcohol and tobacco (one-fifth of the textbook, or at least twenty pages) and designated minimum classroom time to be spent on the subject' (Rosen, 1957, p. 310). Many states required thirty lessons a year in temperance physiology for grades 2 through 10. The result, a deadly repetition of the same material year after year combined with the recitation method, as opposed to the laboratory methods used in botany and zoology courses, adversely affected the popularity of physiology. Furthermore, however effective the temperance textbooks may have been against the evils of alcohol, they were not good physiology textbooks and came under strong attack from scientists. By 1900, the influence of temperance groups on physiology curricula had waned.

The attempts of college and high school physiology teachers to place their course on a plane with botany and zoology contributed to the decline of human physiology because high schools were unable to meet the standards prescribed by Harvard and other influential institutions, particularly in the case of laboratory equipment and facilities. Rosen (1957) summarizes the history of the subject as follows:

> The decline of physiology teaching is especially significant as an example of both the working of social and political forces and the influence of higher-education the high school curriculum ... it became a candidate for oblivion because of legal strictures clamped on the subject through efforts of the Women's Christian Temperance Union and attempts of college lab physiologists to introduce research methods into high school courses. (p. 308)

## General Biology Emerges

Darwin's champion, the great biologist Thomas Huxley, had a three-fold influence on science education in the United States through the textbook he wrote with his student, Henry Martin: *A Course of Practical Instruction in Elementary Biology* (1876). This textbook established Darwinian evolution in the biology curriculum, advocated the use of laboratory work, particularly dissection, and introduced the idea of a general biology course.

Huxley based his idea for a general biology course on the concept that 'the study of living bodies is really one discipline, which is divided into zoology and botany simply as a matter of convenience' (Huxley and Martin, 1876, p. v). The term 'Biologie' first appeared in a work by Lamarck in 1801. 'Almost simultaneously it occurred to Treviranus that all sciences dealing with living matter should be treated as one, and in 1802, he published the first volume of his *Biologie*' (Christy, 1936, p. 180). Biology was defined by Whewell in 1847 as 'the science of life' and by Monroe in 1911–13 as 'general elementary courses of instruction in which both plants and animals are considered in their relation to each other as illustrations of principles that hold true for living things generally' (quoted in Christy, 1936, p. 180).

In the 1870s, Henry Martin brought the concept of a general biology course that would integrate botany, zoology, and human physiology to Johns Hopkins University. From there it quickly spread to other colleges and universities and, soon after, began to appear in high school curricula. The first high school biology course in the United States was offered in Milwaukee in 1881. By 1900, seven other cities were teaching high school biology and the New York Board of Regents had developed a general biology course for use in the state's high schools (Hurd, 1961).

At first, high school biology teachers used college textbooks, such as that by Huxley and Martin, and modeled their courses on college curricula. Thus, Huxley's ideas on general biology and the importance of laboratory work diffused very rapidly into the mainstream of science education, although evolution was much slower to win acceptance (Cretzinger, 1941; Rosen, 1959). One of the problems with establishing biology courses that were truly integrated was that there were no models for such courses and the first textbooks were side-by-side botany and zoology texts with no attempt at consolidation. The usual approach was known as the 'two-type' method, or the fern and worm method, in which these two organisms were studied as prototypes of their respective kingdoms. The first truly blended textbook was *General Biology* by J.G. Needham (1910).

Despite the efforts to make biology an integrated course in life science, in practice many courses and textbooks maintained a tripartite division into units on botany, zoology, and human physiology (Finley, 1926), an organization that still survives today in some curricula and textbooks. The 'divided' approach was evident in the general biology syllabus developed by the New York Board of Regents in 1899 as it was in the first textbook written to conform to the Regents syllabus: *Elements of Biology* (Hunter, 1907). This approach was maintained in New York State until the most recent revision of the syllabus in 1982 (Bureau of General Curriculum Development), in which the treatment of plants and animals was integrated, but human physiology remained as a separate unit. Both the blended approach and the tripartite approach had their advocates, and although by 1936 Christy reported that the former was increasing, there was still controversy over the best approach to take.

Early high school biology courses shared some of the characteristics of their predecessors, botany, zoology, and physiology, in that they were highly academic and emphasized structural detail. Dissatisfaction with the state of the biology curriculum was expressed from several quarters and from several points of view. The American Association for the Advancement of Science pleaded for a natural history approach in 1903, while the Central Association of Science and Mathematics Teachers advocated a strong academic course. One of those who protested against the academic approach was Jean Dawson, a biology instructor at the Normal School in Cleveland, Ohio, who complained in 1909 that

> ... the botany and zoology of our high schools has been from the first undifferentiated from the work of the college. New methods or phases of biology appearing in college soon crop out in the high school ... with but few changes. The appointments of the high school laboratory are also modeled after and even rival those of the college....
>
> The high school textbooks ... are so complete that they form compendiums from which I have seen graduate students studying preparatory to taking an exam for the degree of Doctor of Philosophy (p. 653).

Such courses were judged by Dawson and others to be inappropriate, not only for the majority who were not preparing to enter college, but for the level of maturity of high school freshman or sophomores. For example, as Dawson (1909) describes in one high school:

> The freshman class, little girls with their hair braided down their backs, came into the laboratory ... In a short time they were given cross sections of the corn stalk to study with the microscope. The object of the work was to reconstruct mentally a fibro vascular bundle by means of cross and longitudinal sections and then to make a comparative study of the endogenous and exogenous stems. By means of questions the instructor endeavored to draw from her pupils what they could see under the microscope, but met with no better success than is indicated by such answers as 'they saw what seemed to be many rings', 'a monkey's face' and a 'pansy face' (pp. 654–5).

Dawson concluded that description by saying that 'Certainly no one would thus attempt to teach higher mathematics and advanced physics' to 'children of their age' (p. 655).

In 1909 New York City introduced a general biology course emphasizing the relationships of humans and their biological environments. In addition, the proponents of the course hoped that by integrating the life sciences into one course and without the confusing diversity of courses, biology would be on a par with high school chemistry and physics. New York State published a general biology syllabus in 1910 with four major aims: (i) knowledge of plants and animals; (ii) understanding of life functions; (iii) knowledge of the economic importance of plants and animals and the importance of conserving natural resources; and (iv) understanding of individual and public health.

Biology courses increased in popularity very quickly, while enrollments in botany, zoology, and physiology declined (see table 2). By 1923, 83.8 per cent of high schools offered a biology course, compared to only 26.5 per cent in 1908. Part of the success of biology can be attributed to the increase in the proportion of non-college bound students in high schools that accompanied the increase in the percentage of students attending high school during the first quarter of the twentieth century. The industrial expansion that characterized the period from 1910 to 1920 increased public awareness of science and may have contributed to the popularity of biology. Increasing wealth freed children from labor and the first compulsory schooling law was passed in 1852. In subsequent years there was also an increase in the terminal age for compulsory schooling (Downing, 1925).

*Table 2: Percentage of Schools Offering Biological Science Courses: 1908 and 1923*

| Course | 1908 | 1923 |
|---|---|---|
| Botany | 81.5 | 29.9 |
| Biology | 26.5 | 83.8 |
| Physiology | 69.9 | 34.3 |
| Zoology | 52.2 | 1.8 |

*Source:* Finley, 1926, p. 31

Increasing attendance in high schools was not only a result of a larger population, but of recognition of 'the urgent need to move through public agencies to the support of education' (Barry, 1965, p. 602). This urgency grew out of the breakdown of traditional cultural patterns for transmitting culture, particularly the extended family, which accompanied emigration to the New World and subsequent migration through the wilderness (Bailey, 1960). Public education thus became the major avenue for perpetuating culture and civilization. 'The Puritans transferred the fragments of the shattered family educational pattern to the formally structured institutions of learning' (Barry, 1965, p. 602).

### Defining the Biology Curriculum

High school biology was unusual because 'It represented the first science course in the secondary school curriculum to be planned for the majority of students' (Hurd, 1961, p. 30). As H.E. Walter, a Professor at Brown University who had taught high school for ten years in Chicago said in describing in *An Ideal Course in Biology for the High School* (1909),

> To the great majority of boys and girls the high school, if not the grades, marks the end of school days, and thus any course of study to be ideal, plainly should minister to the majority while at the same time providing suitable preparation and advancement to those who are fortunate enough to go on. (p. 717)

Downing expressed a similar sentiment in 1925:

> Now the schools are serving a new constituency which demands an education as efficient as that of the old classical course, but which deals with the subject matter of life. (p. 52)

In 1909, Linville said that 'it is evident that teachers of biology are desirous of bringing their subject into line with other agencies that are contributing to the improvement of man's well being' (p. 121). He proposed that biology education would help prepare citizens and legislators to make wise decisions about the use and conservation of natural resources. Education about the 'conditions conducive to health should be extended as widely as possible' (p. 124) because 80 per cent of school children 'are suffering from some irregularity of the eye, ear, throat, or nose' (p. 124) and TB was on the increase (p. 125). Finally, Linville called for sex education as a way of dealing with a serious social problem:

> The fight that society has made in the open against the evils of sumptuary excesses has long been accompanied by a desultory or timid struggle against the more gigantic evils of abnormal sexuality. Uncertain as we are still of the best methods of abating these far-reaching evils, we do know that the first steps towards success in it must be the frank and open but methodical teaching of the facts of sexuality and reproduction to the young (p. 126).

Linville's idea of 'frank and open' was not the same as our present-day use of the terms, for he suggested couching sex education in a study of vegetative organs of plants 'thus showing that the rules of hygiene are not arbitrary regulations set by parents and teachers but the expression of laws governing the whole living world of which he [the student] is part . . . he has, as in a parable, been taught his duty to his race' (p. 127).

Educators who supported the movement to make biology relevant to the majority of students attempted to develop a course that would emphasize 'the *practical, ecological, economic, human* welfare aspects of biology' (Finley, 1926, p. 19). Gradually 'the aim in biology teaching . . . changed from "biology for the sake of biology" to "biology in relation to human welfare"' (*ibid*, p. 31), or as H.R. Linville (1910) expressed it, 'Besides teaching people how to think, we need to teach them how to live' (p. 212). High school biology, Dawson said, should be a course that 'furnishes a knowledge that everyone must have concerning the living things about them in order that they may live more efficiently' and schools should 'furnish men and women more capable of coping with their environment and acting intelligently in conserving the biological resources of individual, community, state, and nation' (Dawson, 1909, p. 656). These quotations clearly mark an orientation toward biology for life and living.

The titles of some of the textbooks of the period reflect this practical orientation: *Applied Biology* (Bigelow and Bigelow, 1911); *Civic Biology* (Hodge and Dawson, 1918); *Civic Biology* (Hunter, 1914); *Biology and Human Welfare* (Peabody and Hunt, 1924); and *Practical Biology* (Smallwood, Reveley and Bailey, 1916). Many educators aurged for an orientation toward biology as a science of life, such as H.R. Linville (1910),

> Most biologists will say that this is not biology. It is *not* the subject-matter of conventional biology, but it is the subject matter of life. And if biology can help along in making life better and happier in some concrete way, then it can be a useful servant in the education of the people (p. 213).

There was, however, disagreement about this approach to teaching biology. Dissenting opinions came from professors in the colleges and universities, such as H.E. Walter of Brown who in 1909 said:

> At the present time, it is frequently true that the biological course of the average high school has a strong resemblance to hash. To speak plainly, it too often consists of warmed up left-overs, for example, a little nature study from the grades, some large indigestible chucks of college zoology, a dash of elementary physics and chemistry, a little botany and hygiene, and in certain states where required by law, an intemperate dose of temperance (p. 721).

A similar view was expressed by C.A. Shull (1909) in delineating a program for a beginning zoology course: 'If the course which I am about to outline seems to contain too much matter, let me urge that the time for playing in science in the secondary school is past' (p. 725). John Dewey, himself, expressed opposition to the 'new biology', which he disparaged as 'the scrapbook approach' (Dewey, 1916).

Despite the criticism of academics, institutional acceptance of the new biology courses occurred. In 1913, colleges began accepting biology for admission and a year later the first (twelve) students took a College Entrance Examination in Biology (Rosen, 1959). There was, however, little unity in the biology taught. In 1923 Richards found no standardized course and in fifty-nine cities surveyed, found sixty-seven different texts and reference books in use.

The content of the 'new biology' was influenced by the health conditions in the cities, where populations were swelled by immigrants, rural to urban movements and increasing mechanization (Peterson, 1954). Topics such as the sources and biological importance of food, the relation of organisms to food production and food destruction, hygiene of food preparation and digestion, sanitation, the effects of alcohol and narcotics, the risks involved in patent medicines, the role of living organisms in producing clothing and building materials, conservation, disease, public health, and sex were advocated as proper subjects for a biology course (Linville, 1909).

The First World War focused attention on health problems, which was reflected in a greater emphasis on hygiene in biology courses. For example, the Report of the Science Committee of the Commission for the Reorganization of Secondary Education indicated that the World War had emphasized health as an important goal of education. The Report also indicated that biology should include health instruction as one of its primary goals (Caldwell, 1920).

The increase in laboratory work in science courses received impetus not only from scientists, such as Huxley and Agassiz, but from the influence of the psychological theory of learning known as 'mental discipline' (Del Giorno, 1969). Laboratory work, it was believed, would promote the faculties of observation and will power. Linville described (1910) how earlier educators had thought it possible to train students' powers of observation and that such training could be transferred to other areas of life. 'The mind ... like a muscle or gland, used in any particular way increases its ability to repeat the same process' (Hahn, 1905, pp. 155–6, quoted in Christy, 1936, p. 185). Adherence to the theory of mental discipline resulted in a morphological orientation for biology education. When psychologists demonstrated that there is no general faculty of observation, educators turned to emphasizing thinking skills, with the idea of extending the skills learned in science laboratories to other spheres of life. There was then a transition from an emphasis on mental discipline to one on the scientific method. Gradually also physiology began to become as important as morphology, but science teachers were reluctant to change their approach.

Linville (1910) proposed that by using problems of the everyday world in the classroom, the transfer of thinking skills to situations outside the classroom would be facilitated.

The great and splendid opportunity of all the sciences in the schools appears to be this: They may use the method of the experiment in schools on problems that come up in life itself (p. 212).

The types of problems Linville recommended were the germination and growth of seeds, the preparation and digestion of food and the relationship of bacteria to health. Many people agreed with Linville and the early years of the twentieth century saw a shift away from the goal of biological knowledge and toward the personal/social aim of biology education.

As has often happened in the history of science education, the emphasis on laboratory work seemed to some to be carried too far and a backlash developed. Although praising it as 'emancipation from the old-time bookish slavery of pre-laboratory days', in 1909 H.R. Walter warned against two pitfalls with the use of laboratory work: the danger of spending too much time on it and over-emphasis of the type-study method originally introduced by Huxley for college courses. The latter, Walter said, involves, 'a succession of studies upon an approved series of forms in which certain orthodox observations could be repeated and confirmed by the pupil with the aid of definite directions' (p. 719). Furthermore, the emphasis on laboratory work was in conflict with the practical approach advocated by some educators because the practical 'aspects of biology do not lend themselves so well to laboratory work as did the anatomical, morphological, and microscopic work' (Finley, 1926, p. 19).

## Evolution

Although a general, integrated approach and laboratory work were widely and readily accepted innovations in biology education, the theory of evolution entered the arena of biology education slowly and reluctantly. Following the Civil War there was a wave of anti-evolutionism in this country and some evidence indicates that educators and biology teachers agreed with the grass-roots attitude of anti-evolution. In 1942, Riddle found that the subject of evolution was either avoided or badly treated in most public schools. As recently as 1967, Troost found that only 33.5 per cent of a random sample of Indiana biology teachers considered evolution a fact and that most deemphasized the topic and demonstrated serious misunderstandings of the concepts of evolution. Presently, there is still a strong anti-evolution movement in this country (Nelkin, 1977) which has considerable influence on the content of biology textbooks (Weinberg, 1978; Skoog, 1979; Skoog, 1984).

The first textbook to mention evolution was Sedgwick and Wilson's *An Introduction to General Biology* (1890). Although this text was used in some early biology courses, it was of the old style, modeled on college courses. The first biology textbook written by a high school teacher, *Essentials of Biology* (Hunter, 1911) did not mention evolution. In a monumental study of the treatment of evolution in high school biology textbooks, from 1900 to 1982, Skoog has shown (1979 and 1984) that little attention was given to evolution in textbooks published between 1900 and 1919. He analyzed eight textbooks from that period and found that only three of the eight had chapters devoted to evolution. In one of these, the word evolution was not used and in another, the word was used only twice. Hunter's very popular textbook, *Civic Biology* (1941) had three pages on evolution. Another textbook by Hunter (*Essentials of Biology*, 1911) and *Elementary Biology* (Peabody and Hunt, 1913), both of which were popular books (Frank, 1916) had 1000 to 2000 words on evolution whereas *The Elementary Principles of General Biology* by Abbott (1914), with no evidence of being a popular book, contained eight times as much on evolution. Some comments by textbook authors indicated that they may have considered evolution to be too difficult and abstract for high school students, but that raises the question of why other subjects, such as geometry and classical languages, were not considered equally inaccessible to high school students (Skoog, 1979).

From 1920 until 1925, some authors expressed strong support for evolution and included substantial sections on the subject in their textbooks, for example, *Biology for High Schools* (Smallwood, Reveley and Bailey, 1920). Skoog found that not until the 1960s would statements such as these again become as frequent. Still other textbooks, such as that by Peabody and Hunt (1924), contained virtually nothing on the subject (ninety-four words in that case) (Skoog, 1979) and 'many authors still accepted Lamarack's thesis concerning the inheritance of acquired characteristics' (*ibid*, p. 628).

## Genetics

Genetics was another area of biology that was slow to reach the secondary schools. The rediscovery of Mendel's principles occurred in 1900 and the eugenics movement began in the United States in 1905, but it was not until 1914 that genetics appeared in a high school textbook: *Civic Biology* by Hunter published in 1914. Half of the textbooks published from then until 1940 avoided discussions of human genetics and those that did discuss it did so from the prevailing eugenics position. Such discussions focused on inheritance of physical characteristics, intelligence and feeblemindedness, but not on genetic diseases or on the 'moral, social, and political implications of the overall eugenics movement' (Hurd, 1978, p. 4).

During this same period, however, textbooks devoted considerable attention to infectious diseases of humans. The theory of abiogenesis had persisted in textbooks until 1910, despite the formulation of the germ theory of disease in 1759 by Wolff and proof of that theory in 1861 by Pasteur (Cretzinger, 1941). Some theories, such as epigenesis and metagenesis, were readily accepted and appeared rather quickly in secondary biology textbooks. The reluctance of textbook writers to include certain topics is explained by Cretzinger (1941):

> Early biological textbook writers showed little interest in scientific theories or discoveries that opposed deep-seated established opinions or superstitious beliefs. Such opinions and beliefs caused many scientific theories to be kept out of textbooks for many years until those theories were finally accepted and included in textbook materials of secondary level.... On the other hand, writers seemed willing to present in their books any new discovery of biological science that they thought would be generally accepted by the public. (pp. 311–2)

## Conclusion

Biology was born out of a combination of historical, intellectual, and social developments that occurred during the latter part of the nineteenth century. The principal historical event was the industrialization of America and its attendant effects on population growth, particularly population growth in the secondary schools. The principal intellectual development was the synthesis of botany and zoology into general biology that was articulated by Thomas Huxley. The principal social development was the wave of immigrants that reached this country in the late 1800s and the wave of migrants from the rural to urban areas of the country.

But biology was not only born out of such influences, it also continued to be affected by other historical, intellectual and social forces during the first twenty-five years of its life. Among these were the influence of religion on the teaching of evolution and temperance, and the influence of legislators, who voted into law compulsory education, the teaching of temperance and the exclusion of evolution. Also influential were the committees, such as the Committee of Ten (1894) and the Commission of Reorganization of Secondary Education (1920). Scientific advances influenced the development of biology as well, both directly through advances in the field itself (evolution, genetics, cytology, physiology, etc.) and indirectly through advances in psychology, as in the case of the mental discipline theory. Other strong influences on the development of biology were the colleges and college professors through the training of teachers, the establishment of admission requirements and the writing of textbooks. In all of these areas, the European influence was strong. The idea for biology as a subject and the theory of evolution came from England, the laboratory method from Germany and England and Louis Agassiz himself came from Switzerland.

Those first twenty-five years of biology are not unique in the 100 years of its existence as a secondary school subject. Throughout its history, the biology curriculum has reflected events in the larger society as well as incorporating scientific advances. The story of the emergence of biology is only one example of the intimate and intricate interrelationship among science, society, and biology education that has prevailed for 100 years. One of the major themes of that history has been the explicit or implicit debate about the goals of secondary biology: whether it should be primarily a vehicle for teaching the science of life, i.e., pure science, or whether it should be a science for living, i.e., should serve the individual needs of students and the needs of society.

## References

ABBOTT, J.F. *The Elementary Principles of General Biology*, New York: Macmillan Co, 1914.

AGASSIZ, L. and GOULD, A.A. *Principles of Zoology*, Boston, MA: Gould and Lincoln, 1851.

BAILEY, L.M. *Botany, An Elementary Text For Schools*, New York: Macmillan Co, 1900.

BAILYN, B. *Education in the Forming of American Society*, Chapel Hill, NC: University of North Carolina Press, 1960.

*Dorothy B. Rosenthal and Rodger W. Bybee*

BARRY, D.G. 'Early American science and the roots of modern biology', *The American Biology Teacher*, 27, 8, 1965, pp. 600–6.

BIGELOW, M.A. and BIGELOW, A.N. *Applied Biology*, New York: Macmillan, 1911.

BUREAU OF GENERAL EDUCATION CURRICULUM DEVELOPMENT *Biology Regents Syllabus*, Albany, NY: The State Education Department, The University of the State of New York, 1982.

BYBEE, R.W. 'The new transformation of science education', *Science Education*, 61, 1, 1977, pp. 85–97.

CALDWELL, O. (chair) *Reorganization of Science in Secondary Schools*, Commission on Reorganization of Secondary Education, Bulletin 1920, No. 26, Department of Interior, Bureau of Education, Washington, DC, 1920.

CHRISTY, O.B. *The Development of the Teaching of General Biology in the Secondary Schools*, Peabody Contribution to Education, No. 21 George Peabody College for Teachers, 1936.

COULTER, J.M. 'Chapters in the history of American botany, Part 1', *School Science and Mathematics*, 11, 1911, pp. 814–6.

CRETZINGER, J.I. 'An analysis of principles or generalities appearing in biological textbooks used in the secondary schools of the United States from 1800 to 1933', *Science Education*, 25, 6, 1941, pp. 310–3.

DAWSON, J. 'The essentials of biology in the high school', *School Science and Mathematics*, 9, 1909, pp. 653–7.

DEL GIORNO, B.J. 'The impact of changing scientific knowledge on science education in the United States since 1850', *Science Education*, 57, 4, 1969, pp. 485–91.

DEWEY, JOHN. 'Method in science teaching', *General Science Quarterly*, 1, 1, 1916, p. 3.

DEYOUNG, C.A. and WYNN, R. *American Education*, New York: McGraw-Hill, 1972.

DOWNING, E.R. 'Are the new science subjects crowding out the old in the high school?', *School Science and Mathematics*, 22, 1, 1924, pp. 46–50.

DOWNING, E.R. *Teaching Science in the Schools*, Chicago: University of Chicago Press, 1925.

FINLEY, C.W. *Biology in Secondary Schools and the Training of Biology Teachers*, New York: Teachers College, Columbia University, 1926.

FRANK, O.D. 'Data on text books in the biological sciences used in the middlewest', *School Science and Mathematics*, 16, 1916, pp. 218–9; 354–9.

GLENN, E.R. *Bibliography of Science Teaching in Secondary Schools*, Washington, DC: U.S. Bureau of Education, Bulletin No. 13, 1925.

GRAY, A. *How Plants Grow*, New York: American Book Company, 1858.

HELLMAN, R.A. 'Evolution in American school biology books from the late nineteenth century until the 1930s', *The American Biology Teacher*, 27, 10, 1965, pp. 778–80.

HODGE, C.F. and DAWSON, J. *Civic Biology*, Chicago: Ginn and Company, 1918.

HUNTER, G.W. *Elements of Biology*, New York: American Book Company, 1970.

HUNTER, G.W. *Essentials of Biology*, New York: American Book Company, 1911.

HUNTER, G.W. *Civic Biology*, New York: American Book Company, 1914.

HURD, P.D. *Biology Education in American Schools 1890–1960*, Biological Science Curriculum Study Bulletin No. 1, Washington, DC: American Institute of Biological Sciences, 1961.

HURD, P.D. 'The historical/philosophical background of education in human genetics in the United States', *Biological Sciences Curriculum Study Journal*, 1, 1, 1978, pp. 3–8.

HUXLEY, T.H. and MARTIN, H.N. *A Course of Practical Instruction in Elementary Biology*, New York: MacMillian, 1876.

LINVILLE, H.R. 'The practical use of biology', *School Science and Mathematics*, 9, 2, 1909, pp. 121–30.

LINVILLE, H.R. 'Old and new ideals in biology teaching', *School Science and Mathematics*, 10, 1, 1910, pp. 210–6.

MORSE, E.S. *First Book of Zoology*, 1875.

NEEDHAM, J.G. *General Biology*, Ithaca, NY: Comstock Publishing Company, 1910.

NELKIN, D. *Science Textbook Controversies and the Politics of Equal Time*, Cambridge, MA: MIT Press, 1977.

PEABODY, J.E. and HUNT, A.E. *Elementary Biology*, New York: MacMillian, 1912.

PEABODY, J.E. and HUNT, A.E. *Biology and Human Welfare*, New York: MacMillian, 1924.

PETERSON, O.L. 'A brief look at the history of science education in America: Its past, present, and future', *Science Education*, 43, 5, 1959, pp. 427–35.

RICHARDS, O.W. 'The present status of biology in the secondary schools', *School Review*, 31, 2, 1923, pp. 43–146.

RIDDLE, O. (Ed.) *The Teaching of Biology in Secondary Schools in the United States: A Report of Results From a Questionnaire*, Menasha, WI: Union of American Biological Societies, 1942.

ROSEN, S. 'The decline and fall of high school physiology', *School and Society*, 85, 1957, pp. 308–11.

ROSEN, S. 'Origins of high school general biology', *School Science and Mathematics*, 59, 60, 1959, pp. 473–89.

SEDGWICK, W.T. and WILSON, E.B. *General Biology*, New York: Henry Holt and Company, 1895.

SHULL, C.A. 'A first course in zoology', *School Science and Mathematics*, 9, 1909, pp. 725–30.

SKOOG, G. 'Topic of evolution in secondary school textbooks: 1900–1977',

*Dorothy B. Rosenthal and Rodger W. Bybee*

*Science Education*, 63, 5, 1979, pp. 621–40.

SKOOG, G. 'The coverage of evolution in high school biology textbooks published in the 1980s', *Science Education*, 68, 2, 1984, pp. 117–28.

SMALLWOOD, W.M., REVELEY, I.L., and BAILEY, G.A. *Practical Biology*, Boston, MA: Allyn and Bacon, 1916.

SMALLWOOD, W.M., REVELEY, I.L., and BAILEY, G.A. *Biology for the High School*, Boston, MA: Allyn and Bacon, 1920.

SMELLIE, W. *The Philosophy of Natural History*, Philadelphia, PA: P. Campbell, 1824.

TENNEY, S. and TENNEY, A.A. *Natural History of Animals*, New York: Charles Scribner and Son, 1866.

TROOST, C.J. 'Teaching of evolution in the secondary schools of Indiana', *Journal of Research in Science Teaching*, 5, 1, 1967, pp. 37–9.

WALTER, H.W. 'An ideal course in biology for the high school', *School Science and Mathematics*, 9, 1909, p. 721.

WEINBERG, S.L. 'Two views on the textbook watchers', *The American Biology Teacher*, 40, 9, 1978, pp. 541–54.

# 6  Mathematics Education in the United States at the Beginning of the Twentieth Century

*George M.A. Stanic*

## Abstract

By the late nineteenth century, mathematics had become a central element in the curriculum of schools in the United States. And at the turn of the twentieth century, mathematics education became a professional area of study at institutions of higher education. Ironically, as the professional study of mathematics education grew during the early years of the twentieth century, the traditional place of mathematics in the school curriculum was being threatened.

During this era, mathematics educators had to respond to a complex network of factors affecting the school curriculum: The United States was developing as an industrialized society; the school population grew dramatically; and four general curriculum interest groups argued for their distinct visions of what knowledge is of most worth. In the field of mathematics education, the early years of the twentieth century were characterized by conflict, continuity, and compromise.

By the late nineteenth century, mathematics had become a central element in the curriculum of both elementary and secondary schools of the United States. In fact, the role of mathematics as a school subject had advanced to the point where, at the turn of the twentieth century, mathematics education became a separate and distinct professional area of study at colleges and universities (Jones, 1970).

David Eugene Smith of Teachers College, Columbia University, and Jacob William Albert Young of the University of Chicago did much to help identify mathematics education as a legitimate field of professional study. It is more than a little ironic that as the professional study of mathematics education grew during the early years of the twentieth century, the traditional place of mathematics in the school curriculum was being threatened (Stanic, 1983/1984 and 1986). The development of mathematics education from the turn of the century to the late 1930s is the focus of this chapter. It was a time of growth and crisis.

Mental discipline theory provided a strong justification for the place of mathematics in the school curriculum during the nineteenth century. By the end of the century, however, the idea that the study of mathematics exercised and trained the mind in some general way was challenged by educational psychologists and educators who were attempting to adapt the school curriculum to an increasingly industrialized society and a changing school population. As mathematics educators began to define their field of study, interest groups that sought to shape the twentieth century school curriculum (Kliebard, 1981) were emerging in the general curriculum field. The American report of the International Commission on the Teaching of Mathematics, published in 1911 and 1912, provides evidence of changing justifications for including mathematics in the school curriculum, while the reports of the Committee on Economy of Time in Education, published in 1915, 1917 and 1918, provide evidence of a growing social efficiency ideal which most threatened the traditional role of mathematics in the school curriculum. By the 1930s, mathematics educators perceived a crisis in their field. There was not, however, a simple correspondence between social, political, and economic conditions and what happened to the field of mathematics education during this era. Although the conditions in the wider society had an important impact on mathematics education, there was a network of related influences — including events and ideas in the general curriculum field and the reform ideas and actions of the new professional mathematics educators — which led to the crisis of the 1930s and to which mathematics educators had to respond. This chapter begins with a discussion of mental discipline theory and ends with a description of the complex reform milieu that had developed by the 1930s.

## Mental Discipline Theory and Mathematics Education

The dominant curriculum theory of the nineteenth century was mental discipline theory. Growing out of a not entirely smooth merger between nineteenth century classical humanism with its emphasis on the liberal arts and the psychological theory of faculty psychology and having as ancestors Cartesian and Aristotelian conceptions of the mind, mental discipline theory was based upon a fundamental mind-body metaphor. In the words of Edward Brooks (1883/1970):

> The mind is a spiritual activity and grows by its own inherent energies. Mental exercise is thus the law of mental development. As a muscle grows strong by use, so any faculty of the mind is developed by its proper use and exercise. An inactive mind, like an unused muscle, becomes weak and unskillful. Hang the arm in a sling and the muscle becomes flabby and loses its vigor and skill; let the mind remain inactive, and it acquires a mental flabbiness, that unfits it for any severe or prolonged activity. An idle mind loses its tone and strength, like an unused muscle; the mental powers go to rust through idleness and inaction. To develop the faculties of the mind and secure their highest activity and efficiency there must be a constant and judicious exercise of these faculties. (p. 84)

The faculties referred to by Brooks are capacities 'for a distinct form of mental activity' (p. 78). According to Brooks, the three general classes of faculties which constitute the mind are the intellect, the sensibilities, and the will. Each of these can then be broken down further; for instance, the intellect consists of the faculties of perception, memory, imagination, understanding, and intuition or reason (pp. 78–9).

While various authors used their own unique labels for the faculties, the discussion by Brooks is fairly representative. The basic metaphor which permeates all classifications is to view the mind as if it were a muscle. Just as a muscle requires exercise for development, so does the mind.

Mental discipline theory represents a merger between nineteenth-century faculty psychology and the liberal arts tradition because the metaphor just described does not require a particular subject or group of subjects with which to 'exercise the mind'. Technically, based on faculty psychology, all that is required is sustained, extended, and rigorous study, with the content of study being relatively unimportant. This does not mean that just any study would do. But it does mean that the supporters of the liberal arts were successful in perpetuating the importance of the classical studies (for example, mathematics, Greek, Latin) by formulating the rationale for these studies within the framework provided by faculty psychology.

For the mental disciplinarians, the place of mathematics in the school curriculum was justified based upon its extraordinary potential for improving certain faculties of the mind, especially that of reason. 'The study, *par excellence*, for the culture of deductive reasoning,' said Brooks (1883/1970), 'is mathematics' (p. 86). In his book, *The Logic and Utility of Mathematics with the Best Methods of Instruction Explained and Illustrated*, Charles Davies (1850/1970) quoted approvingly the following passage on the value of mathematics (credited to *Mansfield's Discourse on Mathematics*, no date provided):

> If it be true, then, that mathematics include a perfect system of reasoning, whose premises are self-evident, and whose conclusions are irresistible, can there be any branch of science or knowledge better adapted to the improvement of the understanding? It is in this capacity, as a strong and natural adjunct and instrument of reason, that this science becomes the fit subject of education with all conditions of society, whatever may be their ultimate pursuits. Most sciences, as, indeed, most branches of knowledge, address themselves to some particular taste, or subsequent avocation; but this, while it is before all, as a useful attainment, especially adapts itself to the cultivation and improvement of the thinking faculty, and is alike necessary to all who would be governed by reason, or live for usefulness. (pp. 59–60).

To the mental disciplinarians, then, mathematics provided the primary vehicle through which to improve the reasoning faculty. Furthermore, all mental disciplinarians did not frown upon considering the immediate utility of a particular subject such as mathematics — even though all viewed the general improvement of faculties as the primary criterion of justification for teaching a subject.

As criticism of mental discipline theory grew, various curriculum interest groups began to emerge to provide different justifications for including subjects in the school curriculum. However, mental discipline theory did not suddenly vanish from the scene. Although mental discipline theory did begin to decline in influence at the turn of the century, experiments motivated by it and discussions about it continued for some time into the twentieth century — and it even has present day manifestations (see, for example, comments by teachers in Stake and Easley, 1978).

Of the experiments motivated by a concern over mental discipline theory, those conducted by James (1890), Thorndike and Woodworth (1901), and Thorndike (1924) played perhaps the most important roles in questioning the theory. Yet the very fact that Thorndike was still dealing with the issue in 1924 provides evidence that mental discipline theory did not suddenly vanish at the turn of the century. Thorndike continued to discuss the disciplinary values of subjects even after his 1924 experiment. 'Apparently', said Thorndike in 1925, 'some careless thinkers have rushed from the belief in totally general training to the belief that training is totally specialized' (p. 365). But his discussions did not really present an optimistic picture for justifying school subjects based upon mental discipline theory. 'The advisable course', he said, 'in estimating the disciplinary effect of any study, occupation or the like would seem to be to list as accurately as possible the particular situation-response connections made therein' (Thorndike, p. 421).

Experiments conducted by educational psychologists were not the only or even the most important factor in the decline of mental discipline theory's influence. Such experiments about mental discipline theory may have provided a 'scientific' rationale for making changes in the school curriculum; but, to understand what was happening within schools during the early twentieth century, one must look at the profound changes taking place in society as a whole.

> By the 1890's, nineteenth-century society with its reliance on the face-to-face community was clearly in decline, and with the recognition of social change came a radically altered vision of the role of schooling. No longer was the school the direct instrument of a visible and unified community. Rather, it became a mediating institution between the family and an increasingly distant and impersonal social order, an institution through which the norms and ways of surviving in the new industrial society would be conveyed. Traditional family life was not only in decline; even when it remained stable, it was no longer sufficient to initiate the young into a complex and technological world. (Kliebard, 1981, p. 1)

The rapid growth of industrialization, urbanization, and immigration led people to rethink the role of schooling and to question mental discipline as the most important justification for teaching a school subject.

## The Changing School Population

Had no other changes been taking place, the significant growth of the school population itself would seem to have set the stage for changes in the school curriculum. For example, between 1890 and 1940, the population of the American high school grew from 359,949 students to 7,123,009 students. In 1890, only 6.7 per cent of 14–17-year-olds attended high school; and only 3.5 per cent of 17-year-olds graduated. By 1940, 73.3 per cent of America's 14–17-year-olds were attending high school; and 49 per cent of 17-year-olds graduated (James & Tyack, 1983).

During this period of significant growth, educators spoke as though the great 'army of incapables' described by Granville Stanley Hall as early as 1904 had indeed invaded the schools. Given the flow of students into and out of high schools, even if the percentage of low ability students (however one chooses to define *low ability*) remained the same, increasing the actual number of low ability students by such a significant amount would create a more visible problem (for some educators). However, the assumption that with an increase in the school population comes a decrease in the overall quality or intellectual capability of that population (that is, not just the actual number but also the percentage of low ability students increases) is problematic despite its commonsense appeal. Few people who made this claim provided any documentation (see Thorndike, Cobb, Orleans, Symonds, Wald, and Woodyard, 1923, for one attempt; and Stanic 1983/1984 for a discussion of the figures provided by Thorndike *et al.*); and no one provided convincing evidence that the quality of the school population had indeed declined as the number of students increased.

It is possible, of course, that the quality of the student population was declining. However, it may be that the biggest problem was not so much dealing with a significant change in the overall quality of the high-school population but, instead, dealing with a significant change in the purpose and function of the high school necessitated by the tremendous growth it was experiencing and the changes taking place in the wider society. For students in 1890, secondary education may have been almost a rite of passage to an esteemed place in society. When a relatively small percentage of high-school-age students was attending and graduating from high school, there was little need to be concerned about individual differences in intellectual capability. Society was in a position to reward anyone who completed high school. However, the rite-of-passage idea became less viable as more and more people were attending and graduating from high school; just completing high school was no longer a necessary and sufficient condition for achieving an esteemed position in society because the number of high school graduates outstripped the number of esteemed positions available. In such a milieu, questions about individual differences became more important, at least in part because pointing to individual differences in capability helped to justify and explain the changing purpose and function of high school attendance and graduation.

The point, then, is not that educators were necessarily wrong in assuming that the overall quality of students was diminishing as the school population was increasing; the point is that the situation was complex and cannot be explained easily. Furthermore, suppose there was clear evidence to substantiate the claim that the overall quality of the school population was deteriorating. How would particular changes in the population require changes in the school curriculum? How would such changes interact with the nation's democratic ideals? While these are all interesting and important issues, it does not appear as though they formed the basis for educational discourse at the time the high-school population was increasing so dramatically. Instead, it seems generally to have been assumed that the overall intellectual capability of the school population was, in fact, diminishing and that, because of this decline, something had to be done about the school curriculum. It is not surprising that such an attitude would have a significant impact on the teaching of mathematics.

## The Emerging Curriculum Interest Groups

As mental discipline theory was being questioned, four curriculum interest groups began to emerge at the turn of the century. The ideas and actions of the members of these interest groups were a part of the network of factors affecting mathematics education. Herbert Kliebard (1981) has labelled these groups the *humanists*, the *developmentalists*, the *social efficiency educators*, and the *social meliorists*. Although the humanists were not unwavering defenders of tradition, they were closest to the old mental disciplinarians. Development of the ability to think and reason was important to the humanists, as it was to the mental disciplinarians; however, the humanists, led by people such as William Torrey Harris, began to place more emphasis on passing on the Western cultural herritage. Granville Stanley Hall and the other developmentalists saw in traditional schooling a lack of recognition of the importance of the natural order of development of children; they believed the school curriculum should be based upon scientific findings about child development. Social efficiency educators, with roots linked through Joseph Mayer Rice to the developmentalists, eventually focused their efforts on creating an efficient society through an efficient system of schooling which would prepare children for their predetermined social roles. Like the social efficiency educators, the social meliorists included an explicit vision of society as part of their curriculum reform efforts. Unlike the social efficiency educators who focused on efficiency, the social meliorists focused on justice; Lester Frank Ward set the tone for later social meliorists in his call for equality of opportunity through the fair distribution of extant knowledge.

All the interest groups recognized the importance of mathematics as a school subject, and all believed that rigorous high school courses should be available for students. However, there were important differences in how the interest groups viewed the role of mathematics as a school subject. For the humanists, it was important that students take as much mathematics as possible, since the study of mathematics developed reasoning power and since the discipline of mathematics was an important part of our cultural heritage. For the developmentalists, individual interest and especially native capacity were to set limits on how much mathematics one should study (see Stanic, 1983/1984, for a discussion of the different views of individualization held by Charles W. Eliot, the humanist, and G. Stanley Hall, the developmentalist). Social-efficiency-standard-bearer David Snedden went so far as to suggest that most people needed to study no more than sixth-grade arithmetic to meet the needs of their daily lives and vocations. Finally, the role of mathematics in the social meliorist program of Lester Frank Ward is not entirely clear. On the one hand, Ward (1883) argued that 'the chief means of education are the arts of reading, writing, and calculating'. On the other hand, he was careful to state that 'in learning these several arts the mind is not in any proper sense acquiring knowledge, although to most persons this information is ranked as knowledge'. Therefore, according to Ward, 'while reading, writing, and the calculus can not be dispensed with as potent agencies in acquiring knowledge, the constant aim should be to reduce the amount of work achieved through them; especially should all devotion to them as ends or parts of culture be discouraged, except for those who have shown by their complete educational record that nature has marked them out either for elocutionists, engrossing clerks, or computers of astronomical tables' (p. 626). When viewed in light of other comments made by Ward — for example, 'Mathematicians and astromoners, who deal with the most exact of all the sciences, usually have no patience with anything that cannot be reduced to mathematical precision' (Ward, 1903, p. 47) — mathematics educators interested in defending the already strong place of mathematics in the curriculum might have found some cause for concern in Ward's ideas.

## The Views of Mathematics Educators at the Turn of the Century

At the turn of the century, the United States was clearly becoming an industrialized society; the school population was in the beginning stage of a period of rapid growth; mental discipline theory was called into question; and four general curriculum interest groups began to emerge. It was to this network of factors that the new professional mathematics educator had to respond. There was an atmosphere of reform not just in the general curriculum field, but also within mathematics education. The turn of the century was a significant era in mathematics education in terms of the issues being raised and the ideas being discussed.

Being in their general viewpoint very much in line with the central themes of Charles W. Eliot and the Committee of Ten, the reports of the conference on mathematics of the Committee of Ten — published with the Committee of Ten report (NEA, 1893) — and of the Committee appointed by the Chicago Section of the American Mathematical Society — published with the report of the Committee on College-Entrance Requirements (NEA, 1899) — were not uncontroversial. Both reports embodied criticism of what they saw as traditional mathematics teaching, and both suggested changes. As an example of what was being discussed, consider the conclusions of the Committee appointed by the Chicago Section of the American Mathematical Society, a Committee chaired by J.W.A. Young:

1 To the close of the secondary-school course the required work in mathematics should be the same for all pupils.

2 The formal instruction in arithmetic as such should terminate with the close of the seventh grade.

3   Concrete geometry should be a part of the work in arithmetic and drawing in the first six grades.

4   One-half of the time allotted to mathematics in the seventh grade should be given to the beginning of demonstrative geometry.

5   In the eighth grade the time allotted to mathematics should be divided equally between demonstrative geometry and the beginning of algebra.

6   In the secondary school, work in mathematics should be required of all pupils thruout each of the four years of the course.

7   Wherever, from local conditions, it is necessary to defer the beginning of geometry and algebra to the secondary school, here, likewise, geometry should be begun before algebra.

8   When once begun, the subjects of geometry and algebra should be developed simultaneously, in so far, at least, that both geometry and algebra should be studied in each of the four years of the secondary-school course.

9   The unity of the work in mathematics is emphasized, and the correlation and inter-application of its different parts recommended.

10   The instruction should have as its chief aim the cultivation of independent and correct thinking on the part of the pupil.

11   The importance of thoro preparation for teachers, both in mathematical attainments and in the art of teaching, is emphasized. (NEA, 1899, p. 148)

These ideas are neither original nor revolutionary, but they cannot be considered conservative given the context of the time in which they were written. The controversy embedded in certain of the recommendations has persisted throughout the twentieth century.

Furthermore, with the work of, among others, Felix Klein in Germany, John Perry in England, and Eliakim Hastings Moore in the United States, the emerging field of mathematics education was presented with an agenda of significant issues to consider. During the latter part of the nineteenth century, Klein emphasized in his writings the relationship between the various areas within mathematics, a relationship embodied in the function concept. Klein also emphasized

teaching mathematics by moving from the concrete to the abstract
and by using applications of mathematics, though he warned

> it is possible that through the mere mass of interesting
> applications, the real logical training may be crippled, and
> under no circumstances may this happen, for then the real
> marrow of the whole is lost. Hence: We desire emphatically,
> an enlivening of instruction in mathematics by means of its
> applications, but we desire also that the pendulum which in
> earlier decades perhaps swung too far in the abstract direc-
> tion, should not now swing to the other extreme, but we wish
> to remain in the just mean. (quoted in Young, 1903, p. 54)

In England, Perry (1902) stressed the usefulness of mathematics,
though it must be understood that Perry's conception of the usefulness of mathematics ranged from its role in 'producing the higher
emotions and giving mental pleasure' through 'the aid given by
mathematical weapons in the study of physical science' to 'giving to
acute philosophical minds a logical counsel of perfection altogether
charming and satisfying', with a variety of other examples of usefulness in between (see Perry, 1902, pp. 4–5); in short, it was quite a
broad conception of usefulness. He criticized 'advocates of orthodox
methods' who seemed 'willing to sacrifice every form of usefulness of
mathematics to one form, the emotional or soul-preserving mind-
training inherent in a perfect logical system; a huge complex deduced
logically from simple fundamental truths' (p. 12) and advocated
'assuming more complex things to be true' so that students 'may
know of all the modern discoveries' and use them sooner than they
otherwise would (p. 13). 'Why not', asked Perry, 'put aside ever so
much more, as to let a young boy get quickly to the solution of partial
differential equations and other useful parts of mathematics that only
a few men now ever reach?' (p. 13). Interestingly, he also stressed that
'the proper method of teaching any subject is through some kind of
experimental work' (p. 19) and that teachers should 'refrain from
prosing and the setting of tasks' and instead 'merely make timely
suggestions and answer ... questions', leaving the student to 'find
out things for himself' (pp. 23–4). In addition to his stress on
students 'making discoveries' (p. 8), Perry emphasized the importance of applications of mathematics and the relationship between
mathematics and natural science.

E.H. Moore did a great deal to advance in the United States ideas
like those of Klein and Perry. In his presidential address delivered

before the American Mathematical Society on 29 December 1902, Moore characterized the 'fundamental problem' as *the unification of pure and applied mathematics*' (Moore, 1902/1926, p. 45). He asked: 'Would it not be possible for the children in the grades to be trained in power of observation and experiment and reflection and deduction so that always their mathematics should be directly connected with matters of thoroughly concrete character?' (p. 45). '*Would it not be possible to organize the algebra, geometry and physics of the secondary school into a thoroughly coherent four years' course?*' (p. 47). And Moore believed that Perry was 'quite right in insisting that it is scientifically legitimate in the pedagogy of elementary mathematics to take a large body of basal principles instead of a small body and to build the edifice upon the larger body for the earlier years, reserving for later years the philosophic criticism of the basis itself and the reduction of the basal system' (pp. 47–8). Based on these ideas, Moore advocated a 'laboratory system of instruction in mathematics and physics, a principal purpose being so far as possible to develop on the part of every student the true spirit of research, and an appreciation, practical as well as theoretic, of the fundamental methods of science' (p. 49).

Led by J.W.A. Young of the University of Chicago and David Eugene Smith of Teachers College, Columbia University, mathematics educators responded to the agenda of issues presented by Klein, Perry, and Moore. Given that the movement toward 'unification' of the areas within mathematics and of mathematics with the sciences found its greatest strength in and around the University of Chicago, it is not surprising that Young would be more sympathetic than Smith to the ideas of people like Klein, Perry, and Moore (see, for instance, Young, 1903 and 1906). Young (1906) did warn that 'it would be doubtful gain, even if it were possible, to abolish the distinction between algebra and geometry, mathematics and physics, when breaking down the wall of separation between them which has often been regarded as an insuperable barrier' (p. 102).

Smith was more reluctant to accept the ideas expressed by Klein, Perry, and Moore; but he did not completely reject their ideas. In his response to Perry's address, for example, Smith commented that 'there is a tone running through the address that grates on one who loves mathematics for its own sake'; he added, however, that 'the speaker told a great deal of truth, and if he went to an extreme, it was because in fighting conservatism one must sometimes be ultra-radical' (in Perry, 1902, p. 91).

Smith responded more boldly to some of the issues in an article written in 1905 entitled 'Movements in Mathematical Teaching'. Referring to Moore's 1902 address, Smith claimed that 'it was a fact apparent to all who heard it that the address was not favorably received by many of those present' (p. 135). After describing the response of educators in 'the East' to Moore's ideas, Smith came to the following conclusion:

> The feeling in the East, as I interpret it after much study, is one of earnest desire to make the class in mathematics a workshop, but in the high school it must be a workshop in pure mathematics. In arithmetic, where the field of real application is very large, there is a manifest desire to banish those problems that pretend to relate to business and science, but do not do so, to substitute genuine ones in their stead, but to hold to such an amount of abstract work as to bring that mechanical efficiency that is necessary to fairly rapid and accurate computation. In algebra and geometry, where the field of real applications is very small, the chief effort will be to turn the class into a laboratory in pure mathematics, recognizing that the applied problem shall be used as one of several means for arousing interest, but that this is a mere incident. (pp. 138–9)

Seemingly describing himself as much as his area of the country, Smith claimed that 'while the East thinks slowly it thinks judicially, while it works conservatively it works thoroughly, while it is not given to rash experiment it is not blind to results, and while it is influenced by traditions it is ready to change when it sees other plans proved to be better then [*sic*] its own' (p. 139).

As was true in the case of the ideas presented by the mathematics conference of the Committee of Ten and the Committee appointed by the Chicago Section of the American Mathematical Society, the ideas of Klein, Perry, and Moore were not new; but the state of the American curriculum was such that ideas like those of these committees and individuals became legitimate and significant foci of discussion for people concerned about mathematics education.

## Growing Criticisms and Growing Concern

The turn of the century was, then, an exciting time for the professional mathematics educator. Between the turn of the century and the 1930s, however, criticism of the place of mathematics in the school curriculum grew to a point where many mathematics educators described the situation as a crisis. In 1930, William Betz suggested that 'there probably has never been a time of greater doubt as to ... [the] educational significance [of secondary mathematics]' (p. 104). In 1932, as President of the National Council of Teachers of Mathematics, Betz warned that 'a passive attitude will only aid the negative propaganda emanating from the ranks of the educational iconoclasts and self-styled apostles of the "new education"' (p. 301). As the decade of the 1930s progressed, others spoke of mathematics being a 'forgotten subject' (Glover, 1934); the 'desperate situation' resulting from the public's acceptance of 'the pronouncements of mathematical ignoramuses' (Bell, 1935, pp. 559–60); 'the *offensive* action against mathematics in the secondary schools' (Hart, 1935, p. 72); the need for 'some evangelism' (Hartung, 1935, p. 82); 'the crisis that threatens ... [the] extinction [of mathematics] as a required subject in major curricula of secondary schools' (Hedrick, 1936, p. 112); the need for mathematics educators to 'face the facts and make appropriate adjustments' (Douglass, 1937, p. 62); the need for more 'cooperation between high school and college teachers of mathematics' in order to fight the critics (Kempner, 1938); and 'the expediency of compromise' (Maddox, 1938). Furthermore, in addition to all the individual claims about and responses to the crisis, the National Council of Teachers of Mathematics was sufficiently concerned about the situation to devote three entire yearbooks — *Mathematics in Modern Life* (NCTM, 1931), *Mathematics in Modern Education* (NCTM, 1936), and *The Place of Mathematics in Secondary Education* (NCTM, 1940) — to the defense of mathematics, generally, and its place in the school curriculum, specifically. The responses of the contributors to these yearbooks were not all the same, but the fact of their cooperative and organized response is further evidence òf a general feeling of concern in the mathematics education community.

The excitement that the turn of the century held for the mathematics educator existed along with the seeds of crisis. Responding to their own vision of the changing conditions in American society, the developmentalists, and especially the social efficiency educators, began to suggest that not all students needed to study mathematics throughout their secondary school years. The writings in the American report of the International Commission on the Teaching of Mathematics, published in 1911 and 1912 by the United States Bureau of Education, reflect the diverse ideas about mathematics education prevalent in the early years of the twentieth century. And the reports of the Committee on Economy of Time in Education, published by the National Society for the Study of Education in 1915, 1917 and 1918, are further evidence of the growing social efficiency ideal which most threatened the traditional role of mathematics as a secondary-school requirement for all students.

### The American Report of the International Commission on the Teaching of Mathematics

Although the American commissioners, David Eugene Smith, W.F. Osgood, and J.W.A. Young, were members of the growing mathematics education community and close to the humanist curriculum interest group in their orientation, the various committees that contributed to the American report of the International Commission of the Teaching of Mathematics included people reflecting a wide range of ideas about mathematics education. Most notably, David Snedden, perhaps the predominant twentieth century social efficiency educator (and, at the time, the Commissioner of Education of Massachusetts), served on one of the committees.

The 'General Elementary Schools' Committee on which Snedden served noted early that 'there is a disposition in school circles to deny that the importance of mathematical training is such as to warrant the place it has occupied and still holds' (International Commission, 1911a, p. 17). Furthermore, the Committee stated that 'there is, among school men, and in the public today, an unwillingness to accept the doctrine of formal discipline as it was formerly stated, so that it is no longer possible to justify the retention of any topic or subject by claiming for it merely great disciplinary value' (p. 22) and that 'whereas in the past instruction in mathematics in the elementary grades has been dominated by logical ideas and a disciplinary aim, at the present the leading purpose is to make the instruction as useful in content and as pedagogical in form as the conditions of school work permit' (p. 38).

The subcommittee on 'Mathematics in Grades One to Six' criticized 'logical' (as opposed to 'psychological') methods of instruction. The members of the sub-committee complained that 'teachers still tend to teach future workmen in the lower schools as they themselves were taught by scientific scholars in the universities' (p. 95). With immediate usefulness as the primary criterion of value, the sub-committee criticized teaching the 'whys' of algorithms, claiming that 'the rational needs of a thinker about mathematics may require an understanding of the reasons why we "carry" in column addition, but the effective everyday use demands an accurate habit of "carrying" rather than an accurate explanation' (p. 95).

The subcommittee further explained that not just 'business need' but also 'social situation' 'determine[s] if a fact or a process is worth comprehending, and whether the method of instruction has been effective' (p. 96). In fact, the subcommittee seemed to believe that 'the social aims of education' were most important. 'The sociologist', said the committee, 'usurps the place of the business man as the school's proper critic' (p. 97).

The subcommittee on 'Mathematics in Grades Seven and Eight of the Public and Parochial Schools' agreed that 'the doctrine of formal discipline is accepted now in only a modified form so that it is no longer deemed sufficient to claim for any subject that it has great disciplinary value' (p. 128). However, they also warned that 'as in all reforms, there is a tendency to go to extremes in this, especially with regard to mathematics. The willingness of mathematicians to subject their science to the test of the new doctrine has invited the less sympathetic scrutiny of others who are not interested in the subject. The result is a tendency to demand more of mathematics in this respect than of other subjects' (p. 128).

The subcommittee on 'Failures in the Technique of Secondary Teaching of Mathematics' of the Committee on 'Public General Secondary Schools' also agreed that 'the one-sided doctrine of mental discipline must go'. They asked for 'a fusion of the abstract and concrete, a fusion dictated by common sense and free from radicalism in either direction' (International Commission, 1911b, p. 104).

The *Report of the American Commissioners of the International Commission on the Teaching of Mathematics* (International Commission, 1912) provides an interesting contrast to some of the other comments in the American report. In a discussion on aims, for example, Smith, Osgood and Young presented a unique argument for the benefits of the study of mathematics:

> Workers in mathematics have every reason to be gratified by the progress that is making in the utilization of the mathematical type of thought in the treatment of the problems of psychology and in other complex fields; in the predominance that precise thinking is gaining over vague theorizing in so many domains of the scientific and practical activities of the day they will see added reason for the careful training of the coming generation in habits of precise thinking, beginning with that simple and readily mastered domain, commonly

known as elementary mathematics, which has been and is the inspiration and model of precise thinking in more difficult fields. (p. 31)

While stating that 'mathematicians will accept and take to heart the results of scientific investigations that bear upon their science or its teaching', they warned against accepting 'too readily' the 'results announced by students of a sister science without ascertaining that the conditions really warrant such acceptance' (p. 31). They claimed, for example, that 'there is danger that results of psychologic research may be misunderstood and misapplied by one who accepts it as a settled fact that these researches have "exploded the doctrine of formal discipline as generally stated"' and that 'few, if any, mathematicians who are conversant with the results of such experiments as have been made, and are sympathetic with their spirit, feel that aught has been as yet established which would require them to change their views of the value of the study of mathematics' (pp. 31–2).

The American commissioners also commented on 'the increased emphasis on the utilitarian values of mathematics'. While viewing this 'tendency' as 'praise-worthy', they warned of the 'element of danger' such a tendency carried with it. And in discussing this danger, they presented a classic example of the humanist viewpoint:

The practical aspects of mathematics deserve attention not only on account of their inherent value, but also on account of the additional interest which they may arouse; and the effort to exhibit the role that mathematics plays in the world about us deserves only commendation; the danger connected with this tendency lies not in the introduction of utilitarian applications, but in the attitude of mind which the search for such applications may engender. The very variety and importance of the uses of mathematics in trade and industry may tend to foster the opinion that the learning of such uses is the chief end of the teaching of mathematics. This is, of course, no more the case with respect to mathematics than it is with respect to the less utilitarian subjects of the curriculum. History and English literature are taught not because they can be directly used in earning dollars, but because the educated person should know something of these fields and because the mind of the pupil will grow along desirable lines through thinking their types of thought. Mathematics is taught for quite similar reasons. Its utilitarian possibilities should not cause us to forget that the main purposes of its teaching are to

acquaint the pupil with the content of a portion of a domain
of thought that is fundamentally characteristic of the human
mind as such, and not of any particular time, place, or
civilization, and to cause his mind to grow along desirable
lines by actually thinking in the type of thought that is
characteristic of this domain. (pp. 32–3)

The American report of the International Commission on the
Teaching of Mathematics is, then, a reasonable reflection of the
diverse ideas about mathematics as a school subject prevalent in the
early years of this century. The American commissioners — Smith,
Osgood and Young — expressed their humanist position; but in the
writings of some of the committees and subcommittees and even
in the somewhat defensive tone of the humanist American commissioners, one can see that the humanist position in the mathematics
education was being challenged. The committees and subcommittees
espoused ideas representative of the humanists, the developmentalists, and the social efficiency educators. And in its lack of social
meliorist ideas, the American report reflects a condition which has
characterized the field of mathematics education throughout the
twentieth century.

## The Committee on Economy of Time in Education

The National Society for the Study of Education, in a series of
yearbooks, published reports of the Committee on Economy of Time
in Education, a Committee established by the National Department
of Superintendence of the National Education Association. Though
not exclusively social efficiency oriented (see contributions by Bagley,
1915, 1917 and 1918; and by Marston, McKown, and Bagley, 1918,
for notable exceptions), with educators like John Franklin Bobbitt
(like Snedden, a standard bearer for the social efficiency movement)
serving on the Committee, the reports generally reflect the ideal of
education for social efficiency.

In terms of the arithmetic curriculum in particular, discussions
by Walter A. Jessup (1915), Walter S. Monroe (1917), G.M. Wilson
(1917), and H. Edwin Mitchell (1918) fit in well with the central
social efficiency theme of the reports. Jessup (1915), Professor of
Education at the State University of Iowa, claimed to be presenting 'a
clearing-house of experience, which ... [would] enable any superin-

tendent to know what other superintendents . . . [were] doing' about 'effecting economy of time by means of omitting certain material, redirecting emphasis on certain other material and modifying the time cost' (pp. 117–8). A major purpose of Monroe's (1917) study (Monroe was at the time a Professor of School Administration at Kansas State Normal School) was 'to secure a list of arithmetical problems which arise in human activities and which possess a sufficient degree of utilitarian or socializing value to justify their being designated as minimum essentials of purpose' (p. 112). Monroe searched arithmetic texts for these problems but added that 'the ideal procedure would be to make a complete survey of activities to ascertain what arithmetical problems exist and the frequency of their occurrence' (p. 119).

This is exactly what Wilson (1917), a Professor of Agricultural Education at the Iowa State College of Agriculture and Mechanic Arts, attempted to do. In order to determine 'the actual demand of social and business usage' (p. 131), Wilson conceived of a research plan in which 'the sixth, seventh, and eighth-grade pupils in any system of schools where the plan . . . [was] carried out . . . collect[ed] through a period of two weeks every problem solved by either the father or the mother' (p. 132). Based on his work, Wilson concluded it was 'evident that the necessary work in arithmetic . . . [could] be mastered in much less time than . . . [was] being devoted to it' (p. 142).

Mitchell (1918), who carried out his study under E.L. Thorndike at Teachers College, summarized his work as follows:

> The data presented . . . are taken from four sources, viz., a standard cook book, the pay rolls of a number of artificial flower and feather factories, marked-down sales advertisements, and a general hardware catalog. These data are, accordingly, concrete stuff out of which arise arithmetical problems of housewives, wage earners, consumers, and retail hardware dealers, respectively. The data are typical of the sort which must be gathered from many sources and made the basis of selection of the problems and drill exercises which are to constitute the course of study in arithmetic. (p. 7)

Like Jessup, Monroe, Wilson, and the social efficiency educators, Mitchell believed that the mathematics curriculum should be based upon the mathematics people actually use in their day-to-day lives and vocations.

*George M.A. Stanic*

## The Complex Reform Milieu

In the work of groups like the Committee on Economy of Time in Education, there was a clear challenge to the humanist position in mathematics education which led to the crisis perceived by mathematics educators by the 1930s. However, the situation was not simply one of mathematics educators being 'attacked' by a group of educators not closely associated with mathematics education. For example, Guy Wilson, who wrote for the Committee on Economy of Time, continued to focus his research and writing on mathematics education; any attempt to label him as a member of a group of general educators not associated with mathematics education is problematic. Furthermore, even apart from people like Wilson who expressed a growing interest in mathematics education, much of the push for reform came from people who were clearly part of the mathematics education community.

For instance, writing in the *Mathematics Teacher* in 1909, N.J. Lennes (who considered himself a mathematician and who had a strong interest in mathematics education) combined the humanist faith in the value of the study of mathematics with the developmentalist concern for the child in an article on the teaching of algebra. Lennes discussed principles and characteristics of 'modern pedagogy', including the importance of 'the study of the child itself, — its needs, interests and capacities' (p. 95). He argued that 'the teaching of secondary mathematics . . . [had] adjusted itself more slowly to the requirements of modern pedagogy than that of any other great subject' and claimed that 'this exceptionally tardy conformity of practice to our best principles . . . [was] the reason for the prevailing discontent' about the teaching of the mathematics (p. 98). However, about the teaching of algebra he said that 'while the beginning . . . should emphasize its dynamic rather than its logical aspect, it is by no means intended that it should end there. When the child has become familiar with the main processes of algebra through their dynamic aspect', the processes 'then become legitimate objects of study for their own sake' (pp. 103–4).

So, both because of the difficulty in labelling certain reformers as being outside of mathematics education and because of examples of reform ideas on the part of people who were clearly part of the mathematics education community, the situation in the early years of the twentieth century was not simply one of mathematics educators being 'attacked' by 'outsiders'. What made the situation even more complex was the relationship between reform efforts inside and outside mathematics education. That is, many mathematics educators viewed their efforts at *internal reform* (i.e., reform within mathematics education) as distinct from *external reform* (i.e., reform within the general curriculum field). In the words of William Betz (1908):

> That one has a right to speak of a reform movement in the teaching of mathematics, must be evident to any but a very indifferent observer. The agitation in favor of better teaching is not confined to our own country, and its effects are felt in colleges, universities, secondary and primary schools, with almost equal force. It is unnecessary to recite ... all the details of its origin and progress ... It is sufficient to say that since Prof E. H. Moore's memorable address in December 1902, 'On the Foundations of Mathematics', an ever increasing number of teachers have become actively interested in the pedagogy of mathematics. (p. 625)

Mathematics educators were not unaware of the reform efforts in the general curriculum field; they did, however, stress the tradition of reform in their own field (Stanic, 1983/1984 and in press).

Mathematics educators, then, helped to create and had to respond to a complex reform milieu. By 1920, the National Council of Teachers of Mathematics had been formed in response to 'so-called educational reformers' who had 'tinkered' with mathematics courses and 'in many cases' had 'thrown out mathematics altogether or made it entirely elective' (Austin, 1921, pp. 1–2). The continuing complexity of the situation can be seen in the fact that the NCTM sought to 'help the progressive teacher to be more progressive' and to 'arouse the conservative teacher from his satisfaction and cause him to take a few steps ahead' while at the same time urging that 'curriculum studies and reforms and adjustments come from the teachers of mathematics rather than from the educational reformers' (Austin, 1921, p. 3). The new members of the NCTM were willing to label as progressives only clear supporters of the subject area of mathematics, calling those who challenged the role of mathematics in the school curriculum 'so-called educational reformers'.

When Robert Havighurst asked, 'Can Mathematicians and Educationists Cooperate?' in the lead article of a 1937 issue of the *Mathematics Teacher*, he was referring to the bitterness many mathematics educators ultimately had come to feel toward the 'so-called educational reformers' during the 1920s and 1930s. 'In such cooperation', said Havighurst, 'much must be understood and forgiven. Foibles and minor faults must be overlooked. Cooperation calls for objectivity, broadmindedness, and straight thinking, none of which flourishes when people permit themselves the indulgence of irritation' (p. 212).

There was indeed a high level of irritation felt by many mathematics educators during the early years of the twentieth century. And perhaps no one expressed more irritation than David Eugene Smith when he responded to *The Problem of Mathematics in Secondary Education* (NEA, 1920), which was a Report of the Commission on the Reorganization of Secondary Education (the Commission which had prepared the National Education Association's *Cardinal Principles* Report in 1918). The *Cardinal Principles* Report reflected the growing social efficiency ideal, but it was too moderate in its tone and recommendations for social-efficiency-educator David Snedden (see Snedden, 1919). The Committee that actually prepared the mathematics report consisted of William Heard Kilpatrick, who chaired the Committee and was a Professor of Education at Teachers College; Fred R. Hunter, Superintendent of Schools in Oakland, California; Franklin W. Johnson, Principal of the University High School at the University of Chicago; J.H. Minnick, Assistant Professor of Educational Methods at the University of Pennsylvania; Raleigh Shorling, teacher at the Lincoln School in New York; J.C. Stone, Head of the Mathematics Department at the State Normal School in New Jersey; Milo H. Stuart, Principal of the Technical High School in Indianapolis, Indiana; and J.H. Withers, Superintendent of Schools in St. Louis, Missouri.

The mathematics report essentially reflects the views of a growing social efficiency/developmentalist coalition (Stanic, 1983/1984). The Committee submitted an 'admittedly preliminary report', because it felt 'a detailed plan would have to be based upon a wider range of experiment than in fact exists' (p. 9). Although social efficiency oriented in its attempt to classify students according to future roles and in its concern that 'the value of . . . [a] topic . . . be sufficiently great in relation to other topics and to the element of cost (as regards time, labor, money outlay, etc.) to warrant its inclusion in the curriculum' (pp. 14–16), the Committee was careful to separate itself from exclusive 'bread and butter' (or direct and limited utility) concerns (pp. 12 and 15–16). The Committee endorsed a form of Kilpatrick's 'project method' in its discussion of the teaching of mathematics (pp. 12–13); and, although the Committee did not reject the idea of 'formal discipline', because of the reduced status of 'formal discipline' as a justification for teaching mathematics and because of the lack of agreement on how much transfer one could hope for, the

Committee decided that it would not use 'the factor of "formal discipline" in determining the content of the mathematical courses to be recommended' (pp. 16–17). The Committee discussed the 'needs' of four groups — 'general readers', the group preparing for certain trades, the group preparing for engineering, and the group of specializers — (pp. 17–20) and concluded that all groups should take (in addition to a review of arithmetic and the arithmetic of social activities) a common and required introductory course in the junior high school which would consist of the following:

> A body of mathematical symbols, concepts, information, and processes — commonly thought of as belonging to algebra and geometry or beyond — which the intelligent general reader of high school or college standing will need in order to meet the demands of his social and intellectual life. As a part of this content, it seems safe to suggest the ordinary algebraic symbols, the use of the formula, the simple equation, and the (statistical) graph.
>
> The opportunity for at least a preliminary testing of mathematical taste and aptitude.
>
> Such additional content — relatively small in amount — as may be needed to make effective teaching of the foregoing. (p. 22)

The Committee assumed 'that as a rule all pupils would take [this introductory course] . . . (or at least begin on it), and that no further mathematics would be customarily required for college entrance' (p. 23).

Although the recommendations of Kilpatrick's Committee do reflect the social efficiency/developmentalist coalition that troubled many humanist mathematics educators, they also represent an attempt to create a compromise with humanist mathematics educators. David Snedden, on the other hand, sought no such compromise, suggesting that all mathematics beyond sixth-grade arithmetic be elective (see, for example, Snedden, 1921). However, despite the moderate view presented in the Kilpatrick Report, it infuriated David Eugene Smith, Kilpatrick's colleague at Teachers College.

In a letter dated 20 January 1919 to J.C. Boykin of the United States Bureau of Education (which published the Report) Smith (1919) responded to a draft of the Report which he had reviewed and expressed his concern about the 'effect of the publication of the monograph by the Bureau of Education'. Smith claimed that the Report was the work of one man (presumably Kilpatrick) and was 'in no sense a report of a Committee'. 'It is well understood', said Smith, 'that no Committee was appointed until the monograph was written, that the monograph was rather widely circulated, and that a Committee was finally selected from those who approved it. . . . There was never a meeting of the entire committee. . . . It stands merely as a monograph approved by those who were appointed because they approved it'. Furthermore, Smith felt that the Committee was 'not representative either of the teaching of mathematics or of mathematics as a science'. Smith admitted that Kilpatrick 'at one time taught mathematics in a small southern college', but he also pointed out that Kilpatrick's 'results were such as to cause him to abandon the work and to take up general education' (see Tenenbaum, 1951, for a biography of Kilpatrick which includes a discussion of his reasonably extensive background in mathematics and his time spent at Mercer University as Professor of Mathematics and Astronomy). Smith could not understand how someone could choose as chairperson of the Mathematics Committee 'a man entirely out of touch and out of sympathy with the subject'. About the rest of the Committee, Smith had little better to say: 'Not a single mathematician of recognized scientific standing was placed on the committee, and not more than one or two teachers of the science who can be said to have made considerable names for themselves were asked to serve'.

In addition to his concerns about the composition and deliberative procedures of the Committee, Smith expressed a number of specific concerns about the text of the report. But when one looks closely at Smith's comments, it almost appears as though he was more concerned about the general tone of the report and the manner of presentation of the ideas than he was about the ideas themselves. 'As to most of the large features of the suggestions for relating mathematics to daily life', said Smith, 'no one will find any particular objection. . . . The chief difficulty lies in the way they are set forth.' Furthermore, 'as to the mathematical reforms', he said 'there seems to be nothing that the mathematicians, who know the subject, are not taking care of rather efficiently at the present time'. But Smith was angry about the implication in the report that mathematics educators had attempted to 'shield' themselves from 'scrutiny', saying that the report 'will at once antagonize those whom it hopes to reach, and all to no purpose'. Smith felt it was 'unfortunate' that the report assumed 'an air of superiority over those who know the teaching of mathematics from successful experience. Such a style', he said, 'will antagonize those whose interest in reform should be stimulated, and will make the report the subject of suspicion if not of a feeling even less to be desired.'

Perhaps as well as anything else could, the passages from Smith's letter indicate that the historical actors whose ideas one attempts to interpret were themselves responding to more than each other's ideas. Not just ideas but egos clashed as these characters interacted. However, this point should not be overdrawn. Given Smith's own writings, it is clear that it was not a simple matter of Smith disagreeing with Kilpatrick's style but not the substance of the ideas in the report. For instance, although the mathematics report did not go to the extreme of some social efficiency educators in discussing individual differences and the need for early determination of future roles, Smith's ideas still represented more of the basic humanist faith in human intelligence. Furthermore, although even Smith ultimately spoke of required mathematics only in the junior high school, his suggested junior high program was more rigorous than that of the report. But, while this clash of personalities should not be overdrawn, it should also not be neglected. For it may have something to do with the fact that it was a social efficiency/developmentalist coalition, and not a humanist/developmentalist coalition, that came to dominate educational thought in the years between the World Wars.

## Conclusion

The educational world of the humanists in mathematics education was changing most drastically during the early years of the twentieth century, and they responded to the challenge and the change in a variety of ways. The debate over the proper role of mathematics in the school curriculum took place not just at the level of committee reports and journal articles. High school course requirements in mathematics and the percentage enrollment in traditional mathematics courses in high schools were declining during this period (Stanic, 1986). By 1923, in *The Reorganization of Mathematics in Secondary Education*, a Report prepared by the National Committee on Mathematical Requirements and published by the Mathematical Association of America, the humanists in mathematics education clearly recognized that the battleground over *required* mathematics was shifting to the developing junior high school, and it was there that they defended their stand for a reasonably rigorous mathematics program to be required of all students (Stanic, 1983/1984).

In the spirit of the Committee of Ten report (NEA, 1893) that had preceded its report by thirty years, the National Committee on Mathematical Requirements insisted that 'the separation of prospective college students from the others in the early years of the secondary school is neither feasible nor desirable. It is therefore obvious', said the committee, 'that secondary school courses in mathematics cannot be planned with specific reference to college entrance requirements. Fortunately there appears to be no real conflict of interest between those students who ultimately go to college and those who do not, so far as mathematics is concerned' (MAA, 1923, p. 43).

The NCMR report, while humanist in its basic viewpoint, was, in fact, reform oriented. The Committee spoke of, among other things, eliminating unnecessary elements from the curriculum (p. 11) and abandoning 'the extreme "water-tight compartment" method of presentation' (p. 13). Referring favorably to the work of John Dewey, the Committee criticized the 'excessive amount of time' devoted to 'drill in algebraic technique, without insuring an adequate understanding of the principles involved' (pp. 51–2) and 'recognized that in the earlier periods of instruction the strictly logical organization of subject-matter is of less importance than the acquisition, on the part of the pupil, of experience as to facts and methods of attack on significant problems, of the power to see relations, and of training in accurate thinking in terms of such relations' (p. 11). The reforms suggested were not presented without caveats. For instance, as a follow-up to the comment on the logical organization of subject-matter, the Committee warned that 'care must be taken, however, through the dominance of the course by certain general ideas that it does not become isolated and unrelated details' (p. 11). Such caveats do not diminish the message of reform that permeates the report. (In fact, in the specific caveat just mentioned, the warning is actually very much in line with Dewey's own thinking; see, for example, Dewey, 1902/1964 and 1938/1973).

While the humanists in mathematics education considered the work of the National Committee to be forward looking (see, for example, Slaught, 1920; Smith, 1922), the Report did not at all satisfy the social efficiency reformers. 'As one reads the pages [of the report by the National Committee]', said Franklin Bobbitt (1922), 'one feels one's self wholly within an academic atmosphere, and never at any time does he get a real whiff of the world's actual life, and of the mathematics that actually functions in the real lives of men and women' (p. 65). Responding to Bobbitt's charge, William Betz (1923) said:

> How anyone acquainted with actual high school conditions and with the principles of democratic American education can tolerate the views of Professor Bobbitt, is a mystery to the writer. And yet it is precisely these one-sided proposals for the solution of our educational problems which are disturbing the educational balance of many school administrators and lead to ill-considered and premature readjustments. (p. 459)

Although Bobbitt and others continued to question the place of mathematics in the school curriculum, the humanists in mathematics education, in the years between the World Wars, continued to espouse a basic faith in the benefits of extensive and intensive mathematics study for everyone. As the National Committee Report shows, the humanists were not blind to the changes taking place around them; but, as Bobbitt's response shows, the basic disagreements between the social efficiency/developmentalist coalition and the humanists persisted, despite the impact of social efficiency and developmentalist thought on the response of the humanists.

The emergence of mathematics as a school subject in the United States during the early years of the twentieth century was, then, characterized by conflict, continuity, and compromise. The conflict was largely a result of changes related to the growth of an industrialized society. Although the debate fostered by this conflict centered on mathematics requirements in the secondary school curriculum, even elementary school mathematics instruction was affected (Stanic, 1983/1984). The continuity during these years is evident in the persistent attempts on the part of humanist mathematics educators to justify the teaching of mathematics based on its uniqueness as a vehicle for developing reasoning power and on its place in our Western cultural heritage; in fact, the mental disciplinarians never really faded away in the field of mathematics education. And the compromise can be seen in the various ways the humanists in mathematics education responded to a changing society and school, ways that sometimes led particular individuals away from the basic humanist viewpoint. And as is true of any compromise, few, if any, people were really satisfied with the result.

## References

AUSTIN, C.M. 'The National Council of Teachers of Mathematics', *Mathematics Teacher*, 14, 1921, pp. 1–4.

BAGLEY, W.C. 'The determination of minimum essentials in elementary geography and history', *The Fourteenth Yearbook of the National Society for the Study of Education: Part I*, Chicago: University of Chicago Press, 1915, pp. 131–46.

BAGLEY, W.C. 'Present-day minimal essentials in United States history as taught in the seventh and eighth grades', *The Sixteenth Yearbook of the National Society for the Study of Education: Part I*, Bloomington, IL: Public School Publishing, 1917, pp. 143–55.

BAGLEY, W.C. 'A symposium on the purposes of historical instruction in the seventh and eighth grades (Introduction and summary)', *The Seventeenth Yearbook of the National Society for the Study of Education: Part I*, Bloomington, IL: Public School Publishing, 1918, pp. 97–8 and 120–2.

BELL, E.T. 'Review of *The Poetry of Mathematics and Other Essays*', *American Mathematical Monthly*, 42, 1935, pp. 558–62.

BETZ, W. 'The teaching of geometry in its relation to the present educational trend', *School Science and Mathematics*, 8, 1908, pp. 625–33.

BETZ, W. 'The confusion of objectives in secondary mathematics', *Mathematics Teacher*, 16, 1923, pp. 449–69.

BETZ, W. 'Whither algebra? — A challenge and a plea', *Mathematics Teacher*, 23, 1930, pp. 104–25.

BETZ, W. 'A message from the new president of the National Council', *Mathematics Teacher*, 25, 1932, pp. 300–2.

BOBBITT, F. *Curriculum-making in Los Angeles*, Chicago: University of Chicago, 1922.

BROOKS, E. 'Selections from *Mental Science and Methods of Mental Culture*', in BIDWELL, J.K. and CLASON, R.G. (Eds), *Readings in the History of Mathematics Education*, Washington, DC: National Council of Teachers of Mathematics, 1970, pp. 76–90, (original work published in 1883).

DAVIES, C. 'Selections from *The Logic and Utility of Mathematics*', in BIDWELL, J.K. and CLASON, R.G. (Eds), *Readings in the History of Mathematics Education*, Washington, DC: National Council of Teachers of Mathematics, 1970, pp. 39–54, (original work published in 1850).

DEWEY, J. 'The child and the curriculum', in ARCHAMBAULT, R.D. (Ed.), *John Dewey on Education: Selected Writings*, Chicago: University of Chicago Press, 1964, pp. 339–58, (original work published in 1902).

DEWEY, J. *Experience and Education*. New York: Collier, 1973, (original work published in 1938).

DOUGLASS, H.R. 'Let's face the facts', *Mathematics Teacher*, 30, 1937, pp. 56–62.

GLOVER, I.R. 'Mathematics: A forgotten subject in present-day schools', *Mathematics Teacher*, 27, 1934, pp. 199–204.

HALL, G.S. *Adolescence: Volume II*. New York: Appleton, 1904.

HART, W.W. 'The need for a reorientation of secondary mathematics from the college viewpoint', *Mathematics Teacher*, 28, 1935, pp. 69–79.

HARTUNG, M.L. 'The need for a reorientation of secondary school mathematics from the high school view point', *Mathematics Teacher*, 28, 1935, pp. 80–90.

HAVIGHURST, R.J. 'Can mathematicians and educationists cooperate?', *Mathematics Teacher*, 30, 1937, pp. 211–3.

HEDRICK, E.R. 'Crises in economics, education, and mathematics', *Mathematics Teacher*, 29, 1936, pp. 109–14.

INTERNATIONAL COMMISSION ON THE TEACHING OF MATHEMATICS, *Mathematics in the Elementary Schools of the United States*, Washington, DC: Government Printing Office, 1911a.

INTERNATIONAL COMMISSION ON THE TEACHING OF MATHEMATICS, *Mathematics in the Public and Private Secondary Schools of the United States*. Washington, DC: Government Printing Office, 1911b.

INTERNATIONAL COMMISSION ON THE TEACHING OF MATHEMATICS, *Report of the American Commissioners of the International Commission on the Teaching of Mathematics*. Washington, DC: Government Printing Office, 1912.

JAMES, T., and TYACK, D. 'Learning from past efforts to reform the high school', *Phi Delta Kappan*, 64, 1983, pp. 400–6.

JAMES, W. *Principles of Psychology*, New York: Holt, 1890.

JESSUP, W.A. 'Current practices and standards in arithmetic', *The Fourteenth Yearbook of the National Society for the Study of Educaton: Part I*, Chicago: University of Chicago Press, 1915, pp. 116–30.

JONES, P.S. 'Epilogue: Summary and forecast', *The Thirty-Second Yearbook of the National Council of Teachers of Mathematics. A History of Mathematics Education in the United States and Canada*. Washington, DC: NCTM, 1970, pp. 451–65.

KEMPNER, A. 'On the need for cooperation between high school and college teachers of mathematics', *Mathematics Teacher*, 31, 1938, pp. 117–23.

KLIEBARD, H.M. *Education at the Turn of the Century: A Crucible for Curriculum Change*, Division B invited address presented at the annual meeting of the American Educational Research Association, Los Angeles, April 1981.

LENNES, N.J. 'Modern tendencies in the teaching of algebra', *Mathematics Teacher*, 1, 1909, pp. 94–104.

MADDOX, A.C. 'The expediency of compromise in mathematical curricula and instruction', *Mathematics Teacher*, 31, 1938, pp. 259–63.

MARSTON, L.R., McKOWN, H.C., and BAGLEY, W.C. 'A method of determining misplacements of emphasis in seventh and eighth-grade history', *The Seventeenth Yearbook of the National Society for the*

*Study of Education: Part I*, Bloomington, IL: Public School Publishing, 1918, pp. 90–6.

MATHEMATICAL ASSOCIATION OF AMERICA, *The Reorganization of Mathematics in Secondary Education*, MAA, 1923.

MITCHELL, H.E. 'Some social demands of the course of study in arithmetic', *The Seventeenth Yearbook of the National Society for the Study of Education: Part I*, Bloomington, IL: Public School Publishing, 1918, pp. 7–17.

MONROE, W.S. 'A preliminary report of an investigation of the economy of time in arithmetic', *The Sixteenth Yearbook of the National Society for the Study of Education: Part I*, Bloomington, IL: Public School Publishing, 1917, pp. 111–27.

MOORE, E.H. 'On the foundations of mathematics', *The First Yearbook of the National Council of Teachers of Mathematics. A General Survey of Progress in the Last Twenty-five Years*, NCTM, 1926, pp. 32–57, (original work published in 1902).

NATIONAL COUNCIL OF TEACHERS OF MATHEMATICS. *The Sixth Yearbook of the National Council of Teachers of Mathematics. Mathematics in Modern Life*, New York: Bureau of Publications, Teachers College, Columbia University, 1931.

NATIONAL COUNCIL OF TEACHERS OF MATHEMATICS, *The Eleventh Yearbook of the National Council of Teachers of Mathematics. Mathematics in Modern Education*, New York: Bureau of Publications, Teachers College, Columbia University, 1936.

NATIONAL COUNCIL OF TEACHERS OF MATHEMATICS, *The Fifteenth Yearbook of the National Council of Teachers of Mathematics. The Place of Mathematics in Secondary Education*, New York: Bureau of Publications, Teachers College, Columbia University, 1940.

NATIONAL EDUCATIONAL ASSOCIATION, *Report of the Committee on Secondary School Studies*, Washington, DC: Government Printing Office, 1893.

NATIONAL EDUCATIONAL ASSOCIATION, *Report of the Committee on College Entrance Requirements*, Chicago: NEA, 1899.

NATIONAL EDUCATION ASSOCIATION, *Cardinal Principles of Secondary Education*, Washington, DC: Government Printing Office, 1918.

NATIONAL EDUCATION ASSOCIATION, *The Problem of Mathematics in Secondary Education*, Washington, DC: Government Printing Office, 1920.

PERRY, J. (Ed.) *Discussion on the Teaching of Mathematics*, New York: Macmillan, 1902.

SLAUGHT, H.E. 'Retrospect and prospect for mathematics in America', *American Mathematical Monthly*, 27, 1920, pp. 443–51.

SMITH, D.E. 'Movements in mathematical teaching', *School Science and Mathematics*, 5, 1905, pp. 134–9.

SMITH, D.E. Letter to J.C. BOYKIN, Bureau of Education, available from National Archives, 20 January 1919.

SMITH, D.E. 'The new mathematics of the schools', *School and Society*, 15, 1922, pp. 292–4.

SNEDDEN, D. 'Cardinal principles of secondary education', *School and Society*, 9, 1919, pp. 517–27.

SNEDDEN, D. 'Mathematics in junior high schools', *School and Society*, 14, 1921, pp. 619–27.

STAKE, R.E. and EASLEY, J.A. *Case Studies in Science Education: Volume II*, Washington, DC: Government Printing Office, 1978.

STANIC, G.M.A. 'Why teach mathematics? A historical study of the justification question', (doctoral dissertation, University of Wisconsin-Madison 1983), *Dissertation Abstracts International*, 44, 1984, 2347A.

STANIC, G.M.A. 'The growing crisis in mathematics education in the early twentieth century', *Journal for Research in Mathematics Education*, in press.

TENENBAUM, S. *William Heard Kilpatrick: Trail Blazer in Education*, New York: Harper, 1951.

THORNDIKE, E.L. 'Mental discipline in high school studies', *Journal of Educational Psychology*, 15, 1924, pp. 1–22 and 83–98.

THORNDIKE, E.L. *Educational Psychology: Volume II. The Psychology of Learning*, New York: Teachers College, Columbia University, 1925.

THORNDIKE, E.L., COBB, M.V., ORLEANS, J.S., SYMONDS, P.M., WALD, E., and WOODYARD, E. *The Psychology of Algebra*, New York: Macmillan, 1923.

THORNDIKE, E.L., and WOODWORTH, R.S. 'The influence of improvement in one mental function upon the efficiency of other functions (I)', *Psychological Review*, 8, 1901, pp. 247–61.

WARD, L.F. *Dynamic Sociology: Volume II*, New York: Appleton, 1883.

WARD, L.F. *Pure Sociology*, New York: Macmillan, 1903.

WILSON, G.M. 'A survey of the social and business use of arithmetic', *The Sixteenth Yearbook of the National Society for the Study of Education: Part I*, Bloomington, IL: Public School Publishing, 1917, pp. 9–16.

YOUNG, J.W.A. 'What is the laboratory method?', *Mathematical Supplement of School Science*, 1, 1903, pp. 50–6.

YOUNG, J.W.A. *The Teaching of Mathematics in the Elementary and the Secondary School*, New York: Longmans, Green, 1906.

# 7    Need as Ideology: A Look at the Early Social Studies

## Michael B. Lybarger

### Abstract

The origins of the idea that the 'need' of students was the first criterion in shaping the social studies curriculum. When first advanced by the Committee on Social Studies in 1916, was considered 'a new and most important factor' at least seven members of the Committee on Social Studies had been active in charity organization or social settlement work. The writings of these committee members with settlement and charity organization work, articulating idea of need. As a defect in the mental, moral, and intellectual character of the individual served by the settlement or charity organization worker.

### Part I

1986 was the seventieth anniversary of the publication of *The Social Studies in Secondary Education*, the final Report of the Committee on Social Studies of the Commission on the Reorganization of Secondary Education. At least four elements of the modern social studies curriculum may be traced to the recommendations of the Committee on Social Studies: first, the courses in community civics and vocational civics in the seventh and eighth grades; second, the high school courses in Problems of American Democracy; third, the use of the term 'social studies' to refer to the school subjects of civics, economics, history, political science, and sociology; and fourth, the idea that the 'immediate needs' of students be the major factor in shaping the social studies curriculum. Indeed, it was not until the late seventies that evidence emerged that the scope and sequence of the social studies curriculum established in *The Social Studies in Secondary Education* began to show signs of change (Gross, 1977, p. 196).

In this chapter we will be concerned with the recommendation that the 'immediate needs of students' be the principle of selection in determining the content of this social studies curriculum. Committee members called the adoption of such a principle 'a new and most important element', and claimed the work of John Dewey as warrant for their principle. Moreover, several early supporters of the recommendation found in *The Social Studies in Secondary Education* attributed these to the work of John Dewey (Judd, 1918, pp. 511–2; Johnson, 1917, pp. 192–3). In this study we will seek to locate other, more remote, origins of the Committee's recommendation, by employing the concept of ideology.

In the preface to the English translation of *Ideology and Utopia* Louis Wirth asserts that 'A society is possible in the last analysis because the individuals in it carry around in their heads some sort of picture of that society.' Since this is the case Wirth continued, 'The most important thing we can know about a man is what he takes for granted, and the most elemental and important facts about a society are those that are seldom debated and generally regarded as settled' (Wirth, in Mannheim, 1957, pp. xxiv–v)

While Napoleon I is credited with the first use of the term 'ideology', Karl Mannheim is considered responsible for its modern formulation. In *Ideology and Utopia* Mannheim advanced two conceptions of ideology, the particular and the total. The particular conception of ideology calls into question ideas and representations advanced by an opponent by viewing them as 'more or less conscious of the real nature of a situation, the true recognition of which would not be in his interests' (Mannheim, 1957, p. 56). On the other hand, the total conception of ideology is implied when we speak of the ideology of an age, an epoch, or a group. Total ideology addresses and seeks to understand an individual's statements, norms or beliefs about society and how it works by viewing these as '. . . a function of his existence [and] an outgrowth of the collective life of which he partakes' (*ibid*, p. 57).

Few contemporary scholars employ the concept of particular ideology. Michall Katz implies the particular conception of ideology in his *Irony of Early School Reform*. Katz asserts that the Groton, Massachusetts School Committee used ideology as '. . . a kind of cloak with which they could cover their less idealistic motives' (Katz, 1968, p. 74). Katz's use of the term implies that ideology was a device used by the ruling class to legitimate their stewardship of society.

*Michael B. Lybarger*

Mannheim's view of total ideology is implied in his statement that '... opinions, statements, propositions, and systems of ideas are not taken at face value but are interpreted in the light of the situation of the one who expresses them'. Ideas, Mannheim continues, are '... a function of him who holds them, and [of] his position in the social milieu' (Mannheim, 1957 pp. 58–9).

Until recently, few scholars used the concept of ideology; either particular or general. Ideology has been often used by vulgar Marxists as a pejorative term to characterize the ideas and activities of their opponents. More recently, however, there have been efforts to employ ideology in a more universal, less pejorative sense. Carl Kaestle, for example, uses ideology synonymously with 'social outlook' and defines the former as

> ... a set of compatible propositions about human nature and society that help an individual interpret complex human problems and take action that the individual believes is in his or her best interest and the best interests of society as a whole. (Kaestle, 1982, p. 125)

In forthcoming pages we will endeavor to understand the work of the Committee on Social Studies as reflecting the ideology of two turn-of-the-century philanthropic movements: charity organization societies and social settlements. These groups were choosen for two reasons. First, both charity organizations characterized their work as addressing the 'needs' of their charges. Second, important members of the Committee were associated with one or both groups early in their careers. An examination of the work of both groups may afford us some sense of 'the picture of society', 'the seldom debated facts' about that society as well as 'the compatible propositions about human nature and society' which members of the Committee 'carried around in their heads'.


## Part II

At least seven members of the Committee on Social Studies had experience in charity organization work. The Committee's Chairman, Thomas Jesse Jones, and its first Secretary, William Anthony Arey, were visitors for the New York Charity Organization Society while studying at Columbia University between 1897 and 1904. Clarence Kingsley, the Chairman of the Commission on the Reorganization of Secondary Education, the parent group of the Committee on Social Studies, also worked for the New York Charity Society. At Columbia, Kingsley studied under Edward Devine, one of the founders of the charity organization movement. Kingsley's master's essay at Columbia, *The Treatment of Homeless Men in New York*, reflected an important concern of the New York Charity Organization Society where he was an agent in 1902. James Lynn Barnard, an active Committee member, in 1904 served as an agent for the New York Charity Organization Society. Arthur W. Dunn, the second Secretary of the Committee, and co-author with Barnard and Kingsley of *The Teaching of Community Civics* was active in 'civic philanthropy' while studying sociology at the University of Chicago. Blanch Hazard was associated with Robert Woods' South End House while teaching at the Girls' High School of the Practical Arts in Boston.[1]

The charity organization movement arose as a consequence of the unsatisfactory operation of both private and public charitable work during the depression of 1873–1878. The founders of the movement were concerned about both the rising government expenditures for relief and the attendant political corruption of public relief agencies, holding that private benevolence could meet all genuine demands for assistance.

Private benevolence, however, was in need of reformation. Charity reformers considered it flawed in three ways. First, indiscriminate and ill-thought-out almsgiving had attracted beggars, drunks, and criminals to the cities in order to secure money. Second, with so many charitable agencies providing aid, it was possible for cheats to secure help from two or more. This, according to one scandalized observer, tempted workers to a life of idleness, thus siding with labor against employers. Thirdly, there existed no effective means to help philanthropists distinguish between the deserving and undeserving poor; or deal with '. . . forces of experienced and crafty pauperism' (Bremmer, 1956, p. 168).

According to one historian of charity organization work, the immediate purpose of the movement was '. . . to promote cooperation and higher standards of efficiency among the numerous groups engaged in dispensing relief' (Lubove, 1965, p. 17). Andrew Carnegie was one philanthropist who considered such higher standards necessary. According to Carnegie

> There is something far more injurious to our race than poverty; it is misplaced charity. Of every thousand dollars

> spent upon so called objects of charity, it is not an overesti-
> mate to say nine hundred of it had better been thrown away.
> It is so given as to encourage the growth of those evils from
> which springs most of the misery of human life ... The
> more one studies the question of wealth and poverty the
> more difficult does it appear to interfere with existing
> conditions. (Page, 1969, p. 217)

Thus charity organization societies furnished no direct aid to the
poor and unfortunate. Instead, they acted as bureaus of information
collecting and investigating, usually referring the deserving poor to an
appropriate public or private agency.

  Not only did charity organization societies furnish no direct aid,
but the workers often counseled against indiscriminate almsgiving.
According to one worker, 'We must all remember that it is very easy
to make our well-meant charity a curse to our fellow men.' According to another worker, 'Alms are like drugs, and are as dangerous,
they create an appetite which is more harmful than the pain they
relieve' (Bremmer, 1956, p. 171).

  One historian has claimed that the charity organization worker's
hostility to almsgiving was based upon an '... individualistic interpretation of poverty and a pessimistic view of human nature'. Robert
Bremmer quotes Josephine Shaw Lowell, whom he describes as 'one
of the most enlightened of charity reformers'. In Mrs. Lowell's
social outlook '... the cause of poverty is to be found in some
deficiency — moral, mental, or physical — in the person who
suffers' (*ibid*, p. 169). Richard Ely, the great progressive economist
at the University of Wisconsin, contended,

> Plague, pestilence, and famine together could not work such
> irreparable harm as fifty free soup kitchens. The danger in
> gifts and clothing is that people will cease to exert themselves
> and will become miserable dependents on the bounty of
> others losing their self-respect and manhood. (Ely in Page,
> 1969, p. 227)

Robert Treat Paine would have agreed with Ely. According to Paine,

> ... relief, given in love begets a degenerate craving for more,
> 'shelters' in cities gather crowds of vagrants, where cheap
> rates tempt them to live in prolonged and increasing degrada-
> tion, begging easily from a half educated public the meager
> means for their wretched life. (Paine in Page, 1969, p. 230)

Viewing poverty as the consequence of personal inadequacy, charity organization workers endeavored to give something more precious than money, food, or clothes. According to Robert Treat Paine, the poor needed '. . . self-respect, hope, ambition, courage, character', more than money or aid. While Paine's virtues might not remove the burden of being poor, Washington Galdden thought that the practice of these virtues might put '. . . strength into the character of the sufferer, so that he would be willing and proud to bear his burden' (Bremmer, 1956, p. 169).

## Part III

Charity organization workers were not alone in their efforts to mitigate the lot of the unfortunate city dwellers. Equally important in addressing the needs of the victims of immigration, industrialization, and urbanization were the efforts of settlement house workers. We will next consider the educational and philanthropic work of the two settlement houses: Hull House in Chicago and Columbia University Settlement in New York. These were chosen for different reasons. Hull House, founded by Jane Addams, was probably the most famous settlement, and the one about which we have the most extensive sources. Moreover, Jane Addams was a friend of John Dewey and credited him with helping direct the educational work of Hull House. Columbia University Settlement was chosen because of its association with the early careers of Jones, Kingsley, Barnard and Arey.

With many settlement workers in the last quarter of the nineteenth century, Jane Addams was concerned that the social unity Americans once enjoyed was fractured by industrialization, urbanization, and a great influx of foreigners, whom she called 'densely ignorant' of American customs and institutions. Addams argued that the restoration of social unity required three things. Charity organization and settlement work would mitigate the suffering of the poor. More important, however, such work would also produce a group of people, settlement workers, '. . . whose allegiance was to society as a whole and not to any one part' (Levine, 1964, pp. 30–1). The second requirement for a restoration of social unity, according to Addams, was education '. . . which could show workers reasons for satisfaction in even the most humble task'. Finally, there was the government upon which rested the obligation to provide the necessities of satisfactory living (*ibid*, p. 32).

One of the educational activities at Hull House was a museum. Exhibits in the museum were developed, according to Addams, after 'many talks with Dr. Dewey'. The result of these talks was an exhibit of spinning wheels arranged in historical sequence. Since many of the young women at Hull House were engaged in textile trades, Addams thought they 'needed' to know,

> ... that there is no break in orderly evolution if we look at history from the industrial standpoint: that industry develops similarly and *peacefully* year by year among the workers of each nation. (Addams, 1899, p. 237)

Addams intended that the presentation of history at Hull House would impart to the worker, '... the conception of historic continuity in order to reveal to him the purpose and utility of his work' (Addams, 1915, p. 218). The demonstration of the orderly and peaceful development of labor, Addams hoped, would benefit the worker by raising the quantity and quality of his output and the employer by developing a more contented worker. We may see this more clearly by considering an address Jane Addams made to the National Society for the Promotion of Industrial Education. Addams described her visit to an industrial school for girls. Here girls were trained for work in the sewing trades. These trades, according to Addams, were 'so sub-divided that there is little education for the worker in them'. As a consequence, school officials endeavored to overcome this difficulty by teaching the child to understand the history of her craft and its relationship to her work and the finished product. It schools could do this, Addams concluded:

> ... her product must be a very different thing from that she would produce if she were ignorant of these matters. Her daily life is lifted from drudgery to one of self-conscious activity. (*ibid*, p. 215)

One insight into Jane Addams' social outlook lies in her conception of the source of 'drudgery'. Drudgery does not lie in the quality of the task itself, but rather in the worker's view of that task. Once workers were able to think differently about their tasks, and the place of these in the history of industry, work became self-conscious activity. It is not conditions which make work demeaning, rather it is the worker's conception of his work. Change that conception and, Addams believed, the product of the work 'becomes a very different thing' (*ibid*, p. 218).

It is only fair to point out that Jane Addams spent a great deal of her life seeking to mitigate the harsh conditions under which many of the neighbors of Hull House worked. At least twice she sought to assist striking workers (Levine, 1964, pp. 33–4). Both Addams and her colleague, Julia Richmond, worked tirelessly to secure enactment of the Illinois Child Labor Law and enforcement of factory and work-place codes (*ibid*, pp. 33–4). Indeed, Addams' life testifies to her unselfish interest in and concern for the casualties of industrialism and urbanization. It is clear that her recommendations for industrial education arose out of a concern to help the folk she saw around her. It is equally clear, however, that Addams did not often make any connection between the plight of workers and social conditions.

While Hull House reflected the ideas and values of one person, Jane Addams, the second of our settlements, Columbia University Settlement, (where Thomas Jesse Jones, the future Chairman of the Committee on Social Studies, was acting headworker in 1902) presents us with a more academic and eclectic style. The Settlement often sheltered Columbia faculty, graduate students, and interested outsiders (most of them middle or upper class), all of whom sometimes worked with the institution's clients or lived at the settlement while pursuing other projects. The bulletin of the settlement was subtitled *Social Studies* (in all probability, this was the first time Jones encountered the term). Articles in *Social Studies*, along with Jones' Master's and PhD dissertations, and settlement documents affords us an insight into the world of the settlement worker.

In the first article Jones published after leaving Columbia, he compared the role of a teacher at Hampton Institute (a Black and Indian trade school) to that of a club leader in a settlement (Jones 1903, p. 5). An examination of *Social Studies* indicates that in 1902 the Columbia University Settlement sponsored twenty-four clubs for boys or young men, and sixteen for girls. According to the Bulletin, the work of the boys' clubs was of a three-fold character: literary, social and athletic. Each club met four times a month. Three of the meetings were given to the club's main interest, whether literary, civic or political. The fourth meeting was devoted to social activities at which there was a special program. In addition, each club enjoyed the use of the Settlement's rooftop basketball court for at least one hour for one or two evenings per week.

According to Jones, the aims of the different clubs were determined in no small measure by the settlement workers' perception of '... the needs of the type [of persons] prevailing in the club'. Jones gave one example of this. According to Jones, 'The Jewish people are very prone to develop intellectual keenness at the expense of muscular strength; [and] their meetings have a tendency to cultivate an unpleasantness over small matters.' Accordingly, Jones continued, '. . . it has been deemed wise to restore the equilibrium by emphasizing the robust and a reasonable sacrifice of self for others'. In order to accomplish this, athletics were given a large place in the activities of the clubs with a number of Jewish members. The directors of these clubs were 'large-hearted men'. These men, according to Jones, 'tolerate no quibbling over small points . . . [or] any bickering or playing for place'. Whether in athletics or debate, Jones continued, '. . . the members are expected to be manly, straightforward, and fair in all their relations'. The work of the athletic clubs, Jones concluded '. . . would do much to socialize the naturally individualistic character of the Hebrew boy' (Jones, 1902, p. 148).

The girls' clubs at the settlement were similar to those for the boys. Here again, the directress had to work against the tendency to '. . . waste time over trifles [by] . . . dabbling in literature and aesthetics to the neglect of more domestic activities'. Instead, Jones stated, '. . . it has been the endeavor of the workers to direct the interest of girls into courses more useful to the state of life which they will enter' (*ibid*, pp. 74–5).

Jones and his colleague, James Hamilton, held that settlement work had two aims. The first of these was betterment of the conditions under which the settlement's clients lived. Betterment was the objective of such settlement activities as penny savings banks, public baths, and lectures on topics dealing with health and sanitation. The second and more important objective of settlement work was what Jones called the social evolution of the individual, or 'the transformation of the individual into the Anglo-Saxon ideal' (Jones, 1905, p. 48). This objective was served by such settlement activities as club work, lectures, and most important, association with settlement workers. Jones' superior, James Hamilton, was concerned that residents of the neighborhood which the settlement served, look to the settlement workers of native American stock for assistance in cultural, political, and social affairs. To fail to do this, Hamilton argued, was

> . . . narrow, provincial, and bigoted — and especially undesirable where the neighborhood happens to be composed largely of people of foreign birth. A community of this sort should welcome persons of native stock in their midst and all Americanizing agencies. (Hamilton, 1899, pp. 16–17)

Robert A. Woods, founder of South End House in Boston, (where Committee member Blanch Hazard worked) shared Reynolds' view of leadership for the immigrant. Woods indicated that the results of turn-of-the-century mental tests indicated that large members of immigrants and their children were found in 'the lesser ranges of ability'. These results demonstrated for Woods that settlement clients 'need and crave leadership'. Moreover Woods continued, 'Everything depends upon what sort of leadership they are to have.' Settlement leadership, according to Woods, must impart to poor people 'larger visions and higher ideals. It must put men and women in touch with noble souls' (Woods, 1902, p. 324).

Settlement workers and charity organization workers often shared similar views of their clients. We have seen charity workers cautioned against the forces of 'experienced and crafty pauperism'. Jones' predecessor at Columbia University Settlement, James Reynolds, reported to the Council of the Society that $40,000 raised for relief after a snow storm in January 1898 was not needed because the contributors did not know that 'the winter had been one of unusual prosperity'. Settlement workers organized and paid groups of needy able-bodied men to help clear snow in the neighborhood. Many of those who came lived in Bowery lodging houses and Reynolds contended '. . . were simply the crowd of bummers always ready to take on a short job . . . the only suffering which these people endured was that of walking . . . through the snow to get tickets [for free food and coal]'.[2]

When he was a charity visitor, Jones had an experience similar to Reynolds. He was taking the application of a family which, although not in need, had applied for charity. Jones had difficulty examining the family's application because the mother did not speak English. When the daughter arrived home from school, she was able to '. . . use her knowledge of English to forward her mother's illicit desire'. Thus Jones continued, '. . . the beneficiary of public education used that education to defraud the community' (Jones, 1897, p. 23). This incident, Jones contended, was evidence that the girl's teachers had failed to meet the 'immediate needs and defects of their charges'.

According to Jones the activities of Columbia University settlement had two objectives: social welfare and social evolution. Social welfare was the object of settlement activities such as penny savings banks, public baths and some lectures on sanitation and building codes. The object of these was to teach settlement clients how to make the most of their immediate environment through the use of existing public and private agencies.

The second aim of settlement work was the social evolution of the individual. Social evolution had as its end 'the transformation of the individual into the Anglo Saxon ideal'. In pursuit of social evolution, Jones enjoined

> Every possible agency to change the numerous foreign types ... The impulsiveness of the Italian must be curbed. The extreme individualism of the Jew must be modified. The shiftlessness of the Irish must give way to perseverance and frugality. (Jones, 1903, p. 189)

Jones' early writings indicate that he considered the work of the school and the settlement essentially — if not virtually identical. School and settlement were to serve welfare by teaching either children or adults to make the best of their immediate environment by utilizing existing public and private agencies; and at the same time serve the end of social evolution by devising experiences which might bring their charges to respect and imitate Anglo-Saxon ideals. The objective of school and settlement in addressing 'immediate needs' was to make good citizens of the children of immigrants crowding into urban schools. Linking citizenship with meeting 'immediate needs' affords us an insight into the view of society held by those members of the Committee on Social Studies with backgrounds in charity organizations or social settlement work.

Need in 1916 and need today implies dependency; a defect in the moral, intellectual, or personal make-up of the student or settlement house client which must be addressed by a particular activity (club work in the settlement or civics class in the school). This idea of need suggests that the weak needed the strong to define the characteristics they required to be useful citizens.

Jones' discussion of the similarities between settlement work and education affords us an insight into the idea of fitting activities to the needs of the students; an idea the Committee on Social Studies considered 'new and important' in 1915. At Columbia University Settlement, and the schools discussed in the reports of the Committee on Social Studies, the perception of need did not arise from the people being served, but from the people in charge; teachers in school and club leaders at the settlement. Jones counseled both teachers and settlement workers to consider needs in terms of the next higher stage of race development. Thus, Italian children 'need' educational and club work serving to make them less impulsive and more cautious and deliberate. Jewish children, on the other hand, 'need' educational experiences which will make them more impulsive and less cautious and deliberate (Jones, 1905, pp. 146–8). Need then reflected the social judgment of charity organization, social settlement workers, and civics teachers about what ideals and traits ought be inculcated in the weak by the strong through instruction in the social studies. Thorsten Veblin observed as much,

> ... the solicitude of settlements is in part directed to enhance the industrial efficiency of the poor, and to teach them the more adequate utilization of the means at hand, but it is also no less consistently directed to the inculcation by precept and example of certain punctilious of upper class propriety in manners and customs. (Veblin in Page, 1969, p. 17)

**Part IV**

In this chapter we have sought to understand the recommendation found in *The Social Studies in Secondary Education* that the social studies curriculum reflect the 'immediate needs' of students by viewing it in relation to the interest members of the Committee on Social Studies had in charity organization and social settlement work. From these sources Committee members acquired a conception of need as the reflection of individual personal inadequacy and not institutional shortcomings. Long before joining the Committee, members had articulated a view of society which legitimated some ways of dealing with those in need and denied legitimacy to other ways. This view permitted Committee members to enjoin teachers to approach the needs of immigrant children in much the same ways settlement and charity organization workers had dealt with their parents.

The work of Jane Addams and John Dewey at Hull House represented an effort to adapt historical study to the 'needs' of workers and their children and Hull House museum was developed to impart a sense of history and purpose to the most meaningless of work. Addams and Dewey hoped that workers acquainted with the history of their trade would be happy and content with their lot. On the other hand, the exhibits at Hull house museum implicitly placed the responsibility for the meaninglessness of work on the worker.

The work of Columbia University Settlement and other settlement houses exercised an important influence upon the recommendations found in *The Social Studies in Secondary Education*. Settlement workers viewed the educational needs of immigrants in terms of the requirements of the dominant society. Settlement workers also sought to keep their clients under the influence and tutelage of people who represented and embodied important aspects of the dominant culture.

The adoption of the 'immediate needs' of children as the criteria for selecting material for inclusion in the social studies curriculum may help explain an important problem in our modern social studies curriculum. Lacking any criteria beyond 'immediate need', contemporary professionals have not developed standards of criticism which might help them discriminate between the social studies and other activities, whose pursuit, while valuable, is best left to other institutions. Thus the content of the social studies expands. During the past ten years, for example, the social studies curriculum has included legal and consumer education, world affairs and urban studies, values clarification and moral development, human relations and sex education, and future studies. Such comprehensiveness allows social studies teachers to claim they are responding to changing social conditions and are thus serving the needs of their students. On the other hand, such comprehensiveness might also serve to deflect the criticism by the public of an increasingly vague and trivial social studies curriculum.

## Acknowledgements

Research for this chapter was supported in part by a faculty development grant from Edgewood College. I am grateful to Sister Alice O'Rourke, OP, President, and the Faculty Council of Edgewood College.

## Notes

1 Information on Jones' and Arey's work with the New York Charity Organization Society may be found in the Columbia University Settlement Society Papers housed in the State Historical Society in Madison, Wisconsin. Barnard's charity organization work is documented in *Who's Who* for 1929. Kingsley's charity work is noted in Drost, W.H. 'Clarence Kingsley — The New York years', *History of Education Quarterly*, vi, Fall, 1966, pp. 18–34. For Dunn's affiliation with both charity organization and settlement work see the Arthur W. Dunn Papers, Library Knox

College, Monmouth, Illinois. Columbia University Settlement Papers document the residence of Arey, Barnard, Jones, Kingsley, and James Harvey Robinson at the settlement.

2 JAMES REYNOLDS, 'Report to the Council of Columbia University Settlement: 1898 Columbia University Settlement Papers', State Historical Society of Wisconsin.

## References

ADDAMS, J. 'A function of the social settlement', *Annals of the American Academy of Political and Social Sciency*, XIII, 1899, pp. 237–43.

ADDAMS, J. 'Address', *Proceedings of the National Society for the Promotion of Industrial Education*, XI, 1915, pp. 216–24.

BREMMER, R.E. 'Scientific philantrophy', *Social Service Review*, XXX, 1956, p. 168.

DROST, W.H. 'Clarence Kingsley — The New York years', *History of Education Quarterly*, VI, Fall, 1966, pp. 18–34.

GROSS, R.E. 'The status of social studies in the public schools in the United States', *Journal of Social Education*, XLI, 1977, pp. 191–7.

JONES, T.J. *Social Education in the Elementary School*, Masters dissertation, Columbia University, 1897.

JONES, T.J. 'A day at University Settlement', *Bulletin of Columbia University Settlement: Social Studies*, VI, 1902, pp. 144–9.

JONES, T.J. 'Comparison of the past and present arms of Hampton', *Southern Workman*, XXXIII, March, 1903, pp. 3–7.

JONES, T.J. *The Sociology of a City Block*, doctoral dissertation, Columbia University, 1905.

JONES, T.J. 'The work of the settlement: 1901–1902', *Bulletin of Columbia University Settlement: Social Studies*.

JUDD, C.H. 'The teaching of civics', *School Review*, XXVI, 1918, pp. 511–32.

KASTLE, C.F. 'Ideology and American educational history', *History of Education Quarterly*, XXII, Summer, 1982, pp. 123–37.

KATZ, M. *The Irony of Early School Reform*, New York: Vintage, 1968.

LEVINE, D. *Varieties of Reform Thought*, Madison, WI: State Historical Society of Wisconsin, 1964.

LUBOVE, R. *The Professional Altruist: The Emergence of Social Work as a Career*, Cambridge, MA: Harvard University Press, 1965.

PAGE, C.H. *Class and American Sociology: From Ward to Ross*, New York: Schocken Books, 1969.

ROBINSON, J.H. *The New History*, New York: The Free Press, 1912.

WIRTH, L. in MANNHEIM, K. *Ideology and Utopia*, New York: Vintage Books, 1957.

WOODS, R.O. *The City Wilderness*, Boston, MA: Heath, 1903.

# 8    The First Crusade for Learning Disabilities: The Movement for the Education of Backward Children

*Bary M. Franklin*

## Abstract

There exists among those who work in the area of learning disabilities a widely shared view of the historical development of their field. Learning disabilities, according to this conventional wisdom, is thought to have emerged out of the research of Alfred Strauss and Heinz Werner with brain injured, mentally retarded children during the late 1930s and early 1940s. In this chapter, I argue that this is a flawed history. It is a history that sees learning disabilities as a problem within the individual, the result of a brain injury or other neurological dysfunction. What is missing from this account is any link between the appearance of learning disabilities and events in the larger society, particularly changes in existing political and economic arrangements. In this chapter, I offer a revised history of learning disabilities that traces its origins to the early twentieth century movement for the education of backward children. Looking at the development of the ungraded class program for backward children in the Atlanta public schools during the first two decades of this century, I show how what today we call learning disabilities first appeared on the scene as an educational response not to a problem of brain injury but to serious disruptions and dislocations that resulted from the nation's transformation into an urban, industrial society.

**Part I**

Not unlike other professionals, those who work in the area of learning disabilities are linked together by, among other things, a shared understanding of the historical development of their field. According to this conventional wisdom, which one can easily find in any of a number of the field's introductory textbooks, learning disabilities emerged out of Alfred Strauss and Heinz Werner's studies of so-called brain injured, mentally defective children during the late 1930s and early 1940s. Working at the Wayne County Training School in Northville, Michigan, a school for what today we would call mildly mentally handicapped children, Strauss and Werner identified within the student population two distinct types of mental deficiency. One type, which they labelled as endogencous, referred to a deficiency that was thought to be hereditary in origin and to occur in children who had a family history of retardation. A second type, which they labelled as exogeneous, referred to a deficiency that they postulated as being the result of brain injury or disease occurring before, during, or immediately after birth.

In studying these two groups of children, Strauss and Werner found differences in their perceptual motor and conceptual thinking abilities. They also noted that during their stay at the school, the IQs of the endogeneous children underwent a slight increase while those of the exogeneous children underwent a slight decrease. They argued that these changes in the IQs of these two groups of children indicated that the typical curriculum for the hereditarily mentally defective was inappropriate for those whose retardation was due to brain injury. Based on their studies of these two groups of children, Strauss and Werner identified a syndrome which they argued was the result of brain injury and which manifested itself in perceptual-motor, learning, and emotional problems.

In ensuing years, so this conventional history goes, a number of individuals began to talk about seemingly normal children who, because of a brain injury or neurological dysfunction, exhibited significant learning and behavior problems in school. Some of these individuals, including William Cruickshank, Newell Kephart, and Samuel Kirk, were colleagues of Strauss and Werner and followed their original line of research. Others, including Samuel Orton, Helmer Myklebust, and Marianne Frostig, had a less direct connection to Strauss and Werner but came to what were essentially similar conclusions. In April 1963, at a conference in Chicago sponsored by the Fund for Perceptually Handicapped Children,

Samuel Kirk coined the term learning disabilities to refer to this syndrome (Bryan and Bryan, 1978, pp. 12–20; Hallahan and Cruickshank, 1973, chapter 3; Hallahan and Kauffman, 1976, chapter 1; Haring and Bateman, 1977, chapter 2; Lerner, 1976, chapter 2; Mercer, 1979, chapter 1; Myers and Hammill, 1976, pp. 35–41).

Locating the origins of learning disabilities in the work of Strauss and Werener does make clear why the concept of brain injury has been so important in the field's development. Nevertheless, it is an account which is seriously flawed. Nowhere in this conventional history is any connection made with events in the larger society. We should not, however, be surprised by this oversight. Like most explanations penned by psychologists, and nearly all of those who have written about the history of learning disabilities are educational psychologists, it is a description of individuals and individual minds without mention of any social context (Sarason, 1981, chapters 2–4).

The problem with this historical record becomes apparent when we recognize that educational and psychological research is at root a social activity. Those who carry it out live in particular social settings and bring to their work the values, beliefs, concerns, and interests which they have acquired as participants in those settings (Buss, 1979, pp. 1–24; Gergen, 1973; Popkewitz, 1984, chapter 1). The work of those who built the field of learning disabilities is inextricably linked to events in twentieth-century American society, to changes that have occurred in its political and economic arrangements as well as to attempts of its social institutions to respond to these changes. To write a history of learning disabilities without paying attention to this social context is to stand at risk of missing what is most important in that history. Unfortunately, according to the educational historian Marvin Lazerson, it is this very kind of omission that typifies much of the effort today to write about the history of special education (1975, pp. 33–52).

As it turns out, the field of learning disabilities has been shaped from its inception by concerns over larger societal issues, particularly questions of social deviance and discord. Speaking at the 1963 Conference of the Fund for Perceptually Handicapped Children, where as we already have mentioned the term learning disabilities was coined, John Alderson of the University of Illinois' School of Social Work pointed out that perceptually impaired children often exhibit difficulty in their social functioning (1963, p. 20). One of the earliest government reports on the problem of learning disabilities, the now famous 1966 report of Task Force I, noted that learning disabled children frequently respond to legitimate authority in 'anti social' and 'aggressive' ways (Clements, 1966, p. 12).

The clearest example of the connection between the learning disabilities field and problems of social deviance can be seen in the 1969 hearings before the House of Representative's Sub-committee on Education on the then proposed Children with Learning Disabilities Act. During the first day of the hearings, the Chairperson of the Sub-committee, Roman Pucinski of Illinois, suggested a link between the kind of social disorders that characterized the decade of the 1960s and conditions such as learning disabilities. The nation, he warned, is:

> going to continue spending billions of dollars on public aid programs, on various programs dealing with social disorders, crime in the streets. We are going to see continued havoc and chaos if we don't address ourselves to problems of emotional instability in human behavior. (US Congress, 1966, p. 23)

Pucinski's fear was shared by many of those who presented testimony to the Sub-committee. Harold McGrady of Northwestern University pointed out that if the educational needs of learning disabled children are not met, they will 'join the ranks of the maladjusted'. He noted in this vein a study in which one investigator suggested that Lee Harvey Oswald may have been a dyslexic (p. 56). Mrs. Leon Lock, President of the Pennsylvania Association for Children with Learning Disabilities, also pointed out that learning disabled children often end up in 'trouble with the law' (p. 163).

In a letter to the Sub-committee, a Mrs. Wimberly of Lake Charles, Louisiana, argued that if a learning disabled child was not given an appropriate education, he or she may become 'a drop out, a dope addict, a murderer'. Another letter, this one from L.S. Holmes of Houston, Texas, pointed out that many learning disabled children ultimately end up as school drop outs. He also noted that 85 per cent of the prison population of Texas were school drop outs. 'I wonder,' he asked evidently rhetorically, 'what per cent of these prisoners were brain injured with learning disabilities' (p. 192).

More recently, the Canadian Senate established a sub-committee to investigate the role of early childhood experience in causing criminal behavior. In its 1980 report, the sub-committee identified learning disabilities as one of a number of factors during childhood that could result in 'later deviant behaviour'. The sub-committee concluded that when accompanied by other factors such as poverty and child abuse, learning disabilities may 'set the course of a child's life so that it eventually becomes a violent criminal' (Canadian Senate, 1980, p. 61).

During the last several years a number of researchers have begun to explore the social context surrounding the emergence and growth of the learning disabilities field. Gerald Coles, for example, has noted the growing popularity of hereditary explanations for the existence of learning disabilities. Such efforts, he argues, represent attempts to conceal the societal causes of school failure behind biological explanations. What is, according to Coles, a failure of the nation's social institutions requiring political remedies has become under the rubric of learning disabilities an individual failure requiring psychological or medical remedies (1978 and 1980).

James Carrier (1983a and 1983b) and Christine Sleeter (chapter 9) have argued that the concept of learning disabilities was devised by educators to explain and remedy the school failure of upper and upper middle class white children without calling into question the legitimacy and soundness of America's public schools. A major purpose served by the existence of a learning disabilities field, they both note, is to defuse the kind of popular criticism of the nation's social institutions that may ultimately have disruptive effects.

The problem with the field's conventional history, as I see it, is that it locates the origin of learning disabilities in the wrong place. Strauss and Werner's work does represent a phase in the eventual emergence of learning disabilities. Elsewhere (Franklin, 1980), however, I have argued that at least a quarter century before Strauss and Werner began their work at the Wayne County Training School, American educators had identified the problem that we today call learning disabilities. Writing in 1914, Henry Goddard and Barbara Morgan both noted the existence of children who though not mentally defective were nevertheless not making adequate progress in their school work. Referring to these children as 'backward', both Goddard and Morgan believed that despite their present performance, these children could with special teaching and additional time show improvement (Goddard, 1914, pp. xvi–xvii; Morgan, 1914, pp. 1–4).

Goddard and Morgan were not alone in their concern for these so-called backward children. Other prominent educators of the day, including Arthur Holmes and Lightner Witmer, wrote about these children. Between 1904 and 1921, a national organization, the Conference on the Education of Backward, Truant and Delinquent Children, a forerunner of the National Conference of Social Work, met annually to examine the needs of these children. During the first two decades of this century, a number of the nation's school systems established what they called 'ungraded' classes to serve these backward children. We can, I think, view the years between 1900 and 1925 as the nation's 'first crusade' for learning disabilities. If we are to understand the social role that learning disabilities plays in American society, we must, I believe, recast the field's history. A first step in this direction is to examine this 'first crusade'. It is to this task that I will now turn.

## Part II

Turn-of-the-century American educators used the term backward to refer to a diverse lot of children who were not adjusting to the academic and social demands of the public schools. Often, they used the term as a synonym for mental deficiency. At other times, they used the notion of backwardness to encompass children whose school failure was the result of poor attendance, social malajustment, or the inability to speak English. And on still other occasions, they used the term to refer to intellectually normal children whose reason for failure was somewhat uncertain but who exhibited what they believed were signs of some sort of cognitive dysfunction (Sarason and Doris, 1979, pp. 300–11). It was this third usage of the term which suggests that among these backward children were those who today we would call learning disabled. Speaking at the seventh annual Conference on the Education of Backward, Truant and Delinquent Children in 1910, Howard McQueary of Soldan High School in St. Louis pointed out that these children were not mentally defective:

> By 'backwardness', we refer more to school attainments than to mental status, that is our emphasis is upon failure to make regular process in grades with the average group of children, or unbalanced accomplishments. This may be due to a great many causes, such as late entrance into school; the lockstep in promotion; frequent transfer from school to school, or from teacher, the presence of physical defects, and sickness causing irregular attendance; poor teaching; and home indulgence; in addition to mental incapacity or delayed maturity; so that there may be a general all-round retardation; or backwardness may be manifest only in some particular subject or study. (1910, pp. 122–3)

If these backward children were not mentally defective, what, then, was wrong with them? They were, according to some of these early twentieth century educators, brain damaged. During the discussion of his paper on teaching backward children at the 1905 Conference on the Education of Backward, Truant and Delinquent Children, Charles Krauskopf, Secretary of the Illinois Society for Child Study, stated that backwardness was a problem of children's 'nervous organization'. What was perplexing about these children, he went on to say, was that despite the lack of any physical defect, 'some portion of the brain has not developed fully' (1905, pp. 94–5). A member of the audience, a one Dr. Abbott, noted the difficulty brought about by the inability to actually locate the brain injury:

> When you come to the children that are backward, these children that are not right and we don't know exactly what to do, it is an extremely difficult problem. There may be no defect apparent and still the child may suffer from these mental deficiencies to a greater or lesser degree (Krauskopf, 1905, p. 97).

Writing in 1914, Barbara Morgan took a similar position and described backward children as those exhibiting 'inherent fundamental brain disturbance', a 'sense defect', or a 'slow rate of development' (p. 210). And twelve years later, Annie Inskeep suggested that one of the characteristics of backwardness was word blindness, 'a condition arising because of a lesion of the left, or, if the patient is left-handed, the right angular gyrus or a cellular deficiency in this same region' (1926, p. 39).

Others, however, maintained that the problem was environmental. Henry Goddard pointed out that backward children were those 'who for some cause, local, environmental, physical, or somewhat mental, are slow, dull and cannot progress at the rate that our ordinary school curriculum presupposes' (1914, p. xvi). At the 1909 meeting of the Conference on the Education of Backward, Truant and Delinquent Children, Florence McNeal identified eighteen categories of backwardness, over half of which could be attributed to environmental or social causes. Included among the backward, she noted, were children who could not speak English, who had a poor self concept, whose school attendance was unsatisfactory, who had weak study skills, and who simply could not complete the required school work (1909, pp. 62–3).

One environmental factor that was singled out for particular attention was the school. At the 1905 meeting of the Conference on the Education of Backward, Truant and Delinquent Children, Nelson McLain, Superintendent of the St. Charles School for Boys, argued that backwardness was the result of a school curriculum that 'failed to nourish the mental growth or to engage, employ and direct the physical activities of child life' (1905, pp. 6–7). A year later at the 1906 meeting of the Conference, William Shearer, Superintendent of Schools in Elizabeth, New Jersey, also pointed to the role that the school played in causing backwardness:

> ... I think that it may be shown that the very large proportion (I can't say all) of the so-called backward children are not backward because of inherited mental or physical defects but are considered backward and made to appear backward because of the methods which we are using in our public schools (1906, p. 27).

Shearer went on to claim that for many children the existing curriculum was inappropriate. 'We are stuffing the coming men and women in our school with a lot of matter which is not digestible, which cannot go to build strong brains' (p. 30). In responding to a comment of a conference participant about the ability of backward children to adjust to the demands of adult society, Shearer was even more direct in placing the responsibility on the schools. 'These so-called backward children, when they get out in life, prove they were not backward but very much forward and I believe we are responsible largely for keeping them back when we should not' (p. 39).

Backwardness was not, then, simply a problem within the individual. There was, educators of the day believed, a clear connection between backwardness and events in the larger society. A number of participants at the 1905 meeting of the Conference on the Education of Backward, Truant and Delinquent Children noted that children who were backward in school were likely to be the same children who engaged in delinquent acts outside of school (Bodine, 1905, p. 70; Jackson, 1905, p. 13; McLain, 1905, p. 6). William Bodine, Superintendent of Compulsory Education for the Chicago Public Schools, saw a direct connection between backwardness and changes that were then occurring in American society. Accompanying the nation's late nineteenth and early twentieth century transformation from a rural, agrarian society to an urban, industrial one, he argued, were a host of unwholesome changes that had led to an increase in the incidence of backwardness. There was, Bodine stated, the problem of unrestricted immigration that was allowing the entry into the country of 'illiterates' and others who would make 'undesirable citizens'. Such individuals, he believed, would not recognize the need to send their children to school (1905, p. 64).

Another factor in the increasing incidence of backwardness, Bodine believed, was the ease with which people could marry and have children. 'We forget that there is no uniform marriage law to stop the marriage of the feeble-minded, epileptics, consumptives, habitual drunkards and school girls in short dresses who play with fate to the tune of the wedding march' (p. 65).

There were, Bodine argued, other aspects of modern urban life that were responsible for backwardness. They included the ready access that children living in the city had to liquor, tobacco, cocaine, and opium, the countless opportunities they had to engage in gambling, and the confinement brought about by apartment living. Even the rise of labor unions, he believed, had contributed to increases in backwardness. Bodine maintained that the use of strikes by workers as an organizing tool had taught children a disrespect for law which frequently led to acts of disobedience and defiance in the classroom (pp. 66–7). These were conditions, Bodine pointed out, that were unknown in the nation's rural past:

> Slowly but surely, the home is passing away in the cities — the old fashioned home with its green yards and flowers, its broad porch, and comfort for child life. There are few if any neurotics among country children where they live next to nature and where they grow up into robust manhood and womanhood as nature's own (p. 66).

At another presentation during this same conference a Miss Paul of Nebraska, responding to several comments about the causes of backwardness, echoed Bodine's concerns. 'I hope the gentlemen don't think the majority of these children are of American parentage, for they are not. The majority of them are of foreign parentage' (Krauskopf, 1905, p. 104).

## Part III

Not unlike other early twentieth century school reformers who believed that a curriculum organized along more functional lines could resolve the problems that urbanization and industrialization had created for the nation, educators of backward children embraced the cause of curriculum change. A.J. Hutton, speaking at the 1905 meeting of the Conference on the Education of Backward, Truant and Delinquent Children, argued that if 'extraneous matter' was removed from the curriculum, backward children could be successful. He proposed, for example, that such topics as taxes, insurance, simple and compound interest, and bank discounts be removed from the course of study in arithmetic. 'What remains', he asked? 'Enough for all the needs of the ordinary citizen' (1905, pp. 19–20). At the same meeting, Nelson McLain suggested that the problem of backwardness could be addressed by the inclusion of industrial training within the course of study. Such an addition, he argued, would appeal to those students whose backwardness was the result of boredom with the existing school curriculum (McLain, 1905, pp. 7 and 12).

Some of those who championed the causes of backward children believed that the regular classroom teacher could adequately instruct these children. Lightner Witmer of the University of Pennsylvania suggested at the 1906 meeting of the Conference that if teachers would only individualize their instruction, they could successfully educate those children whose backwardness was not too severe (p. 13). Commenting on Witmer's suggestion, a Miss Briggs of New York recommended a practice then popular in Batavia, New York, in which two teachers were assigned to each classroom. One teacher was responsible for instructing the class as a whole while the second teacher worked with individual students who were having difficulty (p. 14). A year earlier, at the 1905 meeting, Charles Krauskopf argued for something akin to what today we call mainstreaming. Isolating backward children in special classes, he believed, posed the same danger as the creation of segregated institutions for the mentally defective:

> the special teacher will trend away from the conventional instruction so much that the vital connection with the rest of the school system will be lost and will thus tend to prevent transfers to and from the regular classes. Quite a per cent of these slow children can be so strengthened by special instruction that they can enter the regular grade work for certain periods, if not permanently, much to their benefit and occasionally a normal child can be helped greatly by work with the special teacher. This helpful interchange can only be secured by keeping the special classes under the administrative system and making them an organic part of some school. In order to preserve this organic relationship the modifications of the curriculum and methods of instruction for the

sub-normal should be as small as possible, consistent with good results to the individual (pp. 89–90).

It was not, however, proposals such as Krauskopf's for integrating backward children into the regular class that were, at least initially, to influence the nation's educators. What was to have an impact was the suggestion that a new type of special class, the 'ungraded class', was needed for these children. According to Florence McNeal, the ungraded class was a place where backward children's problems could be diagnosed and their course of study modified accordingly. In such a class, she believed, a special teacher could both augment the strengths and remedy the problems of backward children so that they could in time rejoin their regular class (1909, p. 61).

Located as they were in the public schools, these ungraded classes could not be isolated from the political and social events of the day. Examining their development, particularly their relationship with other educational reforms of the day, will provide us with a view of the social context in which this first effort to educate the learning disabled took place. Like backwardness, the ungraded class designation was used loosely by educators to include classes for the backward, the mentally defective, the foreign born, and the socially malajusted (Sarason and Doris, 1979, p. 267). In at least one school system, however, the public schools of Atlanta, Georgia, ungraded classes were in the beginning used primarily for children who could be considered backward. It is to the development of ungraded classes in Atlanta that I will now turn.

## Part IV

As early as 1898, Atlanta educators talked about the need to introduce more functional content into a course of study that was devoted to the goal of mental discipline. In his 1898 report to the Board of Education, Superintendent William F. Slaton noted that a major priority for the city's schools was the introduction of industrial training (Slaton, 1898, pp. 52–3). Two years later, the President of the Board of Education, Hoke Smith, stated that the establishment of a shop work course at Boys' High School and the appointment of a Director of Manual Training marked the beginning of the effort to 'prepare children of our schools for practical work' (Smith, 1900, p. 21). In 1903, the desire to make the curriculum more functional led to the inclusion of a business course and a technology course at Boys' High School (Slaton, 1903, p. 54).

The goal of making the curriculum more functional was one phase, an educational phase, if you will, of a larger reform movement that appeared during the early years of this century. Known as the social efficiency movement, it represented the attempt of many American intellectuals to bring harmony to a society which they saw as being prone to conflict and disruption in the wake of the nation's transformation to an urban, industrial society. It was during the first two decades of this century in the name of social efficiency that Americans embraced such diverse reforms as the scientific management movement in industry, the creation of a system of juvenile courts, the attempt to professionalize social work, and the introduction of a more functional school curriculum in hopes of making the nation more cooperative, more unified, and more stable.

Efficiency minded educators promoted a number of school reforms. One change, which we have already mentioned, was the desire to make the curriculum more functional. Another change which they promoted was that of differentiating the curriculum into distinct courses of study to prepare youth of different abilities for different occupational and social roles. These two reforms, they believed, would increase the ability of the schools to smooth the transition of children to their adult work and citizenship roles in an increasingly interdependent society and minimize the chance of social dislocations and disruptions (Franklin, 1986, chapter 4). The establishment of the ungraded class was one of the approaches that Atlanta educators would adopt to achieve this differentiation.

Reporting to the Atlanta Board of Education in 1912, Superintendent William M. Slaton noted that within the city, there were currently 'a number of deaf and dumb children' who were not presently being educated by the public schools. 'If there were a sufficient number of these children in our town to justify the establishment of a school for them', he went on to say, 'I think we should provide for them at an early day' (Slaton, 1912, p. 43). Two years later, Atlanta established its first special class, a class for deaf children at Ashby Street School (Bell, 1974, p. 208; Ecke, 1972, p. 77). During the next ten years, Atlanta would establish a city-wide program of special education in its segregated white schools that would include classes for the deaf, blind, mentally defective, socially maladjusted, and backward.

Although Superintendent William M. Slaton had noted the problem posed by backward children as early as 1911 (Board

Minutes, 26 January 1911, p. 123), the first effort to establish a program for these children did not take place until 1916. In her report to the Board of Education on special classes in June 1916, Laura Smith, the Primary Supervisor, requested the establishment of three additional special classes for mentally defective children at Luckie, Ashby, and Fraser Street schools to complement the two existing classes for these students. She also called attention to another group of students who were 'over age for their grade' and who were not being efficiently served by existing programs. 'These children', she pointed out, 'are not mental defectives. Most of them are retarded because of lack of opportunity, or illness'. She argued that these children represented the city's 'most serious loss' because they were likely to become disheartened over their lack of progress and leave school. Smith recommended the establishment of an ungraded class where these students could be placed terporarily until they were able with the help of special teachers 'to make their grades more rapidly' and thus catch up with children in the regular classroom (Board Minutes, 22 June 1916).

The following year, two ungraded classes were established at the elementary level, one at Boulevard School and the other at English Avenue School. At Boulevard School, twenty-two so-called 'over age' students were taken from other grades and assigned to one teacher who would work with them until they could perform at grade level and would be returned to their regular class. At English Avenue School, the Batavia Plan was introduced and two teachers would work with students in the ungraded class in those areas where they were having difficulty (Board Minutes, 24 January 1918, p. 7; Ecke, 1972, p. 113). During the next four years, the ungraded program was expanded throughout the city until by 1922 there were ungraded classes in fourteen elementary schools. In 1924, the program was expanded to the secondary level with the establishment of two ungraded classes at Hoke Smith Junior High School (School Directory, 1921–22 and 1924–25).

As was the case with other programs in Atlanta's segregated schools, the special education offered to black children was limited and erratic. In 1920, special classes for black mentally defective children were established at Carrie Steele School and at Pittsburg Night School. The following year, these two classes were closed, and two new special classes were opened at Stoors School. The next year, these classes, too, were closed and no further provision was made for special education for blacks for the remainder of the decade (School Directory, 1920–21 and 1921–22).

Designed for children who required additional help in one or more subjects before returning to a regular classroom, the ungraded program included the basic elementary subjects combined with a number of more functional activities that were thought to be interesting and useful to backward children. We can obttain a picture of the program of the ungraded class from a series of articles on the operation of the Atlanta Public Schools which appeared in the *Atlanta Constitution* in 1927 and 1928 and was later republished in a small pamphlet by the Board of Education. In the ungraded class, 'the boys and girls are first made happy and are then given an opportunity for the kind of activities that give them a feeling of success'.

One of the boys in the ungraded class was unable to do the work of his fourth grade class and in addition exhibited conduct that was 'atrocious'. Assigned to the ungraded class, he was not only given work in reading, arithmetic, and geography, he was also involved in a number of practical activities such as repairing toys for the Junior Red Cross and weaving a rug for his mother's Christmas present. 'Since his placement here', the article noted, 'he has not been absent, nor would he think of leaving his happy schoolroom where his interest is stimulated along "doing lines"'.

A second case cited in the article attested to the apparent success of the ungraded class. In this instance, the student was a female who had completed her elementary work at the age of 14. She was placed in the ungraded class at Thomson Junior High School, and after three years of 'fine work' was sent to Commercial High School to study home economics. 'This girl who could not master the regular course of study has been salvaged for society by special education' (Atlanta Board of Education, 1928, p. 72).

As a special program for backward children, Atlanta's ungraded class was short-lived. In 1923, a number of ungraded classes were renamed 'adjustment' classes and given a new function. They were to serve students who had become 'repeaters'. These were students 'who are not handicapped in any way, but who for sufficient reasons have become temporarily misfits in the school program'. With individual instruction in reading, arithmetic, and other subjects, it was hoped that they would 'soon take their places among the boys and girls of the same mental capacity' (School Directory, 1923–24; Atlanta Board of Education, 1928, p. 73).

The adjustment class was a source of pride for Superintendent Willis Sutton. In his 1924 annual report to the Board of Education, he referred to the adjustment class as a 'great achievement' in Atlanta's effort to reduce its public schools' failure rate (Sutton, 1924, p. 2).

Despite its seeming success, a financial crisis in 1926 led to the discontinuance of the adjustment class (Atlanta Board of Education, 1927; Atlanta Board of Education, 1928, p. 73).

The creation of the adjustment class program left the city in 1923 with two ungraded classes, one at Calhoun Street School and the other at Oakland City School. The following year, however, the city's special classes for mentally defective students were redesignated as ungraded classes. During the next three decades, this special effort to serve backward children disappeared as ungraded classes became the city's vehicle for serving not only children of normal intelligence who could not function in the regular classroom but the mentally defective as well. It was not until 1958 that Atlanta would again offer a special program for backward children when a class for brain damaged and/or emotionally disturbed children was established (Jarrell, 1958, p. 21).

For Atlanta educators, a truly differentiated curriculum had to provide not only for a variety of programs for normal children but also, according to a 1928 article in the *Atlanta Constitution*, 'special classes for unusual children':

> There must be night schools for special needs, 'opportunity schools' for grown-ups whose education has been neglected; technical training in various lines. There are high schools for boys and girls offering academic courses; a technical high school for boys; a commercial high school for both sexes. There are schools and classes for the deficient, classes for the deaf, classes for the blind. (Atlanta Board of Education, 1928, p. 9)

The ungraded class was one of Atlanta's efforts in meeting these diverse needs:

> Atlanta's school system is providing for these by clases [sic] for 'behavior problem' children, ungraded classes for other types, and by grouping within the grades children of the same mental age. (Atlanta Board of Education, 1928, p. 80)

## Part V

Although early twentieth-century educators often attributed back-wardness to certain internal, neurological impairments of one sort or another, they did not divorce the condition from the social environment. A host of environmental factors, including inadequate parenting, an inability to speak English, poverty, poor school attendance, and a failure to meet the academic demands of the school, could, they believed, account for backwardness. Some of these educators argued that the increasing incidence of backwardness among American children was the result of the transformation of the nation into an urban, industrial society. They believed that such features of modern life as unrestricted immigration, widespread vice, unregulated marriages, and a growing lack of respect for authority were responsible for increases in backwardness. Backwardness as a category, then, provided educators of the day with a way of understanding and through the establishment of the ungraded class with a way of responding to the disrupting effects that urbanization and industrialization were having on the lives of children.

Beginning our historical account with the backward child movement, does offer us some insight into the social role that learning disabilities plays in American society. The concept of learning disabilities offers contemporary educators, just as the idea of backwardness offered their turn-of-the-century forebearers, a way of conceptualizing the destabilizing effects of social change, particularly problems of childhood deviance, in educational terms. Fundamental problems of social order which at first glance seem intractable and rooted in existing political and economic arrangements are, when thought of as learning disabilities, converted into more managable educational problems. In other words, large scale social problems that may in fact require significant political change become under the rubric of learning disabilities problems of individuals that can be addressed by existing agencies of social improvement, particularly the schools. Herein may in fact lie the great virtue of learning disabilities.

As an concept, learning disabilities is, I think, quintessentially American. A notion that serves to transform fundamental political and economic problems into educational problems does fit nicely in a society that has from its very beginning seen schooling as its principal route to social betterment. Just as early twentieth century Americans needed, it seems, a category to conceptualize the disrupting effects of social change in educational terms, so too may contemporary Americans. Learning disabilities may, as it turns out, be just that category. Only further historical research along the lines indicated in this chapter will tell.

*Barry M. Franklin*

## References

ALDERSON, J.J. 'Social and community seminar preview', *Proceedings of the Conference on Exploration into the Problems of Perceptually Handicapped Children*, Vol. 1, Evanston, IL: Fund for Perceptually Handicapped Children, 1963, pp. 19–23.

ATLANTA BOARD OF EDUCATION. *School Directory*, Atlanta Public School Archives, 1920–26.

ATLANTA BOARD OF EDUCATION. *Board of Education Minutes*, Atlanta Board of Education, 1911–18.

ATLANTA BOARD OF EDUCATION. *The Functioning of the Atlanta Public Schools*, Atlanta Public School Archives, 1928.

ATLANTA BOARD OF EDUCATION. 'Special report concerning negotiations between the conference committee of the board of education and the citizens advisory committee', Atlanta Public School Archives, 1927.

BELL, W. *Atlanta Public School Directory, 1900–1915*, Atlanta Public School Archives, 1974.

BODINE, W.L. 'The cause and the cure', *Proceedings of the Second National Conference on the Education of Backward, Truant and Delinquent Children*, Plainfield: Indiana Boys School, 1905, pp. 62–8.

BRYAN, T.H. and BRYAN, J.H. *Understanding Learning Disabilities*, 2nd edn, Sherman Oaks: Alfred Publishing Company, 1978.

BUSS, A.R. 'The emerging field of the sociology of psychological knowledge', in BUSS, A.R. (Ed.) *Psychology in Social Context*, New York: Irvington, 1979, pp. 1–24.

CANADIAN SENATE. *Child at Risk: A Report of the Standing Senate Committee on Health, Welfare and Science*, Hull: Canadian Government Publishing Centre, 1980.

CARRIER, J. 'Explaining educability: An investigation of political support for the Children with Learning Disabilities act of 1969', *British Journal of Sociology of Education*, 4, 2, 1983a, pp. 125–40.

CARRIER, J. 'Masking the social in educational knowledge: The case of learning disabilities theory', *American Journal of Sociology*, 88, 5, 1983b, pp. 948–74.

CLEMENTS, S. *Task Force I-Minimal Brain Dysfunction in Children*, Public Health Service Publication No. 1415–1966, Washington, DC: Government Printing Office, 1966.

COLES, G. 'The learning disabilities test battery: Empirical and social issues', *Harvard Educational Review*, 48, 3, 1978, pp. 313–40.

COLES, G. 'Evaluation of genetic explanations of reading and learning problems', *The Journal of Special Education*, 14, 3, 1980, pp. 365–83.

ECKE, M.W. *From Ivy Street to Kennedy Center: Centennial History of the Atlanta Public School System*, Atlanta Board of Education, 1972.

FRANKLIN, B.M. 'From backwardness to LD: Behaviorism, systems theory, and the learning disabilities field historically reconsidered', *Journal of Education*, 162, 4, 1980, pp. 5–22.

FRANKLIN, B.M. *Building the American Community: The School Curriculum and the Search for Social Control*, London, England: Falmer Press, 1986.

GERGEN, K.J. 'Social psychology as history', *Journal of Personality and Social Psychology*, 26, 2, 1973, pp. 309–20.

GODDARD, H.H. *School Training of Defective Children*, New York: World Book Company, 1914.

HALLAHAN, D.P. and CRUICKSHANK, W.M. *Psychoeducational Foundations of Learning Disabilities*, Englewood Cliffs, NJ: Prentice-Hall, 1973.

HALLAHAN, D.P. and KAUFFMAN, J.M. *Introduction to Learning Disabilities*, Englewood Cliffs, NJ: Prentice-Hall, 1976.

HARING, N.G. and BATEMAN, B. *Teaching the Learning Disabled Child*, Englewood Cliffs, NJ: Prentice-Hall, 1977.

HUTTON, A.J. 'The elimination of extraneous matter from the course in schools for backward, truant and delinquent children', *Proceedings of the Second National Conference on the Education of Backward, Truant and Delinquent Children*, Plainfield: Indiana Boys School, 1905, pp. 19–20.

INSKEEP, A.D. *Teaching Dull and Retarded Children*, New York: Macmillan, 1926.

JACKSON, H. 'Advisable modification of usual school courses and methods in schools for backward, truant, and delinquent children', *Proceedings of the Second National Conference on the Education of Backward, Truant and Delinquent Children*, Plainfield: Indiana Boys Schools, 1905, pp. 62–8.

JARRELL, I. *Annual Report of the Superintendent of Schools to the Atlanta Board of Education*, Atlanta Public School Archives, 1958.

KRAUSKOPF, C.C. 'The instruction of backward children', *Proceedings of the Second National Conference on the Education of Backward, Truant and Delinquent Children*, Plainfield: Indiana Boys School, 1905, pp. 85–94.

LAZERSON, M. 'Educational institutions and mental sub-normality: Notes on writing a history', in BEGAB, M.J. and RICHARDSON, S. (Eds) *The Mentally Retarded and Society: A Social Science Perspective*, Baltimore, MD: University Park Press, 1975, pp. 37–51.

LERNER, J.W. *Children with Learning Disabilities*, 2nd ed., Boston, MA: Houghton-Mifflin, 1976.

McLAIN, N. 'Elementary instruction in agriculture in schools for backward, truant and delinquent children', *Proceedings of the Second National Conference on the Education of Backward, Truant and Delinquent Children*, Plainfield: Indiana Boys School, 1905.

McNEAL, F. 'Ungraded schools for backward children as a means for reclaiming delinquent children', *Proceedings of the Sixth Annual Con-*

*ference on the Education of Backward, Truant and Delinquent Children*, Buffalo: Glen Mills School of Printing, 1909, pp. 54–67.

McQUEARY, H. 'The relation of the public school and the special school', *Proceedings of the Seventh Annual Conference on the Education of Backward, Truant, Delinquent and Dependent Children*, Westboro: The Lyman School for Boys, 1910, pp. 119–28.

MERCER, L.D. *Children and Adolescents with Learning Disabilities*, Columbus, OH: Charles E. Merrill, 1979.

MORGAN, B.S. *The Backward Child: A Study of the Psychology and Treatment of Backwardness*, New York: G.P. Putnam's Sons, 1914.

MYERS, P.I. and HAMMILL, D.D. *Methods for Learning Disorders*, New York: John Wiley, 1976.

POPKEWITZ, T.S. *Paradigm and Ideology in Educational Research: The Social Function of the Intellectual*, London, England: Falmer Press, 1984.

SARASON, S.B. *Psychology Misdirected*, New York: Free Press, 1981.

SARASON, S.B. and DORIS, J. *Educational Handicap, Public Policy, and Social History: A Broadened Perspective on Mental Retadation*, New York: The Free Press, 1979.

SHEARER, W. 'Why so many children are backward and how the number can be reduced', *Proceedings of the Third National Conference on the Education of Backward, Truant and Delinquent Children*, Lancaster: Boys Industrial School, 1906, pp. 26–36.

SLATON, W.F. 'Annual report of the superintendent of schools to the Atlanta Board of Education', *Twenty Seventh Annual Report of the Atlanta Board of Education*, Atlanta Public Schools Archives, 1898.

SLATON, W.F. 'Annual report of the superintendent of schools to the Atlanta Board of Education', *Thirtieth Annual Report of the Atlanta Board of Education*, Atlanta Public Schools Archives, 1903.

SLATON, W.M. 'Annual report of the superintendent of schools to the Atlanta Board of Education', *Thirty First Annual Report of the Atlanta Board of Education*, Atlanta Public Schools Archives, 1912.

SLEETER, C.E. 'Why is there learning disabilities? A critical analysis of the birth of the field in its social context', paper presented at the annual meeting of the American Educational Research Association, Chicago, April, and in this volume.

SMITH, H. 'Annual report of the president of the Atlanta Board of Education', *Twenty Ninth Annual Report of the Atlanta Board of Education*, Atlanta Public Schools Archives, 1900.

SUTTON, W. *Annual Report of the Superintendent of Schools to the Atlanta Board of Education*, Atlanta Public Schools Archives, 1924.

UNITED STATES CONGRESS, HOUSE OF REPRESENTATIVES. *Children With Learning Disabilities Act of 1969: Hearings Before the General Subcommittee on Education of the Committee on Education and Labor, House of Representatives, Ninety-First Congress, First Session on H.R. 8660* and *H.R. 9065, a Bill to Provide for Special Programs for Children with Learning Disabilities*, Washington, DC: U.S. Government Printing Office, 1969.

WITMER, L. 'What may we expect of the grade teacher in the discovery, education and treatment of backward children', *Proceedings of the Third National Conference on the Education of Backward, Truant and Delinquent Children*, Lancaster: Boys Industrial School, 1906, pp. 13–15.

# 9  Why Is There Learning Disabilities? A Critical Analysis of the Birth of the Field in Its Social Context

*Christine E. Sleeter*

## Abstract

This chapter presents an interpretation of why the category of learning disabilities emerged, that differs from interpretations that currently prevail. It argues that the category was created in response to social conditions during the late 1950s and early 1960s which brought about changes in schools that were detrimental to children whose achievement was relatively low. The category was created by white middle class parents in an effort to differentiate their children from low-achieving low-income and minority children. The category offered their children a degree of protection from probable consequences of low achievement because it upheld their intellectual normalcy and the normalcy of their home backgrounds, and it suggested hope for a cure and for their ability eventually to attain higher status occupations than other low achievers.

Many school structures are built around accepted categories for children. Categories such as first graders, gifted children, slow children, and learning disabled children all presume to designate 'real' commonalities among children, and form bases on which children are grouped and taught. As educators, we tend to take for granted that these categories accurately reflect differences among children, and that their use enables children to be taught better. After all, many of these categories were discovered and researched by 'experts', so they *must* have validity. But in accepting commonly-used categories for children, we also tacitly accept an ideology about what schools are for, what society should be like, and what the 'normal' person should be like. Far from being objective fact, ideology rests on values and assumptions that cannot be proven, and that serve some people better than others.

This chapter illustrates the hidden ideology in 'scientific' categories and resulting school structures, by examining one category: learning disabilities. The chapter will show that, while discussions surrounding the emergence and subsequent use of the category were ostensibly about similarities in a certain identifiable group of children, the category developed largely on the basis of an ideology regarding the 'good' US economic order, the 'proper' social function of schooling, and the 'good' culture.

Learning disabilities is the newest special education category in the US, having achieved national status as a field in 1963 when the Association for Children with Learning Disabilities was founded. In 1979, learning disabilities overtook speech impairment as the largest special education category. By 1982, 41 per cent of the students in special education in US schools were categorized as learning disabled; they constituted 4.4 per cent of all students enrolled in the public schools (Plisko, 1984).

Learning disabilities is commonly viewed as an organically-based disorder within a small percentage of children that interferes with their ability to learn to read and write normally. Hallahan and Cruickshank (1973) have offered an interpretation of why the field emerged when it did, that has been widely accepted within special education. They date it back to the early 1900s when European physicians began to document behavioral and language patterns of individuals with known brain damage. Kurt Goldstein was one of the earliest of these; he studied the behavior of World War I soldiers who had suffered head wounds. Goldstein's work greatly influenced two German scientists, Heinz Werner and Alfred Strauss, who left Germany in the 1930s and eventually came to the US, where they continued their research on neurological foundations of perceptual-motor dysfunction. Their line of research was extended by William Cruickshank, who studied intellectually normal children with cerebral palsy. Through the efforts of these and other physicians, psychologists, and educators (such as Kephart, Getman, Barsch, Frostig, Orton, Mykelbust, and Kirk), the foundations were laid for a data base about neurological impairment and its effects on learning behavior.

This data base was used by frustrated parents of LD children, who organized and lobbied for the establishment of special classes in schools for the learning disabled. According to Kirk and Chalfant (1984), parents pushed for LD programs in schools for two main reasons: many did not see their failing children as mentally retarded and therefore refused to accept placement for them in classes for the mentally retarded, and schools did not provide services for children with severe reading or language difficulties unless they qualified for an existing special education category. Thus, according to conventional explanations of the field's history, by the late 1950s, medical and psychological research, combined with parental pressure, led to the development of special school programs to meet the needs of a population of children that always had existed but only recently had been recognized.

The ideological message in this interpretation is that schools, supported by medical and psychological research, are involved in an historic pattern of progress. Problems that have always existed are one by one being discovered, researched, and solved. Many problems in schooling result from a lack of responsiveness to individual differences among children, which schools are increasingly learning to accommodate to the benefit of increasing numbers of children. Progress is schooling is brought about mainly by individual thinkers involved in research, and at times by pressure groups who are able to use that research to advance the interests of the underdogs. Once alerted to problems, the American public tends to support their amelioration. The main beneficiaries of such progress are those whose needs are finally recognized and met.

This chapter offers a different interpretation for why learning disabilities exists. It argues that the category emerged for a political purpose: to differentiate and protect white middle class children who were failing in school from lower class and minority children, during a time when schools were being called upon to raise standards for economic and military purposes. Rather than being a product of progress, the category was essentially conservative in that it helped schools continue to serve best those whom schools have always served best: the white middle and upper-middle class. This political purpose, however, has been cloaked in the ideology of individual differences and biological determinism, thus making it appear scientifically sound.

## Learning Disabilities and the Escalation of Standards for Literacy

Learning disabilities in the US is essentially a category for reading failure. Learning disabled children are identified in part by comparing their performance in reading, writing, or oral language with norms for children for their age or grade level. These norms become the standards for helping to determine who is classified as learning disabled. It is important to recognize that low achievers are formally identified by tests that are specifically constructed to give meaning to the notion of 'average', and rank-order children to determine who is performing at an average level and who is not. Thus, one is not learning disabled in some abstract sense, but specifically in relationship to statistically-derived standards for literacy.

Standards for literacy have changed historically with changes in requirements of the race for international supremacy, the American economy, and notions of 'culture' and 'national security'. As Chall (1983), and Resnick and Resnick (1977) have described, before the twentieth century, standards for literacy were much different than they are now. Most Americans were not expected to be able to acquire new information through reading since most necessary information could be exchanged face to face and records were relatively simple. Children with reading difficulties, for the most part, did not present a great social problem. Industrial expansion escalated literacy standards, requiring more and more people who could keep and understand increasingly complex records, pursue advanced professional training, and follow written directions in the workplace. As literacy standards in society were raised and schools responded by emphasizing reading increasingly, most students were able to keep up, at least reasonably so. The higher standards went, however, the greater was the spread in achievement levels, and the farther those on the bottom were from the norms. In the late 1950s, this became a very definite problem.

During the decade and half a immediately preceding the founding of the Association for Children with Learning Disabilities, schools were vigorously pressed to raise their acheivement standards; a brief review of economic, political, and cultural conditions during the 1950s will illustrate why.

America emerged from World War II with an interrelated set of economic and political needs. As Hodgson (1976) has pointed out, a major economic need was to redirect production from war-time to peace-time goods, while at the same time providing employment for returning war veterans. With the Depression still fresh in the minds of many, this was a large concern. Hodgson tells us that 'the answer to the riddle — or so thoughtful Americans in the late 1940s and 1950s thought with startling unanimity — lay in abundance' (p. 51). The American economy was to supply consumers with an abundance of material goods. To do this, markets were to be cultivated among middle class consumers, production of consumer goods was to be stepped up rapidly, and prices were to be held down. Technological inventions that could increase production, and cheap raw materials imported from abroad, were needed.

Both needs affected schooling. Increased automation directly affected schooling because it greatly expanded the white-collar labor market while simultaneously reducing demand for blue-collar labor. According to Gilbert (1981), between 1945 and 1970, 'jobs in manufacturing and construction increased only about 35 per cent, while available positions in government and the retail, finance, and insurance sectors rose by more than 200 per cent' (p. 178). As a result, schools were called upon to produce more workers with skills and attitudes for white collar employment, which meant making sure more children attained increasingly high standards of achievement.

The need for raw materials from abroad coincided with the demand that America step up its defense program in an effort to avoid another war; indirectly these demands also affected schools. Business demanded access to resources from abroad, which meant that the US needed to cultivate allies that could provide both raw materials and eventual market demand for American products. Gilbert has pointed out that America's postwar foreign policy of supporting 'political democracy and economic liberalism' and preventing the spread of Communism were both directly connected to business's need for foreign raw materials and markets (p. 34). The interests of business complemented the military's interest in developing America's defense system. The military establishment after the War was huge and powerful, employing millions of Americans in various capacities, and federal funding for defense and military research was relatively abundant (see Gilbert, 1981, p. 167–75; Hodgson, 1976, p. 129–33).

Thus, both business and the military had a strong interest in schools producing young people trained to carry on military re-search. Military spokesmen criticized schools for their failure to produce enough scientists, although their criticisms were not very fruitful at first. For example, Rear Admiral H.G. Rickover warned the public in March 1957 that,

Our schools do not perform their primary purpose, the
training of the nation's brain power to its highest potential.
The result is an alarming shortage of trained professionals . . .
scientists and engineers to push on with our atomic energy
program . . . (p. 19).

Rickover saw the US and the Soviet Union engaged in a 'cold war of
the classrooms' (p. 19). He saw the two nations competing for
political and economic control over the rest of the world, with
schools being crucial in the production of brainpower for this cold
war.

The Soviet aim is achievement of world scientific and engineering supremacy. She is training more scientists and
engineers than her economy now requires. In the United
States we are not keeping up with the needs of our armed
forces and our industry. (p. 108)

Until the Soviet Union's launching of Sputnik, however, most
white American citizens did not see schools as needing major reform.
Sputnik changed this. It provided a focal point for debates about
schooling, and 'proof' that Americans had allowed schools to be too
soft and lax on young people. One can see a sudden outpouring of
concern over American schools by examining the popular literature
during the late 1950s. Before Sputnik, criticisms of schools were
somewhat sporadic; after Sputnik, a deluge of articles and books
blamed schools for being too soft and lenient. In 1958–1960, the
public read numerous articles condemning schools and advocating
raising standards in such lay magazines as *Good Housekeeping,
Vogue, Life, Ladies' Home Journal, Time, US News and World
Report, Look, Newsweek,* and *Readers' Digest.*

A theme that reappeared in many of these articles was the belief
that schools exist to serve American's race for international control.
Rickover, for example, saw a direct connection between schools and
the cold war with Russia. He told the public in December 1957 that,

Sputnik is, of course, of great significance because of its
relation to missile weaponry and because of the potential
military advantages of outer-space control. In the long run,
the more disturbing fact which emerges from the Russian
satellite program is her success in building in record time an
educational system which produces exactly the sort of men
and women her rulers need to achieve technological supremacy day after tomorrow. (p. 86)

Rickover's view of the purpose of schools was reaffirmed to the public by others, such as Arthur Trace, who asked *Saturday Evening Post* readers in 1961, 'Can Ivan Read Better Than Johnny?'

> What Russian students learn in school and what American students learn in school may do much to determine whether the free world will check and defeat Communism, or whether Communism will check and defeat the free world. (p. 30)

Others did not directly link schools with military interests, but condemned schools for a lack of intellectualism. A major spokesperson on behalf of intellectualism in schools was Arthur Bestor. In an interview in 1958 in *US News and World Report*, he charged that, 'The basic trouble is that the persons running our public school system lost sight of the main purpose of education — namely, intellectual training' (p. 68). He went on to condemn 'anti-intellectualism in the schools', and the

> tendency of professional educationists to 'pooh-pooh' the idea of mental discipline, and to say that the aim of public education ought to be 'life adjustment', instead of training in fundamental fields like science, mathematics, foreign languages, history, and English. (p. 68)

Bestor's definition of the aim of schooling as intellectual training supported the push for military development. Even though he generally did not discuss military needs, his views, like those of many others, accepted and complemented them. After condemning 'life adjustment' education, Bestor reaffirmed his belief in intellectual training by pointing out that, 'We have wasted an appalling part of the time of our young people on trivialities. The Russians have had sense enough not to do so. That's why the first satellite bears the label, Made in Russia' (p. 69).

Dubbed by *Time* magazine in 1958 'Wasteland, U.S.A.', American schools were compared with Russian schools and found wanting. The chief problem, critics believed, was laxity of standards. While American schools were described as soft and undemanding, Russian schools were described as tough. As a feature article in *Life* magazine pointed out in 1958, 'the laggards are forced out [of school] by tough periodic examinations and shunted to less demanding trade schools and apprenticeships. Only a third — 1.4 million in 1957 — survive all ten years and finish the course' ('Schoolboys Point up a US Weakness', p. 27). The public was urged that, 'We should not need the threat of Russia to be convinced that it is time to close the carnival and go to work' (Wilson, 1958, p. 37).

Recommendations for reforming American education were prolific. Among them were the following:

1   Toughen elementary reading instruction. 'Unlike Ivan's first-grade reader with its 2000 word vocabulary, . . . Johnny's reader is likely to have a vocabulary of fewer than 400 words' (Trace, 1961, p. 30).
2   End the practice of social promotion — insist that students master subject matter in order to be promoted, and test students' achievement of higher and uniform standards for promotion through a regular, nation-wide examination system. ('Back to the 3 Rs?', 1957; 'What Went Wrong with US Schools', 1958; Rickover, 1957b).
3   Group students into three groups by ability so the bright students can move through school more quickly ('Famous Educator's Plan', 1958; 'Harder Work for Students', 1961; Rickover, 1958; Woodring, 1957).
4   Assign the most intellectually capable teachers to the top group of students (Rickover, 1957b).

The primary beneficiaries of these reforms were to be business and the military, but Sputnik helped coalesce public opinion in support of them. Business would gain by having a more clearly stratified workforce earmarked and trained differentially for blue-collar, white-collar, and professional or scientific research positions. A diagram in *Life* magazine in 1958 illustrated this: 'bright' students (20 per cent of the student body) would be placed in the top track to learn upper-level math and science, and a foreign language, and then sent to college for more specialized training; 'average' students (60 per cent of the student body) would occupy the general track and leave school to enter jobs such as 'building contractor'; and 'slow' students (20 per cent of the student body) would take simplified academic courses and work experience to prepare for blue-collar employment in places such as 'Joe's Garage' ('Famous Educator's Plan', 1958). The military would gain by having more scientists to conduct research, as well as a public schooled to respect and support science and technological growth. However, these interests were not made explicit. Instead the public was told in article after article that school reform was needed for the good and safety of the average citizen: for the intellectual welfare of the young, for their development of self-discipline, and to avert eventual take-over by the Russians.

To some extent, these reforms were all implemented. Standards in reading and math were raised, and tests revised to reflect raised standards. For example, based on analysis of the readability levels of textbooks over a twenty-eight year period. Chall (1977) found elementary readers to offer progressively less challenge from 1944 until 1962. In 1962, first grade readers appearing on the market were more difficult, and became increasingly difficult into the 1970s, in 'greater vocabulary difficulty, in greater vocabulary diversity, in the varied content, and in the stronger decoding program' (p. 27). In sixth grade readers the changes were not as marked, but the trend toward difficulty showed up in:

> levels of reading stages, the proportionate number of pictures to print, the amount and kind of literature included in the reader — particularly unabridged literature, stories written expressly for the reader, and the ratio of expository to narrative writing. (p. 27)

Raised standards for reading acheivement were built into revised test norms of widely-used acheivement tests. The 1958 version of the Metropolitan Achievement Tests was renormed in 1964. The new norms reflected between 2 and 13 months gain in reading achieve-ment made by students in grades 2–9 (no gain was found for first grade) ('Special Report No. 7', 1971). Similarly, the 1957 version of the Iowa Tests of Basic Skills was renormed in 1964. Hieronymus and Lindquist (1974) report that overall, 'the average change for the composite was 3.0 months at the 90th percentile, 2.3 months at the 50th percentile, and 1.1 months at the 10th percentile' (p. 66). In reading, the average gain was 1.9 months at the 90th percentile, 2.6 months at the 50th, and 1.0 months at the 10th.

Ability grouping and tracking were implemented with vigor, and the raised standards were used to assign students to groups. *US News World Report* told the public in 1957 that the old methods of hetergeneous grouping had 'diluted' the quality of schooling for all children. 'Watered-down instruction for everybody' was replaced by tougher standards and ability grouping, which was to 'enable bright students to forge ahead of others. Until recently this was frowned upon by educators as being "undemocratic"' ('Back to the 3 Rs?', p. 39).

What this means is that, in the name of international political and economic competition, students in the early 1960s were expected to acheive at higher levels than their counterparts in the 1950s, and the public was told in no uncertain terms that this was necessary. Students were tested more to determine whether they were performing, and at least two major achievement tests required them to have mastered slightly higher levels of reading. If they were not performing up to standard, they were less likely to be promoted and more likely to be placed in the low ability group. As articles in popular magazines informed parents, low group children were destined for unskilled labor, and might be deprived of the better teachers.

## Race, Social Class, and School Failure after Sputnik

American big business and the military have always been controlled by economically privileged whites. This was certainly the case in the 1950s and early 1960s. School reforms described above were advocated and supported primarily by white Americans of the middle and upper classes. Reforms were to help schools more efficiently fit every child for a 'place' in society, with some 'places' clearly more desirable and profitable than others. Advocates of school reform envisioned their own children among those who would rank as 'bright' or at least 'average', and therefore would receive the better teachers, beefed-up programs, and more lucrative opportunities.

Of course, it was not new that the more socially privileged receive the better schools and opportunities. But the legitimacy of this was increasingly contested after World War II. Following the war, blacks migrated in large numbers to Northern cities in search of jobs, better housing, and better schooling. Blacks' quest for better schooling received legitimacy with the Supreme Court's 1954 decision in *Brown v the Board of Education*. For the first time, the court system declared that citizens were not to be denied equal access to the 'good life' on the basis of race, and that this specifically meant that whites and blacks were to share schools.

It was not until the mid-1960s that serious efforts were made to desegregate schools. For example, Tyack (1974) has pointed out that in 1954 the New York school board issued a statement supporting desegregation, but a decade later, 'the number of schools with 90 per cent or more Negro and/or Puerto Rican pupils had jumped by more than 200 per cent' (p. 280). But when schools were desegregated, minority children were seen as 'behind' and resegregated within the schools in special programs, which helped retain white privilege. Kirp (1982) has described the desegregation process of California Bay Area school districts during the late 1950s and early 1960s. He found them to vary widely in their interest in desegregating schools, but those districts that desegregated (as well as those that did not) 'held a shared and quite conventional understanding of the mission of public education ... The task of the schools, it was felt, was to provide a differentiated education that matched the varied abilities of a heterogeneous population' (p. 225). To do this, schools at all levels were tracked as described above, with minority children placed in compensatory or remedial classes.

Teachers came to see it as 'natural' that a sizable proportion of the student population would be unable to keep up with requirements of the 'average' child, and to explain this by seeking supposed deficiencies within 'slow' or failing children, or within their home backgrounds. For example, in the first volume of the *Journal of Learning Disabilities*, Park and Linden (1968) noted that,

> In grades two and three, 15 per cent of the children may be unable to do the reading required by the average classroom at that level, and approximately 30 per cent of the pupils in grades four, five, and six show that they have not developed the reading skills necessary to handle the program of the typical school. (p. 318)

It would seem logical to wonder why 'average' and 'typical classrooms' required students to use skills 15–30 per cent had not yet acquired. The article did not raise this question, nor did many people involved in education. Instead, what the article did was to describe psychological, physical, emotional, and environmental problems preventing many children from making the required progress.

Educators had developed four syndromes they used to explain why many lower class and minority children could not keep up. They were less certain how to explain failures of white middle class children. This problem, I want to argue, eventually led to the development of a new category, learning disabilities. Let us first review categories of failure 'explaining' lower class and minority children, then examine how learning disabilities was constructed to explain and protect failing white middle class children by differentiating them from the other four categories in ways that made them seem almost 'normal'.

*Mentally Retarded*

One category into which many lower class and minority children were placed was the mentally retarded. These included children scoring below 70–75 on an IQ test. Only about 10 per cent of the retarded population had known organic damage; the rest did not and were termed 'cultural-familial retardates' (Dunn, 1963). Disproportionate numbers of those considered mentally retarded were from low-income or minority families — these constituted most of the 'cultural-familial retardates'. For example, Wakefield (1964) found about 86 per cent of the retarded students he studied to be from low income homes, although only about 38 per cent of his sample was from such homes. Cultural-familial retardates were believed to suffer 'physical and cultural undernourishment', 'impoverished' language, and 'lack of motivation in schoolwork that arises from the family's apathy or lack of understanding of the purposes of education' (Goldstein, 1962, p. 12). These supposed cultural deprivations were believed to retard neurological development, or retard acquisition of basic skills, concepts, and attitudes needed for learning.

The belief that environmental 'deprivation' causes mental retardation was well enough accepted that it was used, for example, to explain why there were fewer retarded persons in the Soviet Union than in the US. In 1963, Dunn and Kirk wrote that, '. . . slums are being rapidly cleared in the Soviet Union . . . Cultural deprivation may also be reduced for Russian children of lower socio-economic status by the availability and frequent use made of the Palaces of Culture, museums, ballets, operas, summer camps for children, etc.' (p. 301). The prognosis for this group was very pessimistic. For example, Goldstein (1962) predicted that retarded children would rapidly fall behind their peers and would be suitable as adults only for unskilled labor or sheltered workshops. Many of those born into slum areas would be destined to remain there because they were 'less well-endowed intellectually' and therefore would 'have difficulty in competing for well-paying jobs' (Dunn, 1963, p. 66).

*Slow Learner*

'Slow learners' comprised children scoring between 75 and 90 on an IQ test. Johnson, then a leading authority on slow learners, wrote in 1963 that 'slow learners compose the largest group of mentally retarded persons. Among the general school population, 15 to 17 or

18 per cent of the children can be considered slow learners' (p. 9). Like the mentally retarded, slow learners were thought to include disproportionate numbers of low-income children and children of color because of presumed cultural 'deficiencies'. According to Johnson,

> Preferred suburban communities where executive and professional persons reside will have very few slow learners ... The subcultural areas of large metropolitan communities where the children receive little psychosocial stimulation present quite a different picture ... Fifty per cent or more of the children can appropriately be designated as slow learners. (p. 9)

The prognosis for slow learners was almost as poor as it was for the mentally retarded. They could be expected to fall farther and farther behind their 'normal' peers in school achievement, especially reading, and many could be expected to drop out before graduation. For that reason, they should be pulled out of regular classrooms so that 'the slow learner can proceed at his own best rate without holding brighter children back' ('Slow Learners', 1962, p. 53). As adults they could be expected to occupy semi-skilled and unskilled occupations (Goldstein, 1962), and to be followers rather than leaders; as Abraham (1964) explained, they could not be expected to understand the complexities of the social order.

### Emotionally Disturbed

Like the above two categories, large numbers of children classified as emotionally disturbed were from low-income backgrounds. Professionals believed that the lower class neighborhoods produced a larger proportion of emotionally disturbed children than middle or upper class neighborhoods. As Dunn explained (1963), in lower class neighborhoods 'security and stability are often lacking' (p. 245). A sub-category was the 'socially maladjusted', who were concentrated in black, Puerto Rican, and immigrant neighborhoods (Shaw and McKay, 1942). Although mental health specialists viewed the emotionally disturbed as suffering 'psychoses, psychophysiologic disturbances, psychoneuroses, personality disorders ... and transient situational disturbance' (Eisenberg, 1960), educators viewed them mainly as unduly disruptive children (Dunn, 1963). Prognosis for emotionally disturbed children was unclear, but if treatment for mental illness or 'maladjustment' was effective, they could be prepared for jobs in accordance with their IQ levels.

## Culturally Deprived

A fourth category, which overlapped with the previous three, was the 'culturally deprived'. In 1964 the National Conference on Education and Cultural Deprivation identified the culturally deprived as Puerto Ricans, Mexicans, southern blacks and whites who moved to urban areas, and the poor already living in inner cities and rural areas (Bloom, Davis and Hess, 1965). Even those who were not classified as retarded, slow learners, or emotionally disturbed were still believed to suffer learning handicaps due to environmental conditions. Deutsch (1963) described their cognitive development as severely handicapped by lack of environmental stimuli, lack of systematic ordering of stimuli sequences (in other words, he believed their lives were chaotic) and lack of language training at home. Ausubel (1966) informed educators that these lacks within the home produced:

> poor perceptual discrimination skills; inability to use adults as sources of information corrections and reality testing, and as instruments for satisfying curiosity; an impoverished language-symbolic system; and a paucity of information, concepts, and relational propositions. (p. 251)

The language poor and minority children learned at home was often cited as a major culprit retarding their ability to learn. For example, Warden (1968) pointed out that 'a restricted language development places limits on intellectual potential. Thus, socioculturally disadvantaged children may begin school with a deficit, not only in using formal language but in conceptualizing as well' (p. 137). Prognosis was not optimistic. Educators believed that the 'culturally deprived' did not value intellectual work and lacked values necessary for success in school and society, such as delayed gratification, individuality, and the belief that hard work brings success (see, for example, Riessman, 1962). It was hoped that compensatory education might provide them with developmental experiences believed unavailable in their homes, and the motivation to succeed in school, but catching them up to the 'average' child was seen as very difficult (see, for example, Bereiter and Englemann, 1966; Rees, 1968).

All four of these categories accepted the school as being essentially as it should be. Children who did not fit its program and its standardized conception of the 'good student' were held to be inadequate, with either their homes or their organic development, or both, at fault. This view was conveyed in the popular press as well as the professional literature. For example, readers of *Saturday Review* in 1962 were told that all schools have 'slow learners', but that 'slow learners appear most frequently in groups whose home environment affords restricted opportunity for intellectual development ...' ('Slow Learners', p. 53). In a later issue they were told about 'culturally deprived children', who grow up in communities in 'virtual isolation from the rest of society', learning 'ways of living [that] are not attuned to the spirit and practice of modern life', and where 'physical punishment is common'. ('Education and the Disadvantaged American', 1962, p. 58).

All failing children, however, were not lower class or minority. As standards for achievement were raised, more and more white middle class children were also threatened with school failure. What to do about them became the basis for the creation of the category of learning disabilities.

## Learning Disabilities as a Category for White Middle Class Children

Before the 1960s, there was no recognized category called 'learning disabilities'. There were, however, other labels that eventually were consolidated to form the category of learning disabilities. In the US, since the early 1900s, a small number of physicians and psychologists had conducted a limited amount of research on people with brain-injury resulting from trauma to the head, people with severe language disorders, and people with severe difficulties learning to read. One can find early professional writings about people (usually adults) with conditions termed 'congenital word blindness' (see, for example, Hinshelwood, 1900), 'developmental alexia' (see, for example, Bender, 1958), 'specific dyslexia' (see, for example, Hallgren, 1950), 'brain injury' (see, for example, Strauss and Lehtinen, 1949) and 'psychoneurological learning disorders' (see, for example, Myklebust and Boshes, 1960). However, until the late 1950s and early 1960s, as Myklebust and Johnson (1962) put it, 'only minor attention has been given to the porblem of dyslexia in children' (p. 15).

For the most part, these conditions were described as having an organic basis, although there was dispute over this. Professionals who argued for an organic basis suggested diverse organic problems, including minimal brain damage (Strauss and Lehtinen, 1947), a maturational lag in general neurological development (Bender, 1957; Rabinovitch, 1962), a failure of the brain to establish cerebral dominance (Orton, 1937), a failure to progress through stages of neurological development (Delcato, 1959), or a failure of the cortex to focus and sustain attention on specific details (Burks, 1957). Often such professionals explicitly ruled out environmental causation. For example, Burks distinguished between children whose learning difficulties stem from 'impoverished cultural background' and those whose difficulties result from 'an underlying brain dysfunction' (p. 169). Strauss and Lehtinen (1947) differentiated between 'the familial type of mental deficiency ... due either to adverse phychological or physical conditions which restrict growth opportunities' and brain injury 'resulting from faulty genes within the germ plasma, which is the child's biological inheritance' (p. 112). One of the criteria Strauss and Lehtinen recommended for distinguishing the brain injured child from the child with familial mental deficiency is that the brain injured child is essentially 'normal' or comes from a 'normal family stock' (p. 112).

In some early writings, there was also mention of the child or adult's IQ level. Cruickshank has been the main defender of the idea that persons at any IQ level could suffer dyslexia, or processing deficits. As he was still arguing in 1977, 'perceptual processing deficits are to be found in children of every intellectual range' (p. 54). Others have disputed his contention, and their perspective prevailed. For example, Mykelbust and Johnson (1962) argued that 'the [LD] individual is of normal mental capacity' (p. 16), and Bryant (1964) noted that 'dyslexia is not a broad defect in general intelligence; IQs tend to be in the normal range and occasionally reflect very superior ability' (p. 196).

The belief that some sort of organic defect causes some people difficulty in learning to read was not accepted by all professionals. For example, in 1957, Stevens and Birch cautioned against making 'leaps of verbal logic' that are 'only vaguely supported by research evidence'. They pointed out that, 'Much more work will need to be done before differing kinds of perceptual experience can be firmly linked to variations in everyday life behavior and to central nervous system lesions in anything approaching a cause-and-effect way' (p. 348). Capobianco (1964) argued against assuming organic causality on pragmatic grounds: the diagnosis of brain injury is of little help to the teacher and may suggest that this is a child who cannot learn.

The idea that reading difficulty among children with normal or above IQs had an organic basis held appeal, however. One reason was that the nature of the presumed organic cause for learning disabilities suggested it might be curable, in contrast to more general organic defects thought to characterize other categories of failure, especially retardation. Americans were well aware of medical successes in treating various diseases, and were generally optimistic that diseases could not cured. Minimal brain injury as an organic defect was not exempt from that optimism. The cure was hypothesized as involving the training of healthy brain cells to take over functions of damaged cells (see, for example, Cruickshank *et al.*, 1961; Frostig and Horne, 1964; Strauss and Lehtinen, 1947), the promoting of overall neuro-logical development (see, for example, Doman, Delcato, & Doman, 1964), the training of the brain to assume greater hemispheric dominance (Orton, 1937), or the altering of chemical balances through diet or drugs (see, for example, Feingold, 1975; Sroufe and Stewart, 1973). So far these hypotheses have proved less fruitful than hoped (Kavale and Forness, 1985). But in the early 1960s this optimism, especially in the popular press, was quite alive.

For example, in 1959, *Newsweek* readers were told about 'Johnnies who can't read' due to inherited neurological conditions. These children were described as 'often hav[ing] very high IQs'. They were also described as educationally treatable using the Gillingham reading method: 'Of the seventy-nine Parker students taught under the method so far, 96 per cent have become average or above average readers' ('Learning to Read', p. 110). In 1964, Maisel, writing in *Reader's Digest*, gave another optimistic account of a treatment for 'brain-injured' children. Case descriptions of children who were brain-injured at birth and experienced difficulty learning language, physical movements, and reading were provided. A new treatment developed by Delcato and the Doman brothers, involving having the child daily complete prescribed patterned motor movements, was reported to 'activate the millions of surviving [brain] cells to take over the functions of the dead ones'. Prognosis was reported excellent: 'Hundreds of other brain-injured children have traveled the same path toward normal or superior development, under an unconven-tional, and controversial, form of medically supervised home treat-ment' (p. 137); readers were told that this treatment even helped affected children learn to read.

A second reason the idea of organic damage had appeal was that it explained reading problems of white middle class children without raising questions about the cultural integrity of middle class homes, or the demand by white middle class business and military leaders that standards in certain areas of school achievement be raised. It was simply easier to believe that some children suffered minor neuro-logical damage through nobody's fault, than it was to question a culture that required economic expansion and economic imperialism, and social institutions that would shape the young for a stratified labor market.

A third reason was that it provided a way of differentiating between the learning disabled and the mentally retarded while at the same time locating both problems within the child. Gould (1981) has argued that many people throughout history have justified a stratified and segregated society by believing people have innately different capacities for learning, and due to their own biological inheritances, can be expected to achieve at different levels.

By borrowing from the ideology of biological determinism, educators and parents gave the ideology some legitimacy, but at the same time elevated those they classified as learning diabled from those classified as slow or retarded by specifying that the organic damage affected specific areas of learning, not learning in general.

This perspective is still quite prevalent. For example, Cruick-shank and Johnson (1975) have presented the trainable and educable mentally retarded as two categories on a continuum, and discussed both in terms of organic causes and physical characteristics. They also described children with specific learning disabilities in organic terms, as 'those who have experienced a disturbance of some sort in normal cephalo-caudal neural maturation' (p. 247). The implication is that learning difficulties can be rank-ordered, with severe retardation at one end and learning disabilities at the other, and all are wholly or in part caused by organic deficiencies.

To underscore the hierarchical distinction between mental re-tardation and learning disabilities, Kirk (1972) has explained:

> To some, the term 'learning disabilities' is confusing since mentally retarded children also have difficulty learning, but it should be noted that their [the retarded] disability is a general difficulty in learning rather than difficulty in a more limited area. (p. 44)

Many parents with failing school children accepted the idea that their children were neurologically impaired or brain injured because it explained the problem in a way they could accept. For example, in 1962, Barsch reported a study of explanations parents offered for the failings of their 'brain damaged' children. The sample consisted of parents of 119 children reported to have organic damage, although the article did not explain how it was known they had organic damage. Barsch found 72 per cent of the parents to use the term 'brain injured' when explaining their children's problems to others. Fifty-seven of the eighty-five parents who used the term reported feeling better when using it. They reported, for example, that it explained the child's deviant behavior and made people stop asking questions, it elicited sympathy, and it helped differentiate the child from the mentally retarded. Parents did not use the term if the child's behavior was near normal, or if they had experienced adverse reactions from neighbors when using it before. Quite likely they found brain injury to be an acceptable explanation because it absolved the home from blame, it gave the problem a disease-like causality, and it fit within prevailing notions about what 'normal' children can do. The 'brain injured' were abnormal but only partially so, and no one could be blamed for their abnormality.

Accepting the idea of brain damage, many middle class parents used it as the basis for organizing to advance the interests of their children. Persons from advantaged social class backgrounds are most likely to organize a pressure group in response to a problem they see as threatening to their own interests. For example, Presthus (1974) found about 80 per cent of the members of American interest groups to come from middle and upper middle class backgrounds (p. 110). So it was with the organization of a pressure group on behalf of 'brain injured' children. It was middle class parents of children who seemed almost 'normal' but were failing in school who lobbied the hardest for the creation of a nationally accepted diagnostic category for their failing children.

Before 1963, parents in various states had banded together to form organizations with names such as 'Minnesota Association for the Brain-Injured Child', 'Fund for Perceptually Handicapped Children', and 'Michigan Children's Neurological Development Program'. These organizations served as support groups for parents, networks for disseminating information, and pressure groups for making physicians and educators more aware of 'normal' children with severe reading problems.

In 1963, the Fund for the Perceptually Handicapped in Evanston, Illinois, sponsored a conference for parents from these various organizations. The announced purpose of the conference was:

> to obtain information, share ideas, and open channels of communication with all groups who are interested in the PERCEPTUALLY HANDICAPPED CHILD. We will

move toward investigation of the child who has average or above average intelligence but is not learning (*Conference Proceedings*, 1963).

In the first major address of the conference, Samuel Kirk opened his remarks by specifying which children the conference was not concerned with, and by implication which children it *was* concerned with: 'As I understand it, this meeting is not concerned with children who have sensory handicaps, . . . or with children who are mentally retarded, or with delinquent or emotionally disturbed children caused by *environmental factors*' (my emphasis, *Conference Proceedings*, p. 1). He went on to propose that the children be called 'learning disabled' because this term directs attention toward a school problem without specifying that there be a firm diagnosis of organic damage. The term stuck, and the Association for Children with Learning Disabilities was founded. By 1966, it had enough members that it was able to sponsor a large, very well-attended international conference in Oklahoma. Two years later the first volume of the *Journal of Learning Disabilities* appeared.

For purposes of obtaining funds for special classes and teacher training, the category required a legal definition. The definition that was accepted in 1968 incorporated elements that helped differentiate the LD child from categories of failure described earlier, and that reaffirmed the belief that this was an organically based problem. The National Advisory Committee on Handicapped Children (1968) defined LD children as exhibiting disorders in one or more of the following: 'listening, thinking, talking, reading, writing, spelling, or arithmetic'. (Since then, the main way to determine whether the child has a disorder has been to give a standardized reading test; oral language tests and standardized math tests are also used.) It specified that 'these disorders are *not* due primarily to visual, hearing or motor handicaps, to mental retardation, emotional disturbance or to environmental disadvantage'. (In other words, this category does not include children who can be classified as mentally retarded, slow learner, emotionally disturbed, or culturally 'deprived'.) The types of conditions that were said to be the same as learning disabilities were mainly organic: 'perceptual handicaps, brain injury, minimal brain dysfunction, dyslexia, developmental aphasia, and so forth'.

Thus, by the mid-1960s, white middle class parents and educators had borrowed from medical research the notion of minimal brain injury to explain why their children were unable to keep up with the schools' raised achievement standards. How do we know the category was really created for white middle class children?

The literature did not specify the family background or kind of neighborhood believed most likely to produce learning disabled children, although it was very explicit about the kinds of the neighborhoods most likely to produce other categories of school failure. But there is evidence that the great majority of students placed in LD classes during the category's first ten years (1963–1973) were, in fact, white and middle class. This was born out by an investigation of the race and social class composition of subject samples of research studies of students classified as learning disabled during that period. Of a total of 460 subjects in the samples of twelve research studies, 98.5 per cent were white. Of a total of 588 subjects in sixteen studies, 69 per cent were middle class or above (Sleeter, 1986).

Similar findings have been reported in studies of the composition of special classes in Westchester County, New York and Missouri (Franks, 1971; White and Charry, 1966). For example, White and Charry found students in Westchester County who were labeled 'brain damaged' had no significant IQ or achievement differences from those labeled 'culturally deprived', but were from significantly higher social class backgrounds.

If the category of learning disabilities was used primarily for white middle and upper class children, this use was tacitly sanctioned by professionals. Many professionals believed that LD children were distinct from 'culturally deprived' children, even though the two shared similar learning characteristics. This can be seen in the professional literature, which treated the two categories as if they were distinct. Volumes 1 and 3 of the *Journal of Learning Disabilities* (1968 and 1970) contained twelve articles about culturally 'deprived' or 'disadvantaged' children. Most of these were reported studies; none of the subjects were reported to be in LD classes (many were in Head Start programs), nor did the authors suggest they could or should be. Authors of just two of the twelve articles criticized the practice of distinguishing between LD and culturally 'disadvantaged' students, arguing that a significant proportion of such students probably belonged in LD classes (Grotberg, 1970; Tarnopol, 1971). In 1973, the *Journal of Learning Disabilities* featured a symposium questioning the distinction between the disabled and the disadvantaged. Although the symposium did not resolve the issue, two authors suggested it was wise to keep the two groups separate for funding purposes. As Myers and Hammill pointed out,

... disadvantaged pupils who read significantly below MA expectancy or who evidence basic linguistic disorders could be considered learning-disabled. Many professionals in the field of learning disabilities are reluctant to accept this because it would mean that between 25 per cent to 50 per cent (or more) of urban center-city school children would qualify for learning disability programs when adequate funding and personnel are not available. (p. 409)

I have argued that learning disabilities emerged in response to increased pressure on schools to raise the achievement levels of students, and to group students for instruction and eventual occupational distination based on achievement and ability. The fact that many children were not able to reach those standards was explained in terms of deficiencies within children rather than the social system that was pressuring schools to treat children in certain ways. Learning disabilities was created to explain the failure of children to meet those standards when existing explanations based on mental, emotional, or cultural deficiency did not seem to fit. Learning disabilities seemed to explain white middle class children particularly well because it did not level blame on their home or neighborhood environment, it upheld their intellectual normalcy, and it suggested hope for a cure and for their eventual ability to attain relatively higher status occupations than other low achievers.


### Learning Disabilities Today

In the last ten years, there has been a shift in who is classified as learning disabled and how the category is used. During the late 1960s and early 1970s, pressure on students to achieve at increasingly high levels seemed to wane, as various test score patterns indicate (such as scores on the SAT or the Iowa Test of Educational Development). This probably caused some parents from advantaged backgrounds who had children experiencing difficulty in school to feel somewhat less need for having their children placed in a special category. At the same time, minority groups exerted pressure on educators to discard the notion of cultural deprivation and stop classifying disproportionate numbers of minority children as mentally retarded. As a result, children of color have recently been classified increasingly less as retarded, emotionally disturbed, or slow, and more as learning disabled. Although the majority of LD students are still white, the proportion of minority students in LD classes has climbed. Tucker (1980) examined the racial composition of LD and MR classes in over fifty school districts between 1970 and 1977. He found the proportion of black students in classes for the mentally retarded to decrease, while at the same time their proportion in classes for the learning disabled increased. In school year 1978–1979, nationwide, 15 per cent of the LD students were black, 8 per cent were Hispanic, 1 per cent were Native American, 1 per cent were Asian, and 75 per cent were white (DBS Corporation, 1982), while enrollment in the public schools was 15.7 per cent black, 6.8 per cent Hispanic, 1.4 per cent Asian, 0.8 per cent Native American, and 75.3 per cent white (Grant and Eiden, 1981). By 1980, LD students were 16 per cent black, 8 per cent Hispanic, 1 per cent Native American, 1 per cent Asian, and 74 per cent white, almost identical to the racial composition of public schools during that year (DBS Corporation, 1982).

However, it appears that LD classes are still disproportionately middle and upper middle class. Gelb and Mizokawa (in press) have analyzed recent national data on the social class composition of various special education categories. They found that students classified as learning disabled are disproportionately middle class and above, while those classified as retarded are disportionately lower class.

So far analyses of race and social class have been done separately, but it appears that middle class parents of color may be using the category increasingly as a way of distinguishing their children who are having difficulty in school from lower class children of color, who are still being overclassified as retarded. It also can be suggested that some districts may be using the category increasingly as a 'dumping ground' for minority students, similar to the way other categories had been used previously, while other districts still reserve the category primarily for middle to upper class white students.

As schools currently are being called on again to raise standards, it is not clear yet how white middle class parents of failing children will protect their children. A new category (such as the 'gifted disabled' or the underachiever) may be created and defined to suggest high expectations for success if certain modifications are made for them in the school program. Or, learning disabilities may regain this function by being redefined to make it more restrictive. Some professionals are in fact, advocating restricting who is classified as learning disabled to ensure that the category once more serves those for whom it was originally intended. For example, in 1984 Kirk warned that:

> In this country we seemd to have confused those children who are educationally underachieving because of extrinsic reasons (economic and cultural disadvantage, lack of opportunity, inadequate instruction) with those children who are underachieving for intrinsic reasons (mental retardation, sensory handicaps, serious emotional disturbance, learning disabilities).

He went on the express concern that 'the needs of the real learning disabled child are neglected' (p. 9). This must cause one to wonder who the real learning disabled child is. A strict conception of who is to be served in LD programs may lead to programs that once more serve primarily white middle class children.

## Conclusion

School structures are created and used by someone to serve the interests of someone with a particular context. This may be done with excellent intentions, but it may also reaffirm existing assumptions about who deserves what and why. Learning disabilities in the US was constructed as a way of understanding certain kinds of low achieving children by those who accepted the need to push children to achieve in specific areas at increasingly high levels. It was a category that was used politically by concerned parents and educators who believed white middle class failing children should not be failing, or at least should suffer the consequences of school failure as little as possible.

The category affirmed the necessity for the US to engage in international technological competition, and for schools to sort and select the young for future work roles. It also affirmed the use of class and race biased procedures and beliefs for conducting schooling and for distinguishing among children. This was not accomplished by a top-down mandate, but by parents and educators who were attempting to make the best possible life for their children within a social context they accepted. Rather than being a discovery of science and an instance of progress, learning disabilities has represented an attempt to maintain race and class stratification (although probably not consciously so by many who were involved in it), but to do so in

*Christine E. Sleeter*

a way that appears to be based on innate human variation and objective assessment of individual characteristics.

## Acknowledgements

I would like to thank Michael Apple, Carl Grant, Thomas Popkewitz, and James Ysseldyke for their helpful and constructive comments on earlier drafts of this chapter.

## References

ABRAHAM, W. *The Slow Learner*, New York: Center for Applied Research in Education, 1964.

AUSUBEL, D.P. 'Effects of cultural deprivation on learning patterns', in WEBSTER, S.W. (Ed.), *The Disadvantaged Learner: Knowing, Understanding, and Educating*, San Francisco, CA: Chandler, 1966.

'Back to the 3 Rs?' *US News and World Report*, 42, 15 March 1957, pp. 38–44.

BARSCH, R.H. 'Explanations offered by parents and siblings of brain-damaged children', *Exceptional Children*, 27, 1961, pp. 286–92.

BENDER, L. 'Specific reading disability as a maturational lag', *Bulletin of the Orton Society*, 7, 1957, pp. 9–18.

BENDER, L. 'Problems in conceptualization and communication in children with developmental alexia', *Psychopathology and Communications*, 1958, pp. 155–76.

BEREITER, C. and ENGLEMANN, S. *Teaching Disadvantaged Children in the Preschool*, Englewood Cliffs, NJ: Prentice-Hall, 1966.

BLOOM, B.S., DAVIS, A. and HESS, R. *Compensatory Education for the Culturally Deprived*, New York: Holt, Rinehart, and Winston, 1965.

BRYANT, N.D. 'Characteristics of dyslexia and their remedial implications', *Exceptional Children*, 31, 1964, pp. 195–9.

BURKS, H.F. 'Brain pathology', *Exceptional Children*, 24, 1957, pp. 169–74.

CAPOBIANCO, R.J. 'Diagnostic methods used with learning disability cases', *Exceptional Children*, 31, 1964, pp. 187–93.

CHALL, J.S. *An Analysis of Textbooks in Relation to Declining SAT Scores*, Princeton, NJ: College Entrance Examination Board, 1977.

CHALL, J.S. *Stages of Reading Development*, New York: McGraw-Hill, 1983.

CRUICKSHANK, W.M., *et al.* *A Teaching Method for Brain-Injured and Hyperactive Children*, Syracuse, NY: Syracuse University Press, 1961.

CRUICKSHANK, W.M. 'Myths and realities in learning disabilities', *Journal of Learning Disabilities*, 10, 1977, pp. 51–8.

234

CRUICKSHANK, W.M. and JOHNSON, G.O. (Eds) *Education of Exceptional Children*, Englewood Cliffs, NJ: Prentice-Hall, 1975.

DBS CORPORATION 'Elementary and secondary schools civil rights survey', unpublished paper prepared for the US Office of Civil Rights, Washington, DC, US Department of Education, 1982.

DELCATO, C.H. *The Treatment and Prevention of Reading Problems*, Springfield, IL: Charles C. Thomas, 1959.

DEUTSCH, M. 'The disadvantaged child and the learning process', in PASSOW, A.H. (Ed.), *Education in Depressed Areas*, New York: Teachers College Press, 1963, pp. 163–79.

DOMAN, G., DELCATO, C., and DOMAN, R. *The Doman-Delcato Developmental Profile*, Philadelphia, PA: Philadelphia Institutes for the Achievement of Human Potential, 1964.

DUNN, L.M. *Exceptional Children in the Schools*, New York: Holt, Rinehart, and Winston, 1963.

DUNN, L.M. and KIRK, S.A. 'Impressions of Soviet psycho-educational service and research in mental retardation', *Exceptional Children*, 29, 1963, pp. 299–311.

'Education and the disadvantaged American', *Saturday Review*, 45, 19 May 1962, p. 58.

EISENBERG, L. 'Emotionally disturbed children and youth', *Children and Youth in the 1960s*, 1960.

'Famous educator's plan for a school that will advance students according to their ability', *Life* 44, 14 April 1958, pp. 120–1.

FEINGOLD, B.F. *Why Your Child is Hyperactive*, New York: Random House, 1975.

FRANKS, D.J. 'Ethnic and social status characteristics of children in EMR and LD classes', *Exceptional Children*, 37, 1971, pp. 537–8.

FROSTIG, M. and HORNE, D. *The Frosting Program for the Development of Visual Perception*, Chicago: Follett, 1964.

GELB, S.A. and MIZOKAWA, D.T. 'Special education and social structure: The commonality of "exceptionality"', *American Educational Research Journal*, in press.

GILBERT, J. *Another Chance: Postwar America, 1945–1968*, New York: Alfred A. Knopf, 1981.

GOLDSTEIN, H. *The Educable Mentally Retarded Child in the Elementary School*, Washington, DC: National Education Association, 1962.

GOULD, S.J. *The Mismeasure of Man*, New York: W.W. Norton, 1981.

GRANT, W.V. and EIDEN, L.J. *Digest of Educational Statistics 1981*, Washington, DC: US Government Printing Office, 1981.

GROTBERG, E.H. 'Neurological aspects of learning disabilities: A case for the disadvantaged', *Journal of Learning Disabilities*, 3, 1970, pp. 25–31.

HALLAHAN, D.P. and CRUICKSHANK, W.M. *Psychoeducational Foundations of Learning Disabilities*, Englewood Cliffs, NJ: Prentice-Hall, 1973.

HALLGREN, B. 'Specific dyslexia (congenital word blindness): Clinical and genetic study', *Acta Psychiatry Neurological*, Supp. 65, 1950, pp. 1–287.

'Harder work for students' *US News and World Report*, 51, 4 September 1961, p. 45.

HIERONYMUS, A.N. and LINDQUIST, E.G. *Manual for Administrators, Supervisors, and Councelors, Forms 5 & 6, Iowa Tests of Basic Skills*, Boston, MA: Houghton Mifflin, 1974.

HINSHELWOOD, J. 'Congenital word blindness', *Lancet*, 1, 1900, pp. 1506–8.

HODGSON, G. *America in our Time*, New York: Garden City, 1976.

JOHNSON, G.O. *Education for the Slow Learners*, Englewood Cliffs, NJ: Prentice-Hall, 1963.

KAVALE, K. and FORNESS, S. *The Science of Learning Disabilities*, San Diego, CA: College-Hill Press, 1985.

KIRK, S.A. 'Behavioral diagnosis and remediation of learning disabilities', *Proceedings of the Conference on Exploration into the Problems of the Perceptually Handicapped Child*, Vol. 1, 1963.

KIRK, S.A. *Educating Exceptional Children*, 2nd edn, Boston, MA: Houghton-Mifflin, 1972.

KIRK, S.A. 'Where are we going in learning disabilities?', *The DLD Times*, 2, 1984.

KIRK, S.A. and CHALFANT, J.C. *Academic and Developmental Learning Disabilities*, Denver, CO: Love Pub. Co, 1984.

KIRP, D.L. *Just Schools*, Berkeley, CA: University of California Press, 1982.

'Learning to Read' *Newsweek*, 54, 1959, p. 110.

MAISEL, A.Q. 'Hope for brain-injured children', *The Readers Digest*, 85, 1964, pp. 135–40.

MYERS, P. and HAMMILL, D. 'Deprivation or learning disability: Another dilemma for special education?', *The Journal of Special Education*, 7, 1973, pp. 409–11.

MYKLEBUST, H.R. and JOHNSON, D. 'Dyslexia in children', *Exceptional Children*, 29, 1962, pp. 14–25.

NATIONAL ADVISORY COMMITTEE ON THE HANDICAPPED. *First Annual Report*, Washington, DC: US Government Printing Office, 1968.

ORTON, S.T. *Reading, Writing, and Speech Problems in Children*, New York: W.W. Norton, 1937.

PARK, G.E. and LINDEN, J.E. 'The etiology of reading disabilities: An historical perspective', *Journal of Learning Disabilities*, 1, 1968, pp. 318–30.

PLISKO, V.W. *The Condition of Education*, 1984 edn, Washington, DC: US Government Printing Office, 1984.

PRESTHUS, R.V. *Elites in the Policy Process*, New York: Cambridge University Press, 1974.

*Proceedings of the Conference on Exploration into the Problems of the Perceptually Handicapped Child*, Vol. 1, 6 April 1963, Chicago.

RABINOVITCH, R.D. 'Dyslexia: Psychiatric considerations', in MONEY, J. (Ed.), *Reading Disability: Progress and Research Needs in Dyslexia*, Baltimore, MD: Johns Hopkins Press, 1962.

REES, H.E. *Deprivation and Compensatory Education*, New York: Houghton Mifflin, 1968.

RESNICK, D.P. and RESNICK, L.B. 'The nature of literacy: An historical exploration', *Harvard Educational Review*, 47, 1977, pp. 370–85.

RICKOVER, H.G. 'Let's stop wasting our greatest resource', *Saturday Evening Post*, 229, 2 March 1957a, pp. 19+.

RICKOVER, H.G. 'A size-up of what's wrong with American schools', *US News and World Report*, 43, 6 December 1957b, pp. 86–91.

RIESSMAN, F. *The Culturally Deprived Child*, New York: Harper and Row, 1962.

'Schoolboys point up a US weakness' *Life*, 44, 24 March 1958, pp. 26–37.

SHAW, C.R. and MCKAY, H.D. *Juvenile Delinquency and Urban Areas*, Chicago: University of Chicago Press, 1942.

SLEETER, C.E. 'Learning disabilities: The social construction of a special education category', *Exceptional Children*, in press.

'Slow learners' *Saturday Review*, 45, 17 February 1962, pp. 53–4.

Special Report No. 7 'Guidelines for standardization sampling', *Metropolitan Achievement Tests Special Report*, 1971.

SROUFE, L.A. and STEWART, M.A. 'Treating problem children with stimulating drugs', *New England Journal of Medicine*, 289, 1973, pp. 407–13.

STEVENS, G.D. and BIRCH, J.W. 'A proposal for clarification of the terminology used to describe brain injured children', *Exceptional Children*, 23, 1957, pp. 346–9.

STRAUSS, A.A. and LEHTINEN, L.E. *Psychology and Education of the Brain-Injured Child*, New York: Grune and Stratton, 1947.

TARNOPOL, L. 'Delinquency and minimal brain dysfunction', *Journal of Learning Disabilities*, 3, 1971, pp. 200–7.

TRACE, A.S., Jr. 'Can Ivan read better than Johnny?', *Saturday Evening Post*, 234, 27 May 1961, pp. 30+.

TUCKER, J.A. 'Ethnic proportions in classes for the learning disabled: Issues in nonbiased assessment', *Journal of Special Education*, 14, 1980, pp. 93–105.

TYACK, D.B. *The One Best System*, Cambridge, MA: Harvard University Press, 1974.

WARDEN, S.A. *The Leftouts*, New York: Holt, Rinehart, and Winston, 1968.

'Wasteland, USA' *Time*, 71, 1958, p. 72.

'What went wrong with US schools: An interview with Prof. Arthur Bestor, University of Illinois' *US News and World Report*, 44, 24 January 1958, pp. 68–75.

WHITE, M.A. and CHARRY, J. *School Disorder, Intelligence, and Social Class*, New York: Teachers College Press, 1966.

WILSON, S. 'It's time to close our carnival', *Life*, 44, 1958, pp. 37–8.

WOODRING, P. 'Reform plan for schools', *Life*, 43, 2 September 1957, pp. 123–36.

# 10 Outside the Selective Tradition: Socialist Curriculum for Children in the United States, 1900–1920

## Kenneth Teitelbaum

### Abstract

During the 1900–1920 period, American socialists not only critiqued and attempted to influence the nature of public school practice but also organized alternative educational activities for working-class adults and children. After describing some of the socialists' main criticisms of public school instruction, this chapter focuses on a group of Sunday schools for children that were established and staffed by grass-roots American socialist activists. Attention is placed in particular on the nature of the curriculum that these schools adopted. The claim is made that these socialist educational efforts can be viewed as 'outside' the 'selective tradition' in three related ways: first, generally speaking, as a tradition of radical educational practice about which most of us are wholly unfamiliar; second, as an alternative social and educational perspective that in myriad ways has been directly 'selected out' of mainstream educational debate and practice; and third, as a concrete body of school knowledge that stands in contradistinction to the dominant messages of the public schools.

Scholars of culture and curriculum in the United States, England, and elsewhere have noted the existence of a 'selective tradition' in

Western culture generally and in schools in particular (Williams, 1961; Williams, 1977; Eagleton, 1976; Apple, 1979; Apple, 1982). Such a focus recognizes that there is a virtually unlimited range of human history and culture, and yet only certain historical and cultural traditions and meanings are kept alive and transmitted in social institutions, for example in public schools. The knowledge, skills and values that are legitimated are not random. A selecting process prevails which is the result of and at the same time provides continuity and support for dominant ideologies and contemporary economic and cultural relations. In addition, the particular knowledge and ways of knowing are generally presented as the natural, commonsensical order of things, rather than as deliberate and purposeful choices with far-reaching consequences for social and cultural definition and identification. The selective tradition appears to many as a diffuse and widely accepted sense of tradition, culture and history. To question or contest such a perspective in educational circles is to appear to be 'impractical' in one's concerns or to be 'introducing politics' into the schooling arena.

Recent examinations of the treatment of labor, women, minorities, and other subordinate groups in the school curriculum have highlighted the ways in which the histories and cultures of these groups are included, for example with reference to stereotypes and distortions, as well as omitted, especially with regard to what could possibly (theoretically) have been included that was not (for example, Reynolds and Reynolds, 1974; Fitzgerald, 1979; Anyon, 1979; Taxel, 1978/79; Taxel, 1981; Sadker and Sadker, 1982). Whether or not functional linkages between the logic of capital and the selective tradition in school curricula have been substantiated (Liston, 1984), there has been considerable clarification and documentation of patterns of curriculum inclusion and exclusion that serve to reinforce dominant perspectives and unequal social relations.

However, there has been a missing element in much of this scholarship on the selective tradition in school curriculum: a concrete sense of the contested nature of curriculum development. Perhaps this is in part because discovering the sources of alternatives to hegemonic practice is a very complex and difficult task, for the selective tradition is a powerful process that is linked to many practical continuities that we directly experience in our everyday lives (for example, family, institutions, language). It may be the case that 'the most accessible and influential work of the counter-hegemony' is in fact historical in nature: 'the recovery of discarded areas, or the redress of selective and reductive interpretations' (Williams, 1977, p. 116).

This chapter contributes to the recovery of a heretofore neglected part of our history, specifically the educational analyses and activities of American socialists during the Progressive era (1900–1920), the very time that the linkages between the country's corporate structure and the public schools were becoming entrenched (Katz, 1971; Spring, 1972; Tyack, 1976; Violas, 1978). While they were by no means the 'victors' in the evolution of our social institutions, the efforts of these socialist activists are a part of our educational history (Leslie, 1984). Those involved were optimistic that their overall efforts would eventually lead to the inclusion of their perspectives on ideas, people, and events in public school classrooms (and in other social institutions). They provided their own formal weekend educational experiences for working-class children to supplement the public school curriculum until that time came. The curriculum they struggled to develop comprised materials and activities that explicitly opposed the dominant ideological messages found in mainstream schools, media, churches, and elsewhere. It represents a body of alternative educational ideas and activities that for the most part have been excluded from public school classrooms in the United States but that once *actually existed*, albeit outside of the public schooling arena.

In essence, then, the focus here is not on the winners of the conflicts over school curriculum or the 'imagined' losers, but the real losers, both people and curriculum, in the struggle to establish legitimate public school knowledge. At the same time that this is an historical endeavor, linkages to current interests should also be noted. For example, a familiarity with this 'discarded' history may help to dispel the myth that what constitutes school knowledge today has been the result of a consensual and neutral selecting process. The efforts of these radical activists underscore the political nature of schooling, reminding us that what is presented in schools is not reality but a *particular* version of it. They also represent a heretofore neglected radical tradition of social education from which educators attempting to cut a similar path today may draw (Teitelbaum, 1986). As E.P. Thompson (1981) has observed, 'the past is not just dead, inert, confining; it carries the signs and evidences also of creative resources which can sustain the present and prefigures possibility' (pp. 407–8).

## American Socialists and Public Schooling, 1900–1920

During the 1900–1920 period, socialism was considered a viable alternative to the capitalist organization of society by millions of American laborers, businessmen, farmers, teachers, and others. In 1912, about 1200 socialists were serving as elected public officials in 340 municipalities, including seventy-nine mayors in twenty-four states. Within the next several years, socialists from Milwaukee and New York City were elected to the United States House of Representatives. Additionally, over 300 socialist periodicals were published in 1912, one of which, the *Appeal to Reason*, had a circulation of over 700,000 (Weinstein, 1969). With the assistance of the Socialist Party's national office in Chicago, radical activists organized party locals in all areas of the country, in large and small cities and towns. Political and social committees were established in every local so as to keep members active and interested in party affairs and to help recruit new allies to the movement. Members helped to run hard-fought political campaigns; aided striking workers by publicizing grievances, helping on picket lines, organizing fund-raising events, and donating food, clothing, and money; and spoke on streetcorners from Schenectady to San Francisco about the need for radical change. For radicals who essentially felt 'outnumbered but destined to win' (Buhle, 1981, p. 6), it all seemed 'a small price to pay for utopia' (Morgan, 1964, p. 1).

In addition, American socialist writers and organizers focused considerable attention on aspects of everyday social life that were perceived to be basically capitalist-controlled and thus unprogressive influences on the current and future conditions of the vast majority of American workers. The public school, as well as the mainstream press, religious organizations and mass entertainment, were discussed and written about in numerous lectures, articles, pamphlets, and books.

Most socialists during this period regarded the public school system as a real gain for the working class. For example, Carl D. Thompson (1908), who served in the Wisconsin state legislature, stressed that the public school system itself represented an application of the principles of socialism because it is 'publicly owned and publicly managed serving all the people, giving an equal opportunity to all ... [It is] the very best institution we have in the country'. Unlike those from wealthy families, children from the working class could not afford private schooling. Thus, the expansion of public schools in the United States was 'an especial advantage to the working class' (p. 36). Likewise, in his 1903 book, *Class Struggles in America*,

Algie M. Simons claimed that working-class activists had been able to utilize free (public) schools in their struggle against the capitalist class (Pawa, 1971). And soon after the 1915 election of Meta Berger as president of the Milwaukee School Board, editorials of the socialist *Milwaukee Leader* (of which her husband, Victor Berger, was the editor) proudly announced that, 'The public schools more than any other public institution exemplify the spirit of socialism'. It was logical, then, that 'the socialists have stood as the bulwark of the public schools' (7 and 12 July 1915).

There was thus considerable support among party members for the institution and expansion of public schooling. It was vital to guard against a dimunition of financial support for the public schools and to wage an aggressive campaign to convince working-class children to take better advantage of educational opportunities. Socialist activists engaged in numerous and sometimes successful battles to win seats on local school boards. In 1914, for example, there were 126 socialist school officials (*Socialist Party Congressional Campaign Book*, 1914). Socialists also entered the schoolteaching profession, hoping to introduce socially aware instruction into the public school classroom. And, often in league with liberal progressives and other radicals, party activists agitated for additional school buildings, free textbooks, smaller class size, school lunch programs, and a broad conception of trade education.

Especially during the first years of the century, this support for the institution of public schooling, mixed with a demand for improved resources and a narrowly-conceived notion of equal educational opportunity, tended to deflect the attention of American socialists away from the schools' actual teaching and curricular content. In their emphasis on public versus private (including church-sponsored) education, some socialists accepted the generally constructive value of public schooling as a given. However, as the dissemination of progressive education ideas became more widespread and the ties between the interests of the corporate structure and schools became clearer, a number of more sophisticated radical educational critics began to focus on the actual content and form of school knowledge. While they may have embraced the rather mechanistic view of the relationship between capital relations and schooling that predominated in radical circles at the time, a more comprehensive and critical examination of the internal dynamics of public schools was initiated.

Socialist educational critics during the 1900–1920 period were influenced by progressive critiques of public schooling but their perspectives differed from child-centered progressives in several significant ways. In particular, they linked the problems of the public schools more directly to their capitalistic nature and maintained a constant emphasis on what was of benefit to the country's millions of skilled and unskilled laborers. Classrooms were viewed as not just teaching academic skills to individual children but preparing (or not preparing) groups of children for their role in the struggle to eliminate the inequalities of the class structure and to establish a more active and truly democratic form of citizenship. Schools were perceived not just in relation to the wider society but also to the revolutionized society which socialists sought to bring about.

More specifically, American socialists increasingly criticized public schools for fostering knee-jerk patriotism and militarism, intense competition, the glorification of the profit motive, a hierarchially-based division of manual and mental labor, and uncritical thinking in general. They expressed views similar to those of George Bartlett, Socialist Party candidate for County Superintendent of Schools in Milwaukee: 'their [the capitalists'] idea of our common schools . . . is to reduce them to institutions to make of the children more efficient tools for profit making' (*Milwaukee Leader*, 19 March 1915). Likewise, at the same time that he urged workers to elect socialists to the local school board in 1917, Milwaukee Assemblyman H.O. Kent delivered a scathing attack on the current character of public school instruction:

> The capitalistic interests desire to continue their hold on the schools in order that the workers' children shall not be taught the economics that will lead ultimately to greater justice and freedom.
>
> They want the young mind to be taught to respect the law and institutions under which the present masters of industry may continue to exploit, rob and oppress the many
> . . .
>
> We must not allow the minds of our boys and girls to be filled with capitalist class economics; we can not afford it; it will impede the way in securing speedier justice to our class.
>
> The working class must get control of the educational institutions — the grammar and high schools, the colleges, the universities, and likewise the schools for industrial and vocational education (*Milwaukee Leader*, 31 March 1917).

American radicals were becoming more aware that working-class viewpoints were being systematically eliminated from public schools when they stood in opposition to dominant capitalist interests. The political slant of school materials and instruction was hardly sympathetic to the forces of reform, let alone radical change, in American society. This was especially the case in the emerging social studies field. For example, a 1903 labor union report demanded better social studies textbooks and accused public school officials of failing to inculcate the dignity of manual labor and to give due importance to the service of labor to American society. Too much emphasis was placed on workers being content with their lot and, as a form of delusion, too much attention was spent on exceptional laborers who rose out of their class (Curoe, 1969). Socialist garment unions, such as the ILGWU and ACWA, observed that the public schools had 'serious gaps', in particular with regard to an ignorance of the economic foundations of American life and of the existence and importance of such figures as Nat Turner, Mother Jones, and Eugene Debs. Terms such as 'free enterprise' went unchallenged and unanalyzed despite the realities of the corporate structure. The valuable contributions of organized labor were ignored; indeed, schools seemed to be generally hostile to labor, often using it as a scapegoat for societal problems (Schaefer, 1951). And Francis Gill, a teacher in socialist children's schools in New York City, wrote about the public schools this way:

> Awe and respect for the great and deferential attitude towards superiority of rank or station is inculcated, if not directly at least by implication. But the collective name of the man — worker — who has borne all the burdens of the world and has made all its greatness possible, is never heard. Historically, if considered at all, it is an aspect of inferiority (*The Worker*, 7 March 1908).

Party activists urged others to become more active in local school affairs because of the public school's role in educating future wage workers in 'a habit of slavish obedience to capitalist rule and of prejudice against the working class movement'. It was argued that American workers 'have need to watch schools where the minds of their children are in danger of being perverted to capitalist purposes' (*The Worker*, 6 October 1901). More specific complaints and protests against public school teaching were lodged as well. For instance, a pageant at North Division High School in Milwaukee in 1919, entitled 'The Land of Opportunity', was severely criticized by local socialists as 'a vicious slam at organized labor . . . [that] holds up to the approval of the children the ideal of militarism' (*Milwaukee Leader*,

19 November 1919). Another dispute in Milwaukee centered around the schools' use of the *Current Events* newspaper. The socialist *New York Call* had earlier criticized the paper's 'propagandistic' depiction of Bolshevik rule in Russia. The *Milwaukee Leader* complained that it was nothing more than 'a staunch defender of the capitalist system [that] is systematically poisoning the minds of our children' (*New York Call*, 28 October 1919; *Milwaukee Leader*, 7 March 1921). In 1902, the Yonkers Social Democratic party protested the procurement of $1100 by the local board of education to buy guns for the high school cadet corps. The socialists viewed the measure as a ploy to train students in the military spirit, in particular so that later they would be able and willing to help the state militia when called on to suppress strikes (*The Worker*, 12 January 1902).

Along with their criticisms of public school practice, socialist educational critics also suggested ways in which American education might look different in a socialist society, although these observations were often rather briefly and vaguely expressed. The *Milwaukee Leader*, for instance, put it this way:

> It is their [the Socialists'] purpose that the schools shall equip the children to cope with their environment and to bring out the best that is in them — not by grinding them through an educational mill as sausages are ground from a machine, but by giving the individual opportunity to develop to his fullest capacity in the direction that his talents are most promising. But in giving the individual opportunity, at the same time they recognize the need for cultivating the social consciousness and community spirit (5 March 1917).

Another *Milwaukee Leader* editorial criticized schools for being 'dominated by the forces of standpattism and reaction[,] . . . by men and women who have the stocks-and-bonds outlook upon life'. In contrast, 'Socialists do not want to teach the children Socialism. They only want to teach them to think for themselves — to lead their minds out, which is the true meaning of education — and protect them from the deadening effects of prejudice and falsehood' (19 March 1923). Dr. Charles P. Steinmetz, a party member from Schenectady, suggested that under capitalism 'our children are taught that their main mission in life is to make a living', while under socialism 'they will be taught that the only thing worth working for or worth living for is to make this a better world to live in' (*Appeal to Reason*, 8 August 1914). And Scott Nearing stressed the need to inculcate a sense of social morality along with individual morality.

Social responsibility and cooperation rather than individualism and competition should be stressed. With reference to the growing distinction being made in the preparation of mental and manual laborers, Nearing further suggested that although 'the people cannot all be scholars', that in fact there was no necessity for that to be the case, 'they can all be intelligent upon the great issues of life' (Nearing, 1920, p. 25; Tien, 1972). Once proud of the public school as an evolving socialistic institution, increasing numbers of socialist writers, speakers, and organizers were denouncing what May Wood Simons (1908) of Chicago referred to as 'the tendency among educators to make the interest of society identical with the interest of the property owning class' (p. 7), and attempting to provide a hint of what a socialist alternative might look like.

However, despite all of the serious criticisms directed against public schooling, the American socialist movement generally maintained a faith in the efficacy of the institution. Thus, one observer could argue on the one hand that 'the greatest foe to any real progress in the art of human living today is our empirical, tyrannical educational system', and then emphasize the possibility and necessity of 'capturing the schools ... so that we may be sure of introducing truth and fairmindedness in the elementary grades in place of the false and distorted teaching that now goes on' (*New York Call*, 19 August 1917). While it was evident that significant obstacles in the way of progressive change in the public schools existed, socialists generally continued to view the public school as an important arena in which to work. They never lost hope in the institution's potential to help usher in the Cooperative Commonwealth.

## American Socialist Schools for Children, 1900–1920

The foregoing discussion is intended to reveal past socialist educational activity about which most of us are quite unfamiliar. But besides commenting on the state of public schooling, running for local school board office and entering the teaching profession, and agitating for a variety of school reforms, Socialist Party activists also attempted to develop their own radical educational practice, in which a socialist perspective could more overtly be provided to adults and children. For adults, numerous study classes, lecture series, correspondence courses, 'educational' reading materials, and even colleges were organized by various segments of the socialist movement during the early 1900s. Their purpose was to foster a fuller understanding of the true nature of industrial capitalism, the class struggle, socialist economics and philosophy, and the benefits that would accrue to the vast majority of Americans once the nation turned away from the capitalist stage of development and toward socialism. Of course, they were also intended to recruit new members to the radical cause.

A minority of grass-roots radical activists were also keenly interested in the next generation of laborers, the children from working-class families. Given the pervasiveness of conservative influences in society, these children needed to be educated about the unjust conditions endemic to industrial capitalism and convinced of the value of allying themselves with the socialist movement. Children's camps, choruses, and clubs were established in socialist locals across the country (Teitelbaum, 1985). While the emphasis of these endeavors was placed on the social and the recreational, the learning of socialist tenets and the development of an allegiance to the radical movement were viewed as natural by-products of joining with other youth (under the competent direction of a local party member) to discuss relevant readings, sing radical songs, perform plays with working-class themes, and so forth. For similar reasons, children were encouraged to take part in socialist parades and to attend socialist rallies and meetings. Such exposure to the activities of adult socialists would presumably provide them with valuable lessons on the nature and benefits of allying with the socialist cause.

A small number of socialist youth activists insisted that there was a need to go beyond these rather loosely organized, informal endeavors. They struggled to establish weekend (Sunday) schools, for the purpose of providing children with a formal, systematic education unlike the one that they received in the public schools. These Socialist Sunday schools, as they were most often called,[1] were intended to directly counteract the individualistic, competitive, nationalistic, militaristic, and anti-working class themes that seemed to be prevalent in contemporary public schools. Although in most cases only meeting for two hours a week, the work that went into organizing and running these schools was prodigious for a working-class political movement that was constantly low on funds and bedeviled by internal disputes and external threats. Despite the sundry problems that were encountered, in particular the lack of active support from the vast majority of party members, these American socialist educators succeeded in establishing a tradition of socialist education for children that has been barely mentioned in our historical and educational literature.

Organized by grass-roots activists who were members of the

Socialist Party, the Socialist Sunday schools were English-speaking[2] and intended for children who were about 6–13 years old. There is evidence that at least 100 of these schools were organized in sixty-four cities and towns in twenty states and the District of Columbia (Teitelbaum, 1985; Teitelbaum and Reese, 1983). The most prominent ones were established in New York City (which had fourteen schools in 1912), Rochester, Hartford, Newark, Buffalo (two in 1918), Philadelphia (two in 1912), Pittsburgh (two in 1916), Cleveland (three in 1912), Chicago (eight in 1919), Milwaukee (three in 1915), and Los Angeles. Schools varied in size from a handful in one class, as in the case of the Newport, Kentucky school, to 1000 students in dozens of classes at the school that met at the Brownsville Labor Lyceum in Brooklyn and 400 children in twenty classes in Rochester. The average enrollment was probably between fifty to 100 students. Most schools existed for several years, although there were schools opening and closing in the same year and others that lasted for more than a half-dozen years (for example, the East Side Socialist Sunday School in Manhattan, the Williamsburg and Brownsville schools in Brooklyn, and the International Socialist Sunday School in Milwaukee). In most cases, schools met during the same months as the public schools and the two-hour school sessions consisted of age-divided classes and general assembly times (with announcements, recitations, songs, and remarks by visitors).

It is important to emphasize that the Socialist Sunday schools were established by grass-roots party activists for the purpose of providing a supplementary, two-hour-a-week education for working-class children. In other words, they were never conceived as replacements for public school practice or models of socialist educational practice that would be appropriate for a more diverse student population in full-time daily schools. Furthermore, while some Socialist Sunday School (SSS) staff members (for example, Bertha Mailly, Benjamin Glassberg and David Berenberg of New York City, Kendrick Shedd of Rochester and Milwaukee, May Wood Simons of Chicago, and Carl Haessler of Milwaukee) had college or public school teaching experience, many teachers in these socialist children's schools did not. They were either like Edmund T. Melms of Milwaukee, Frederick Krafft of Newark, Edward Perkins Clarke of Hartford and Lucien Saniel of Manhattan in that they came to SSS work from a lifetime of socialist agitation rather than from a longtime interest in teaching; or like Edna Peters of Milwaukee, Isadore Tischler of Rochester and Gertrude Weil Klein of Brooklyn in that they themselves were barely in their teens and were eager to do more for the socialist movement than just be active members of the Young People's Socialist League. A majority, though not all, of the SSS teachers were women, perhaps encouraged to do little else in the way of socialist agitation by (predominantly male) party stalwarts (Buhle, 1981).

Prominent SSS proponents tended to be knowledgeable about progressive education ideas and practices, and they attempted to infuse the movement with creative, flexible, and humanistic teaching styles and curriculum materials. For example, Kendrick Shedd, a popular and nationally known SSS organizer from Rochester and Milwaukee, argued: 'Make things interesting every minute. Don't lecture the children to death! . . . Make them feel that they are loved . . . Get live comrades to supervise and teach. Tell your dead ones to take a long vacation' (*American Socialist*, 27 March 1915). But appropriate lesson materials were generally not made available to local SSS teachers. The Party's national office and the state party organizations provided very little support for their development and dissemination during most of this twenty-year period. Since most instructors and other staff members labored hard during the week at the workplace and/or at home, they had little available time to prepare their own lessons. Lacking experience and training as well, at times they overrelied on the adaptation of adult reading materials for school use.

The history of the Socialist Sunday School movement tended to mirror the evolution of the political party with which it was associated during these twenty years. Although the German-speaking socialist community organized similar schools for young children in the late 1800s, the first non-ethnic, English-speaking Socialist Sunday schools were initiated soon after the organization of the Socialist Party in 1901. For instance, the San Jose school was established by members of the local socialist women's club in 1902, and schools in Chicago, Boston, and Omaha were organized in 1903 (*The Worker*, 13 July 1902, 9 August 1903, 29 November 1903, 20 December 1903, and 24 January 1904; *The Arena*, July 1903). However, while the Party hit a peak in 1912–1913 and then slid downward until World War I, when it attracted renewed support for its strong anti-war stand, the SSS movement experienced a slow but continuous expansion during the first nineteen years of the century. By the end of the second decade, inter-city school conferences were being held, a national organization of Socialist Sunday schools was being planned for better coordination and development of curriculum materials, and the national Party's Young People's Department was focusing more attention and money on the schools than had been the case earlier.

However, the Socialist Party of America faced severe repression from federal, state, and local government officials and private citizen groups from 1918 to 1920. This development, mixed with a devastating split in party ranks in 1919–1920, basically dealt the SSS movement its death blow. By 1923, the Socialist Party was a shell of what it once was, with 26,766 members in 1920 and 11,277 in 1922 compared to more than 100,000 in 1919. Almost all of the 300 socialist periodicals that had existed in 1912 were gone by 1923 (Weinstein, 1969; Shannon, 1955). After a nationwide tour at the start of the new decade, party activist Ida Crouch Hazlett captured the general atmosphere when she reported the existence of 'a vast amount of discouragement, listlessness, not to say hopelessness, both in the the skeleton-like condition of the organization and in the attitude of thousands of the old rank and file' (Cornell, 1976).

Loyal party members now had to deal with internal and external threats to the organization's very existence. In such an atmosphere, weekend schools for children, which never received extensive attention, time, and money from the party organization before, now could command none. By 1921, so many members had left the ranks of the movement, either joining the new Communist parties or dropping out of radical politics altogether, that, except in a few neighborhoods in New York City and Milwaukee. There were few adults and children who could even be interested in the work of such schools. Eventually, when the Party experienced a resurgence in the early 1930s, about a dozen schools were reorganized in New York City. But gone were any prospects for a national movement and the optimistic spirit that had marked the earlier phase of these radical educational experiments. By the end of 1936, when the Party experienced another serious split in its ranks, there were no Socialist Sunday schools left in the United States. With the passage of time, as well as the tendency in our culture to 'select out' from our traditions the past efforts of radical groups, the attempt to establish a socialist education for children in the United States has by and large been wiped clean from the slate of our collective consciousness.

## Socialist Perspectives on Teaching

The Socialist Sunday School movement in the United States was marked by a lack of uniformity and a paucity of inter-school communication. Still, generally speaking, SSS instruction as a whole included a perhaps surprising variety of teaching methods and materials: lectures, question-and-answer discussion formats, socialist and non-socialist readers and magazines, recitations, tests, essay writing, games, field trips, songs, plays, and pageants. While specific schools differed with regard to the teaching methods they adopted, they basically had common goals. Prominent SSS activist Bertha Mailly (1911), who helped to organize schools in Omaha, Boston and New York City, described their focus this way: 'to teach the children *what* is not just and true and beautiful in things as they are, *why* there is no justice, truth and beauty in people's live, [and] *how* to bring justice, truth and beauty into the world'. Children needed to be freed 'from the many prejudices' and introduced to 'a new social ethic founded upon the conception of society in which profit and wage slavery are to be removed' (p. 6). Kendrick Shedd stressed: 'We want our socialist children to have their eyes and their ears open. What are those instruments for? Let other kiddies sleep through life, if they are so brought up, but let our working class children be inspired to hate the slavery of their fathers and to be filled with an irresistible longing to get out and fight the working class battle to a finish' (*New York Call*, 29 June 1915). These schools emphatically did not seek to socialize children to the inequalities and injustices of the existing workplace and society. On the contrary, children were encouraged to prepare for participation as adults in the struggle for a more egalitarian and democratic social order.

Some participants were more cognizant than others about the inadequacies and possible dangers of attempting to teach children the complexities of the socialist perspective in part-time weekend schools. Differences regarding teaching methods tended to reflect diverse viewpoints of the educational enterprise in general. For example, activities that encouraged children 'to think for themselves' were strongly advocated by some participants. Frances Gill, a prominent SSS organizer in New York City, sounded current when she wrote of the need to develop 'inquiry on the part of the child' and to not treat 'the mind as a blank piece of paper, nor yet as a vessel to be filled with whatever a teacher may see fit to pour into it'. She went on: 'we do not intend to dogmatize on anything whatever, neither Socialism nor anything else' (*New York Call*, 26 February 1911). Likewise, Samuel Meyerson stressed that the schools were in fact utilizing a 'unique system of teaching of facts', one that involved 'the asking of questions rather than the stating of facts themselves'. Such a method allowed the teacher to draw 'the children on from stage to stage, setting their minds working, [and] forc[ing] them to do some thinking' (*New York Call*, 21 March 1913). Like-minded socialist educators warned against SSS instruction that would engender not willful and informed support for socialist tenets but a kind of blind allegiance to them.

Other SSS directors and teachers adopted an approach that was more attentive to the transmission of particular content. This was especially the case during the early years of the movement but it continued throughout its lifetime. Frank Cherdron of Milwaukee, for instance, proudly proclaimed that the children who attended a Socialist Sunday School there were 'being molded into class-conscious Socialist kiddies. We are filling them with a spirit of rebellion against the system that robs the laborers of the fruits of their toil' (*Milwaukee Leader*, 28 June 1915). Given the conditions of working-class life in capitalist America and the pervasiveness of conservative dominant influences, the direct teaching of a socialist vision to children was perceived by Cherdron and others as not only necessary but desirable. As Jeanette Pearl of New York City observed: 'As long as our children are being taught by the church and the public schools to be loyal to their country — the plutes' country — we must teach them loyalty to class — the working class.' In response to criticisms that children were too young to teach about social injustice, Pearl countered, 'make no mistake, children of 10 and over know much of the sadness and sorrow of life which this system of capitalist exploitation inflicts upon them. Our children are the workers' children; and they have imbibed the suffering and privations of the working class with their mothers' milk.' It was especially necessary to counter the 'lies, false economics, false history, false morals, false ethics' and the 'docile and submissive mentality' that marked the public schools (*New York Call*, 29 October 1911). Esther F. Sussman of Hartford agreed, stressing that it was *only* by teaching the children 'the fundamentals of scientific socialism . . . that when they grow up they may be able to face and overcome the social problems of the day with intelligence and broadmindedness' (*Young Socialists' Magazine*, September 1911).

The Socialist Sunday School movement as a whole placed a dual emphasis on the teaching of the fundamentals of and need for socialist relations on the one hand and a more general encouragement of thinking with broadmindedness and a critical intelligence about the social problems of the day on the other. Most teachers attempted to somehow address both goals. Examining the available evidence about individual schools, however, it appears that socialist teachers in general tended to stress the former. The Party's National Education Committee even warned in 1913 that there was some propensity in the schools to teach 'stilted economics and dogmatic exercises to children' (*Party Builder*, 26 July 1913).

Throughout this twenty-year period, socialists did struggle to resolve the dilemma of the appropriate perspective to take toward the teaching of young children. Socialist Sunday School teachers were in the midst of developing and clarifying their educational assumptions and practices, with plans for a national federation of schools, when the SSS movement collapsed. If one is allowed to speculate, it appears that prominent SSS activists were becoming increasingly influenced by the ideas of child-centered progressive educators. Socialist educators would never have abandoned their more comprehensive and radical theory of social formation and their belief in the need to foster an emancipatory social vision. But, if allowed additional time and resources, they may have come up with an interesting blend of radical political theory and progressive educational practice, and of curricular content and form, from which later educators could have perhaps drawn. Instead, their ideas never became clearly formulated and never gained a serious audience outside of their own circle of fellow socialist youth activists.

### Socialist Curricular Themes

While the Socialist Sunday School movement was marked by disagreements over the specific form that the teaching would take, there was little doubt in the minds of proponents that teachers should go beyond the 'negation' of dominant ideas and practices. What was needed was the presentation of an alternative body of knowledge and values to counter the messages of the public schools, mainstream press, churches, etc. One general expression of this agenda was contained in an introductory statement about the schools' purposes prepared by the Socialist School Union of Greater New York:

> to foster a questioning mental attitude; to show that labor creates all and should receive what it creates; to teach that no natural resources should belong to any single person or group; that none should be permitted to eat their bread by the sweat of another's brow; that there should be as inviolable a property right in the things created by labor as is now guaranteed to other forms of property; that the command-

ment against theft should be as operative against the stealing of such property as against any other forms of property; to show how the industrial system is destined to replace the present property system; to trace through history the struggles and progress of the human race and the part that the lowly have played in its course; to teach that sin is an unsocial act, that good and bad acts build a character structure either beautiful or hideous; to teach that life here and now may, and should be, happy and good, and not that a future bliss is compensation for material suffering; to teach sex facts in a wholesome and cleanly way, by analogy from plant and animal life, and to develop whatever may be true, good, or desirable in conduct and behavior because of its social value (McFarland *et al.*, 1915).

Thirteen specific curricular themes predominated in the Socialist Sunday School curriculum as a whole (i.e., not necessarily in the curriculum of any one school). Some themes were emphasized more and taught more directly than others but they all were prominent elements of this radical curriculum. Although not easily separated out from each other, these themes are briefly summarized below.

The first theme involved a reaction to the concept of 'the abstract individual'. Michael W. Apple (1979) has recently described it this way: 'it is the case that our sense of community is withered at its roots. We find ways of making the concrete individual into an abstraction and, at the same time, we divorce the individual from larger social movements which might give meaning to "individual" wants, needs, and visions of justice' (p. 9). The life of the individual, as an economic and social being, is not situated within the structural relations that play an influential role in determining the level of comfort that one does or does not enjoy. In contrast, the SSS curriculum was strongly infused by a perspective of the place of the individual in the world, and in particular of our interdependence and indebtedness to the work of countless others. Such was the focus, for instance, when Bertha Mailly took children from an Omaha socialist school to a shoe factory and pointed out how the guide only spoke of the machinery and not of the workers who were vital to the children being able to buy decent shoes for themselves (*The Worker*, 24 January 1904).

The second curricular theme involved a consciousness of the students as part of the working class community and, following on that, as part of the class struggle. The dignity of labor (if not all laborers) was constantly stressed and virtually every social issue or problem was viewed primarily from the perspective of its effects on workers. For example, two former students of the International Socialist Sunday School in Milwaukee have recollected that many school lessons included a positive portrayal of the important role to be played by workers in the lengthy nonviolent struggle to overthrow the capitalist system (Friebert and Friebert, 1981).

Cooperative and collectivist rather than competitive and private ownership and management was a third theme in the SSS curriculum. A number of lessons focused on the nature and advantages of social property and common ownership (at a time when public ownership and management of utilities, let alone industry, was considered a radical demand). This sense of cooperation and collectivism was extended to social relations in general, so that 'working together' in a variety of ways was stressed as the key to more congenial personal relationships as well as to working-class success in overturning capitalist economic relations. John Spargo's illustration of this perspective in his book, *Modern Socialism*, was indicative of the approach taken in the Socialist Sunday schools. Spargo, a prominent socialist theorist who also authored a book entitled *Socialist Readings For Children* that was used in several of the schools, wrote about a wise teacher who placed a beautiful rose in the classroom 'to brighten the day for her children'. Before long, 'the boys and girls began to clamor for the rose, each begging the teacher for the sole possession of it'. The teacher explained that to give it to any child 'would be unjust to all the others ... Besides, it would be unwise, for whoever obtained it could not get more of its beauty than now'. The teacher went on to explain that she could not divide it, 'for if I do the rose will be destroyed and each child will have a worthless petal only; there will be no rose. Together, we can enjoy it; in a real sense each of us owns the rose' (*New York Socialist*, 25 July 1908).

A fourth theme was a strong emphasis on internationalism, the sense of viewing oneself as closely linked to the interests of others (especially workers) in other nations. Correspondence with schools and youth clubs in other countries (for example, Canada, England, Scotland) was not just to gather information but also to encourage a connectedness with youth and radical political movements in other countries. International songs and flags were a part of the lessons at all schools. Future workers in America needed to realize that the workers in other countries shared a common enemy, the capitalist system, and a common aim, its overthrow.

Anti-militarism, especially after World War I began and the

United States massed troops along the Mexican border during the middle years of the second decade, was also a theme of the SSS curriculum. This was associated with what David Greenberg (1913) of New York City referred to as 'anti-sham patriotism'. Militarist adventures were viewed as primarily hurting the lives of workers (who had to fight in such endeavors), breaking down a feeling of internationalism, and taking attention and funds away from important domestic needs. The association of some of the schools with protest rallies and with the Socialist Party's Prison Comfort Clubs provided the children with active involvement in anti-militarist efforts.

A sixth theme can be explained as a 'revisionist' interpretation of economics, history, and sociology. Socialist Sunday School children were taught lessons that transformed the typical school social studies so that the laboring class was perceived as an instrumental motor for social progress. Birthday celebrations were held for such heroes and heroines as William Lloyd Garrison, Susan B. Anthony, Mother Jones, Eugene Debs, William Morris, Karl Marx, and other national and international social critics and activists. Radical agitators were portrayed not as a lunatic fringe of bombthrowers, as was the case in most textbooks of the time (Elson, 1964), but rather as important allies in the workers' struggle to significantly improve their lot in the United States. Moreover, the traditional glorified account of the American past was counterposed with a consideration of other factors (for example, many of the Founding Fathers owned slaves), and the plight of the poor was viewed not as the result of defective skills or character on the part of individuals but rather as caused primarily by the capitalist organization of society.

A related focus involved the study of anthropology and in particular the evolution of the human race. What was portrayed was the progress of people from the stone age to the iron age to feudalism to capitalism, with the logical next stage in 'the struggle for existence' being socialism. It was an optimistic message, and one that embraced a liberal notion of progress, but it subverted conventional teaching by positing the necessity and inevitability of a next, socialist stage of human civilization. Anthropological teachings were further guided not as much by a sense of how 'primitive' early people were but by the cooperative and collective spirit that had stood them well. This spirit was viewed as in essence 'natural' to humankind but as having been distorted and suppressed by pre-capitalist and capitalist social relations.

Social equity was another important theme of the SSS curriculum. Because American socialists at this time generally embraced a political vision that held class struggle to be pre-eminent, that is, that racial and sexual struggles could not be fully addressed until capitalist relations were eradicated, the vision of equity adopted concentrated primarily on economic issues. Most of the focus revolved around the poverty, threat of unemployment, disease, poor working conditions, and so forth that had to be endured by millions of laborers because of capitalist exploitation. True equity and equality of opportunity meant that workers had to have the same advantages in life as managers and owners, that in essence 'wage slavery' had to be abolished. Adequate levels of food, clothing and shelter were emphasized time and again as the most vital ingredients of human life, from the beginning of civilization to the present, and that only a socialistic society could guarantee that all individuals would not suffer from the want of them.

This does not mean that race and gender issues were never addressed, for prejudicial attitudes were sometimes directly attacked. According to Edward Friebert (1945), who had been a staff member at Milwaukee's International Socialist Sunday School, 'tolerance was strongly stressed'. During the general assembly time of one lesson, for example, about a dozen children were summoned to the hall platform, with a sign placed around the neck of each one. The signs were labelled 'American', 'English', 'German', 'French', 'Russian', 'Negro', and so on. The Director of the school asked the children what would happen if he cut the veins of the American child: 'What would flow?'. The children answered that 'blood' would come out. The Director then asked its color, and the students answered, 'Red'. He continued to do this for each child except the 'Negro' one. After he addressed that child, he cried out, 'You mean to tell me that the same red blood would abound from this negro child as from these white children?!' What happened next is not known, but the lesson serves as an example of how one school dealt with the issue of race relations.

A ninth theme revolved around an awareness of significant social problems. What differentiated the approach of the socialist educators from a more mainstream social problems approach was their constant emphasis on specific social problems (such as poverty, unemployment, unhealthy and unsafe work conditions, child labor, alcoholism, crime, poor housing and sanitary facilities, and the despoliation of nature) being endemic to industrial capitalism. In other words, such social ills could not be fully comprehended or eliminated without taking into consideration the oppressive nature of the capitalist system. Thus, the aim of the staff of the 3rd Assembly District

Socialist Sunday School in the Bronx 'to develop the children into useful citizens' did not refer merely to voting and to participating in uncontroversial social service activities (*New York Call*, 6 December 1918). It meant assisting in the long struggle to eradicate serious social problems in the only realistic way possible, by agitating for the end of capitalist control of economic and social life.

The SSS curriculum also placed considerable emphasis on the everyday lived conditions of workers and in particular their children. Teachers sought to expand the children's awareness and appreciation of the need for good hygiene, healthy diets, proper exercise, safety, nature outings, and so forth. Significantly, these aspects of everyday life were perceived as not just for the benefit of the individual but also with regard to the interests of the community. After all, sickness can spread to others and nature can be enjoyed by others. It was the responsibility of everyone not just for themselves but for the community to take care of these matters.

An eleventh theme involved the portrayal of the Cooperative Commonwealth as embracing the ideal conditions of human life. In other words, a utopic society was presented as a goal for which all progressive people should strive. Such a socialist world would be marked by shared ownership and management of industry and public property, greater economic equality, the elimination of the class structure, and more congenial and satisfactory living conditions and personal relationships in general. Associated with this emphasis was the notion that socialism should be identified with 'happiness'. This was sometimes used as an argument for broadening and relaxing the curriculum to include more games, trips, concerts, pageants, picnics, and the like. While some of these activities were utilized for fund-raising purposes, SSS supporters also stressed that as a by-product the children would be having 'fun' and would thus think of being part of the socialist community as an enjoyable experience.

Education (and self-education) was another important theme of the SSS curriculum. However, it was accompanied by the view that education was only part of the overall program to fundamentally transform the organization of social life. This perspective is in some contrast to that of the later social reconstructionists, whose views tended to embrace the notion that schooling by itself could in fact propel significant social change. Socialist educators never embraced such a perspective. They stressed not only the need to be well educated about the problems of capitalist America and the nature of the coming socialist society, but also that political work outside of the educational arena was crucial to the realization of 'the new social order'.

The thirteenth curricular theme that was embedded in the Socialist Sunday School curriculum involved the encouragement of a generally critical attitude toward everyday life, dominated as it was by capitalist social institutions. For example, public schooling was not portrayed as a neutral site and SSS students were discouraged from accepting at face value what their public school teachers taught them. While no one recommended that these children outrightly reject the messages and practices that they were learning in the public schools, the entire content of the SSS curriculum was developed to remind them that if 'truths' existed, and they certainly did for these socialists, their weekday schools (and the mainstream press, mass entertainment, etc.) were rarely guided by them. It was not just a matter of focusing on different heroes and different interpretations of important historical events. In some of the lessons, even alternative notions of everyday concepts were discussed. For instance, Kendrick Shedd's 1912–1913 lesson outlines for the Rochester Socialist Sunday School included the following guidelines for the treatment of the topics of 'success' and 'justice'[3]:

> What is necessary for it [success]; are the following:
>      Possession of Money? High Position? Power?
> Was Abraham Lincoln Successful?
> Compare the work of Abraham Lincoln and Karl Marx.
> Do successful persons always realize their success?
> Name some who did not.
> Can true success be gained at the expense of one's brothers?
> What is success?

> Is competition just?
> Do the workers get justice?
> Have we political justice?
> Name some instances of political injustice.
> Are these things just:
>      Child wage workers?
>      Mothers employed outside of their homes?
>      Use of militia to settle strikes?
>      War? Capitalist courts? Capitalist Press?
>      Suppression of Free Speech and Assemblage?
> What is justice?

These lessons were thus intended to begin with a discussion that related the general topic to present social conditions and then conclude with a definitional question. Children were encouraged to view commonsensical everyday notions critically and then, in the light of the unsatisfactory character of prevailing views, to adopt alternative perspectives of them. What might be considered as abstract, philosophical constructs were linked to the social context in which they are lived out. Thus, success, happiness, justice, and the like only have meaning in relation to who benefits when certain people are 'successful', 'happy', or 'justly treated' in an unequal capitalist society.

It is clear that the curriculum of the American Socialist Sunday School movement is inadequate as a critical pedagogy today. It would be somewhat ridiculous to expect otherwise, considering that it was developed over sixty-five years ago, when public ownership of utilities and unemployment insurance were considered radical demands and when progressive educational ideas were first being introduced. In particular, the approach taken by SSS teachers too often resembled the kind of 'banking approach' to schooling that Paulo Freire and others have criticized (Freire, 1970; Giroux, 1983). Relatedly, the lessons of these schools generally lacked a participatory element. Although the social vision presented strongly emphasized an active participation in political affairs in general and in the struggle for radical social change in particular, the activities planned for the children (especially the class lessons) were lacking in opportunities for creative self-expression, self-criticism, and collaboration.

Indeed, despite (or because of) the fact that the radical movement at this time was wracked with disputes, the socialists' educational strategies rarely included a critical perspective toward their own ideas and practices. Socialist knowledge itself was often presented authoritatively. And other serious criticisms of the SSS curriculum can be leveled at its devaluing of other social categories of domination besides class, most notably race and gender, and its overly economistic emphasis.

On the other hand, the Socialist Sunday schools presented students with values to believe in and with social goals to strive for, ones that challenged the central assumptions of dominant economic and cultural relations. An explicit vision and commitment to emancipation, in the sense of ushering in a new age of social democracy, was encouraged. Children were taught that 'to make this world a better place in which to live',[4] and in particular to strive for the elimination of rampant individualism and competition, the glorification of the profit motive, and gross economic and political inequities, was an appropriate goal not just for the socialist schools but for their own lives as well. Given recent survey results that indicate high school students' minimum commitment to 'working to correct social and economic inequalities' — approximately 13 per cent classified it as a 'very important' goal compared to 33 per cent for 'having lots of money' and 86 per cent for 'being successful in my work' (Hepburn, 1985) — and our country's (and the world's) growing rather than lessening problems with the homeless, the hungry, the unemployed, and the gap between rich and poor, this was certainly a noteworthy educational goal to have adopted.

If the question in teaching is not whether to advocate or not but rather the nature and the extent of one's advocacy, then perhaps the thirteen curriculur themes of the Socialist Sunday School curriculum are still worth reflecting about today. If specific ones (for example, interdependence of indivdiuals; the dignity and contributions of different kinds of labor; cooperative and collectivist social and personal relations; internationalism; anti-militarism; revisionist social sciences; social equity; serious social problems as inherent in capitalist relations; and a critical perspective toward everyday life) are not deemed appropriate for public school adoption today, at least a consideration of them and the democratic socialist ideals that guided their development may instigate a more extended debate on the knowledge, skills, and values that can and should take their place. The essential point is that for those educators who seek to encourage a more just and humane society, proposals for critical discourse in schools which include little indication of what we should be discoursing about provide us at best with only half of a very large puzzle.

## Outside the Selective Tradition

Part of our difficulty with constructing alternative ideas and practices is that we have lost a sense of past efforts in this direction. Indeed, the ideas and varied educational activities of American socialists during the early 1900s essentially stand *outside* the selective tradition that has such a powerful impact on the way that we think and act. This is the case in three significant ways.

First, the educational perspectives and activities of American socialists during the Progressive era, and in particular the Socialist Sunday schools, are 'outside' in the sense that educators and others today are not aware of their having existed. One reason among many that this has resulted is indicated by a recent analysis of the ideological nature of popular United States history school textbooks. Jean Anyon (1979) found, for example, that of the seventeen widely used textbooks, twelve do not describe the Socialist Party of America or its platform, nor do they mention the existence of various other radical groups. Of the five books that do discuss the Socialist Party, all but one contain disparaging comments about the socialists' intentions, and four of the five minimize the extent to which workers were attracted to radical ideas. In our schools and elsewhere, then, a clear sense of the existence of a respectable American socialist tradition has in large part been eradicated from our collective consciousness. It is hardly surprising that an awareness of socialist educational perspectives and experiments has also been lost to us. Indeed, as one of the characters in the film *Northern Lights* observes, there are parts of our history that have been forgotten or rewritten, leaving us without a knowledge of our own 'rebel roots'.

Besides the homogenizing nature of school materials, another way that the mechanism of the selective tradition is operationalized involves the suppression of efforts to introduce a more critical perspective into our social institutions. This suppression is most overtly manifested during what Gramsci called a 'crisis of authority', for example during World War I and its aftermath. Numerous specific examples of the everyday difficulties faced by public school teachers and students who held radical sympathies during the 1900– 1920 period could be offered (Teitelbaum, 1985; Murray, 1955), but perhaps one particular example will help to clarify this point.

A former student of the East Side Socialist Sunday School in Manhattan graduated from elementary school in 1915 and then attended Washington Irving High School. Three years later, she and her classmates were given an assignment by their English teacher that asked them to read the lead editorial in their favorite newspaper at home and then to bring in 'a little resume of what you read'. Her family received the *New York Times, New York World*, and her favorite, the socialist *New York Call*. She used the *Call* editorial, which dealt with the war, to complete her homework assignment. When she brought in her resume, the teacher was furious at the views presented and reported her to the Principal. Although sympathetic, the Principal warned her about getting into trouble with the teacher again (Goldman, 1981). In such a way in our distant and recent history, multiplied many times over, has a more critical perspective of society been in large part selected out of our public schools. A comprehension of how the selective tradition operates thus needs to take into account the historical dimension of its development. The past does not determine present practice, but it indeed weighs heavily upon it.

At the same time, while we should guard against a romanticization of their efforts — after all, they were hardly successful in creating a strong allegiance to the socialist vision — the efforts of American socialist activists during the early 1900s represent the flip side of such hegemonic practice, that is, the contestation of it. Within and outside the public school arena, these radicals contested the messages and practices of the public school curriculum and attempted to foster an allegiance to an alternative, more socially responsible body of knowledge and values. The particular curriculum for school children that they developed, then, also stands outside the selective tradition. Although many of the ideas presented in the Socialist Sunday School curriculum may seem outdated or even wrongheaded today, as a curricular package it comprises an ideological perspective of the social world which stands in contradistinction to the dominant messages of the public schools. It represents our most concrete indication of the educational views of American socialists, of the specific ideological messages that they believed were not but should be included in public school classrooms.

Former teachers at Commonwealth College, an adult residential labor college in Mena, Arkansas in the 1930s, observed that the basic premise — 'and you may call it a dogma if you will' — of workers' education was 'the acceptance of social revision as axiomatic'. While such education may turn out individuals with widely differing views regarding the exact nature and means of such revision, 'it will turn out no strikebreakers' (Koch and Koch, 1972, pp. 58–65). In essence, that is what most SSS proponents sought. Not that the children would become mindless followers of socialist doctrine when they reached adulthood but that they would comprehend the need for and seek to enlist in the battle against exploitation, prejudice, and social inequalities. Whatever the results or lack of results that can be claimed for the educational activities of American socialists during the Progressive era, they should not serve to obscure or obliterate from our consciousness the reasons for and nature of the efforts that were made.

### Notes

1 Although commonly referred to as 'Sunday schools', few of these Socialist Party-associated schools professed any religious or ethnic character at all.

They met on Sundays because that was the only day off for most workers. Also, several of the schools were actually known by other names (for example, the Children's Socialist Lyceum in Los Angeles and the Arm and Torch League in Cincinnati). No doubt local factors at particular times may have encouraged the adoption of different names. But all the schools referred to as 'Socialist Sunday schools' in this chapter were basically considered as such at the time.

2 Before and after 1900, various radical ethnic groups established their own children's schools. Most prominent were those initiated by the Germans, the Finns, and the Jews. The most significant difference between these schools and the Socialist Sunday schools discussed in this chapter was the former's adoption of an overtly ethnic character, which often included instruction in a second language. The Socialist Sunday schools adopted the general stand of the Party in eschewing such ethnic identification, which was viewed as counterproductive to worker solidarity. The radical ethnic schools are briefly discussed in Teitelbaum, 1985, especially chapter 4.

3 Shedd suggested that teachers in different grades could adapt the guidelines for appropriate use in their classes.

Kendrick Shedd's curriculum materials can be found in 'Rochester Socialist Sunday School Scrapbooks, Vol. I–IV', in the *Kendrick Philander Shedd Papers*, located at the University of Rochester, Rush Rhees Library, Rare Books Department (Special Collections), Rochester, New York. Other curriculum materials were found in a wide assortment of socialist newspapers, journals and other archival papers, and through interviews with former participants.

4 This passage is from a group of short 'red rebel' recitations, located in a folder of miscellaneous materials, in the *Kendrick Philander Shedd Papers*. The whole recitation went like this: 'I shall always remain a Red Rebel as long as there is any poverty in the world, and I will do all I can to abolish poverty and make this world a better place in which to live.'


## References


The following list does not include unauthored newspaper and journal publications, and archival papers, which are cited in the text and notes of this chapter.

ANYON, J. 'Ideology and United States history textbooks', *Harvard Educational Review*, 49, 1979, pp. 361–86.

APPLE, M.W. *Ideology and Curriculum*, London: Routledge and Kegan Paul, 1979.

APPLE, M.W. *Education and Power*, Boston, MA: Routledge and Kegan Paul, 1982.

BUHLE, M.J. *Women and American Socialism, 1870–1920*, Urbana, IL: University of Illinois Press, 1981.

CORNELL, F. *A History of the Rand School of Social Science — 1906 to 1956*, unpublished PhD dissertation, Columbia University, 1976.

CUROE, P.R.V. *Educational Attitudes and Policies of Organized Labor*, New York: Arno Press, 1969. (Originally published in 1926)

EAGLETON, T. *Marxism and Literary Criticism*, Berkeley, CA: University of California Press, 1976.

ELSON, R.M. *Guardians of Tradition: American Schoolbooks of the Nineteenth Century*, Lincoln: University of Nebraska Press, 1964.

FITZGERALD, F. *America Revised: History Schoolbooks in the Twentieth Century*, Boston, MA: Little, Brown and Co, 1979.

FREIRE, P. *Pedagogy of the Oppressed*, New York: Seabury Press, 1970.

FRIEBERT, E. *Autobiography*, unpublished manuscript, Milwaukee, WI, 1945.

FRIEBERT, J. and FRIEBERT, JR., E., Interview, Milwaukee, WI, 1981.

GIROUX, H.A. *Theory and Resistance in Education: A Pedagogy for the Opposition*, South Hadley, MA: Bergin and Garvey, 1983.

GOLDMAN, J.Y. Interview, Putnam Valley, New York, 1981.

GREENBERG, D.S. *Socialist Sunday School Curriculum*, New York: The Socialist Schools Publishing Association, 1913.

HEPBURN, M.A. 'What is our youth thinking?: Social-political attitudes of the 1980s', *Social Education*, 49, 1985, pp. 670–4.

KATZ, M.B. *Class, Bureaucracy, and Schools: The Illusion of Educational Change in America*, New York: Praeger, 1971.

KOCH, R. and KOCH, C. *Educational Commune: The Story of Commonwealth College*, New York: Schocken, 1972.

LESLIE, W.B. 'Coming of age in urban America: The socialist alternative, 1901–1920', *Teachers College Record*, 85, 1984, pp. 459–76.

LISTON, D. 'Have we explained the relationship between curriculum and capitalism? An analysis of the selective tradition', *Educational Theory*, 34, 1984, pp. 241–53.

McFARLAND, J.T., et al. (Eds) *The Encyclopedia of Sunday Schools and Religious Education, Volume III*, New York: Thomas Nelson and Sons, 1915.

MAILLY, B.H. 'The socialist schools of Greater New York', *Little Socialist Magazine For Boys and Girls*, 4, 1911, pp. 6–7.

MORGAN, H.W. (Ed.) *American Socialism 1900–1960*, Englewood Cliffs, NJ: Prentice-Hall, 1964.

MURRAY, R.K. *Red Scare: A Study in National Hysteria, 1919–1920*, New York: McGraw-Hill, 1955.

NEARING, S. *A Nation Divided (or Plutocracy Versus Democracy)*, Chicago: Socialist Party of the US, 1920.

PAWA, J.M. 'Workingmen and free schools in the nineteenth century: A comment on the Labor-education thesis', *History of Education Quarterly*, 11, 1971, pp. 287–302.

Kenneth Teitelbaum

REYNOLDS, D.A.T. and REYNOLDS, N.T. 'The roots of prejudice: California Indian history in school textbooks', in SPINDLER, G.D. (Ed.). *Education and Cultural Process: Toward an Anthropology of Education*, New York: Holt, Rinehart and Winston, 1974.

SADKER, M.P. and SADKER, D.M. *Sex Equity Handbook for Schools*, New York: Longman, 1982.

SCHAEFER, R.J. *Educational Activities of the Garment Unions, 1890–1948: A Study in Workers' Education in the International Ladies' Garment Workers' Union and the Amalgamated Clothing Workers of America in New York City*, unpublished PhD dissertation, Columbia University, 1951.

SHANNON, D.A. *The Socialist Party of America*, Chicago: Quadrangle, 1955.

SIMONS, M.W. 'Vocational education', *Progressive Journal of Education*, 1, 1908, pp. 1–8.

*Socialist Party Congressional Campaign Book*, Chicago: Socialist Party of America, 1914.

SPRING, J.H. *Education and the Rise of the Corporate State*, Boston, MA: Beacon Press, 1972.

TAXEL, J. 'Justice and cultural conflict: Racism, sexism and instructional materials', *Interchange*, 9, 1978/79, pp. 56–84.

TAXEL, J. 'The outsiders of the American revolution: The selective tradition in children's fiction', *Interchange*, 12, 1981, pp. 206–29.

TEITELBAUM, K. *Schooling for 'Good Rebels': Socialist Education for Children in the United States, 1900–1920*, unpublished PhD dissertation, University of Wisconsin-Madison, 1985.

TEITELBAUM, K. *Citizenship Education, The Socialist Version: A Case Study in American History*, paper presented at the annual meeting of the American Educational Research Association, San Francisco, April 1986.

TEITELBAUM, K. and REESE, W.J. 'American socialist pedagogy and experimentation in the progressive era: The Socialist Sunday School', *History of Education Quarterly*, 23, 1983, pp. 429–55.

THOMPSON, C.D. *The Constructive Program of Socialism*, Milwaukee: Social-Democratic Publishing, 1908.

THOMPSON, E.P. 'The politics of theory', in SAMUEL, R. (Ed.). *People's History and Socialist Theory*, London: Routledge and Kegan Paul, 1981.

TIEN, J.S. *The Educational Theories of American Socialists, 1900–1920*, unpublished PhD dissertation, Michigan State University, 1972.

TYACK, D.B. *The One Best System: A History of American Urban Education*, Cambridge, MA: Harvard University Press, 1976.

VIOLAS, P.C. *The Training of the Urban Working Class: A History of Twentieth Century American Education*, Chicago: Rand McNally, 1978.

WEINSTEIN, J. *The Decline of Socialism in America, 1912–1925*, New York: Vintage, 1969.

WILLIAMS, R. *The Long Revolution*, Harmondsworth, England: Penguin, 1961.

WILLIAMS, R. *Marxism and Literature*, Oxford, England: Oxford University Press, 1977.

## 11 Harold Rugg and the Reconstruction of the Social Studies Curriculum: The Treatment of the 'Great War' in his Textbook Series

*Herbert M. Kliebard and Greg Wegner*

### Abstract

In the period between 1929 and 1939, the social studies textbook series developed by Harold O. Rugg enjoyed wide popularity in the United States. In contrast to other social studies textbooks, its content was distinctly leftist in terms of political orientation.

The outbreak of World War Two combined with organized conservative opposition to the textbooks diminished the success of Rugg's work. Nevertheless, it remains a remarkable, if only temporary, example of a successful reconstruction of a school subject both in terms of form and content.

If one were to judge the changes in the American curriculum from the turn of the century to the present by the extent to which certain subjects actually replaced others or by the addition of major new subjects to the curriculum, one is likely to find only moderate alterations. From a list of subjects alone, one might note, for example, that what was once a heavy emphasis on Latin and a lesser emphasis on Greek has been replaced by the study of modern foreign languages. Perhaps the single most dramatic curriculum change in the course of the twentieth century was the massive entry of vocational education in its various manifestations into the school curriculum accompanied by such satellite additions as business English and commercial arithmetic. It would be misleading, however, to judge the extent of the transformation in the American curriculum by such readily visible changes alone. Perhaps the most significant, albeit the most subtle, changes occurred within the context of some of the individual subject areas. English, for example, in 1900 was not the same subject that is taught under the same name in the 1980s.

One of the most significant of these internal transformations involves not simply a name change (from history and other individual disciplines to social studies) but a massive reconceptualization of a subject area. The reconstruction of the social studies took place essentially in two stages. One involved the work of Thomas Jesse Jones of Hampton Institute during the first two decades of this century to redirect the social studies along practical lines in keeping with the dominant curriculum doctrine of social efficiency. It was that effort that constituted the first serious challenge to the traditional academic emphasis in the teaching of the social studies and made civic virtue and efficiently functioning individuals the dominant ideal. The second line of reform, proceeding in a very different direction was spearheaded by the work of Harold Rugg, beginning in the 1920s and extending into the early 1940s, to change both the form and the ideological direction of the social studies. His great ambition was to create a fused social studies out of the several individual disciplines that had traditionally characterized its presence in the curriculum in an earlier era and at the same time to inject into that study a vision of a new America and indeed a new world. That effort reached its peak in the 1930s with the growing popularity of his textbook series, *Man in a Changing Society*.

Rugg's career virtually represents in miniature the panorama of educational ideologies that characterized twentieth-century curriculum reform in America: scientific curriculum making, child-centered education, and, most notably, social reconstructionism. Rugg's first major change in direction occurred when he abandoned his original studies in civil engineering to undertake a doctorate in education at the University of Illinois studying with William Chandler Bagley. After being awarded the degree in 1915, he accepted an appointment in the Faculty of Education at the University of Chicago, which, under the leadership Charles Hubbard Judd, aspired to become the citadel of the scientific study of education. Six years later, now an Associate Professor at Teachers College, Columbia University and an educational psychologist for its Lincoln School, he undertook a massive campaign to reconstruct the social studies.

Although Rugg had long been interested in the social studies as a school subject, his particular ideas on how it should be reconstructed were undoubtedly influenced by his new associations in New York. Rugg himself notes that his move to Teachers College, Columbia University represented 'a sharp turning point in my life marking the beginning of a new period — many years of unlearning and an exciting search for understanding' (1941, p. 186). Something of this transformation in Rugg's thinking had been foreshadowed two years earlier by his contact with Arthur Upham Pope, a remarkable intellectual who had given up a career as a professor of philosophy to devote himself to the study of Persian art, eventually becoming one of the world's foremost scholars on that subject. It was Rugg's meeting with Pope in 1918 (while working on an army project) and their later friendship that first led Rugg into a new domain of social criticism and ultimately to take stock of the 'one long orgy of tabulation' (*ibid*, p. 182) that had been so central to his earlier work. He was later to reflect on 'how seldom most of us fact finders really found the "right" facts' (*ibid*, p. 183). His removal to Teachers College and his associations with New York intellectuals and artists helped nourish the seed that Pope had planted. In Rugg's words, he 'left [Charles Hubbard] Judd's ordered team of "scientists" and joined [Otis W.] Caldwell's company of creative individualists' (*ibid*, p. 188).

Like Pope, many of these intellectuals with whom Rugg now associated combined left-wing social criticism with avant-garde artistic interests. The new humanism of Waldo Frank, the unflinching pacifism of Randolph Bourne, the reinterpretations of America's literary traditions as advanced by Van Wyck Brooks seemed to mesh in Rugg's mind with artistic trends that were being advanced at that time by such innovators in the arts as Georgia O'Keefe and Alfred Stieglitz, who were then among the Greenwich Village 'bohemians' with whom Rugg came into contact in his new setting. Malcolm Cowley, one of Rugg's New York contemporaries once defined bohemia as 'a revolt against certain features of industrial capitalism' (1951, p. 55) which, in its New York manifestation, fought a running battle with *The Saturday Evening Post*, then considered the epitome of the 'business-Christian ethic' (p. 61). By 1920, Cowley reports, Greenwich Village had become not simply an off-beat way of life, but 'a system of ideas' that included among its fundamental tenets the idea of the salvation of the child, the idea of self-expression, the idea of female equality, and the idea of the world as a changing place (pp. 60–1). The influence of Rugg's friendships with these New York intellectuals led him to reevaluate his earlier commitment to a 'science' of education in the direction of a new appreciation of creative artistry combined with social criticism. Were it not for the stimulating new associations that Rugg found in his new environment, his work in general, and, in particular, his attempt to create a new social studies would surely have taken a decidedly different turn.

Early in the 1920s, Rugg (1921a) seems to have begun to consider a reconstruction of the form of the social studies curriculum as well as its content. In particular, he conceived of the idea that a social studies course could be developed around 'the great principles or generalizations in history, economics, industry geography, etc.' (p. 692). These principles, of course, were consistent with the ideas that he found in the New York intellectual environment. Additionally, in Rugg's mind, the existence of these separate subjects as representative of the social studies was a prime example of unwarranted fragmentation in the curriculum. As against such rigid compartmentalization in the organization of the curriculum, Rugg held out the ideal of a unified social studies that would be constructed around the major generalizations as enunciated by leaders in various branches of the social studies:

> Rather than have teachers attempt the almost impossible task of correlating history, geography, civics, economics and sociology (taught as separate subjects), we postulate that more effective outcomes will be secured by weaving together lesson by lesson the facts, movements, conditions, that depend upon one another and that can be fully comprehended only when they are woven together (1921b, p. 127).

Rugg was thus searching for a way of conceptualizing the social studies that would integrate them rather than have them appear in the school curriculum as a disjointed series of separate entities.

One early manifestation of the direction he was to take was reflected in his response to an address delivered by Henry Johnson to the Teachers College faculty. Johnson spoke on behalf of the American Historical Association and the Joint Committee on History and Education for Citizenship, one of several bodies convened by the American Historical Society to explore improvement in the history curriculum. Those committees had been set working intermittently on the history curriculum ever since the Committee of Seven delivered its recommendation is 1899 (Report, 1900, pp. 3–21). The brunt of Rugg's (1921b) criticism of the Joint Committee's recommendations was that the defense of the traditional subject matter triad of history, civics, and geography by the American Historical Association evaded any real reform in the social studies. Reflecting his early faith in a science of curriculum-making, he chided the Joint Committee for making proposals 'without controlled and measured experimentation' (pp. 184–9). But along with Rugg's call for the use of scientific method in the creation of the social studies curriculum there was a strongly voiced expression of need for more activity on the part of children with less compartmentalization in the curriculum. Significantly, Rugg also cited 'social worth' as the basis from which curriculum makers could develop materials for the classroom in light of the vital problems of contemporary life. Rugg's conception of what was socially worthy put him directly at odds with other major curriculum leaders of the period such as Franklin Bobbitt, W.W. Charters and David Snedden.

Some of those ideas on the reconstruction of the social studies curriculum may have been fermenting in Rugg's mind since 1916 when Rugg and Bagley undertook an examination of twenty-three American history textbooks used in junior high schools. Not surprisingly, Bagley and Rugg discovered that textbook writers placed a heavy emphasis on political and military affairs. In combination with the growing standardization of the elementary textbooks, they felt that the social studies were presenting a narrow focus on political developments at the expense of larger social and economic issues in world affairs. Their study concluded with a statement on the implications of the nationalistic view of history in the social studies curriculum:

> The fact is that the obvious influence of the elementary textbook in history today is distinctly toward the promotion of nationalism through giving to all the pupils who reach the seventh and eighth years of school life a common stock of information regarding national development. The important question at the present juncture would seem to center on the desirability or undesirability of making the development of nationalism the primary function of seventh and eighth grade history. This is an issue that is fraught with consequences far too fundamental to be settled by any single group of individuals (Bagley and Rugg, 1916, pp. 58–9).

It was this kind of deficiency that Rugg later sought to correct in his own Junior High School Course which was to gain widespread acceptance in the 1930s.

In 1921–22, Rugg embarked on an ambitious effort to replace the tame and frankly nationalistic social studies textbooks of the day with a series that would embody the basic principles of social worth as to content and integration of previously separated fields in terms of form. The actual task of extracting the needed generalizations from the works of the leading political and social progressives of the day fell to his doctoral student, Neal Billings. From a list of works that were written by what Rugg called 'frontier thinkers', Billings (1929) identified no less than 888 generalizations from such diverse disciplines as sociology, economics, political science, and geography. History, as a discipline was not mentioned by name, although the works of Charles Beard as well as other historians appeared on the final list (*ibid*, pp. 99–209).

One of Rugg's principal points of attack on the traditional history curriculum centered on the memorization of specific facts. It was not Rugg's intention to ignore historical facts. On the contrary, the Rugg social studies curriculum sought to maintain a strong continuity with other programs in terms of building up a mastery of concepts, facts and meanings (cf. Rugg, 1929, with Burnam and Smith, 1926, pp. 273–5 as cited in Wilson, 1933, pp. 162–8). What placed the Rugg's series apart from the other curricula of the day was the special emphasis given to the relationships among the facts, a process which Rugg felt was definitively expressed by what he liked to call generalizing, 'that process of recognizing in a series of situations, events, objects, etc. one or more characters, traits or items that are alike, common to all' (Billings, 1929, p. 34; Rugg and Mendenhall, 1929, p. 19). If repetition was to play any role in social studies education, as Rugg told the American Historical Association in 1921, it was to be in making the interconnections between the great economic, social and political laws, movements and causal relations (Rugg, 1921b, p. 188). Thinking was something a student needed to practice, and the generalizations were presented as the 'glue' in teaching higher thought processes.

The treatment of the Great War in his textbook series provides one dramatic illustration of Rugg's attempt to rescue the teaching of the social studies from the dry memorization of facts on one hand and, on the other, to infuse socially progressive ideas into the curriculum. The starting point for that task was the key generalizations on the subject that Billings had culled from the works of the 'frontier thinkers'. In this regard, Rugg's approach to curriculum design marked another sharp departure from what had become conventional wisdom among the scientific curriculum makers such as

Bobbitt and Charters. They sought to reform the traditional curriculum through the technique they most commonly called activity analysis, an approach borrowed directly from Frederick Winslow Taylor and the widely admired scientific management movement. The basis of activity analysis was first to create a catalog of actual human activity groups under functional categories such as citizenship activities or leisure activities. The minute behaviors, presumably collected through scientific observation, would then become the objectives of the curriculum. In this way, the scientific curriculum makers argued, the teaching of the various subjects could be rescued from the dry and inert teaching that characterized the typical academic curriculum. By basing what was taught on actual observed behavior, the curriculum presumably could be made directly functional in terms of the lives of students.

Rugg recognized, however, that basing the curriculum on the actual activities that people were already engaging in would most likely lead in the direction of a social status quo. He reacted against the idea that the curriculum should primarily be concerned with preparing youth to perform efficiently in predetermined adult roles. Instead, he sought to equip the next generation with the cutting edge of ideas and principles, ideas that Billings had extracted from the principal works of major scholars. In this way, rather than a curriculum tied to the world as it was, Rugg sought to equip the youth of the nation with the concepts and generalizations that could transform existing social conditions.

## Rugg's Treatment of World War I

Inevitably, Rugg's left-wing political commitments found their way into the social-studies textbook series. To some extent, this was dictated by the choice of 'frontier thinkers' in the first place and to some extent by the way in which Rugg chose to integrate the generalizations into the overall treatment of the various topics he included in his textbook series. In few other areas was Rugg's protest against existing social conditions greater than in relationship to militarism and war. In particular, Rugg felt compelled to challenge the student's thinking on the legacy of World War I and to call attention to the prospects for human survival through international cooperation. (Billings, 1929, pp. 122, 155 and 174–6).

In order to illustrate the prevalence of certain concepts in the 888 generalizations, Billings calculated a combined 'cause' and 'result' score for each concept appearing more than once among the mass of generalizations. The concepts, Billings claimed, 'must be built up' in order to make effective use of generalizations in the thinking process. The building to which Billings referred involved a series of calculations in which each concept, either as a cause or effect factor in the historical process, was assessed one point for each time it appeared in either the generalizations or was mentioned more than once in books written by the 'frontier thinkers' (*ibid*, pp. 242–5). Given this system of calculation, out of a total of 505 concepts, war ranked twenty-first, military conquest fifty-seventh, and militarism seventy-second. Interestingly, war was viewed more often as a cause than a result in the generalizations, whereas the reverse was true for military conquest. Militarism, understandably, was most likely to appear in the Billings scheme as a cause for war (see generalization 589 in Billings, p. 175).

Billings's own categories of war and international relations, imperialism, diplomacy, boundaries and international trade are used below to group ideas taken from the 'frontier thinkes'. The source of the generalization is included along with the number of the generalization (Billings, 1929, p. 24; Rugg and Mendenhall, 1929, p. 19):

### War and International Relations

592. 'Other things being equal, that society will stand the best chance of survival which has the largest population.' C.A. Ellwood, *Sociology and Modern Social Problems*, p. 168.

593. 'Political coordination and war are alternative in determining the relations which chief population groups must sustain to each other in order mutually to satisfy their wants by access to resources that only one or the other can supply.' Isaiah Bowman, *The New World: Problems in Political Geography*, p. 59.

594. 'Climate, no doubt, is the key to many of the invasions and conquests which have bent the current of history again and again.' Edward A. Ross, *Principles of Sociology*, p. 68.

595. 'The causes of war are many, some underlying factors leading to war are: Psychological factors of human nature — hatred, rivalries, ambitions and the like. Graham Wallas, *Human Nature in Politics*, p. 16.

> Ellsworth Huntington, *Principles of Human Geography*, p. 98.
> R.H. Tawney, *The Acquisitive Society*, p. 42.
> Ellen Semple, *Influences of Geographic Environment*, p. 552.
> Isaiah Bowman, *New World Problems in Political Geography*, pp. 1, 11, 305.
> Ignorance of past history.
> Harold Stearns, *Civilization in the United States*, p. 307.
> Struggle for food supply.
>> Ellwood, p. 48.
>> Semple, p. 586.
> Increase in population.
>> Ellwood, p. 48.
>> Bowman, p. 502.
> Tariff tinkering.
>> R.T. Ely, *Outlines of Economics*, p. 360.
> Imposition or attempted imposition of ideas and power of one people on another.
>> Bowman, p. 565.

596. 'A treaty which is not signed by the representatives of the people whom the treaty affects does not of itself settle disorder or kill political ambitions.' Bowman, p. 61.

597. 'In general, the more nearly matched are two combatants, the more prolonged and exhausting their conflict is likely to be.' Ross, p. 178.

598. 'The consciousness of a common purpose in mankind, or even the acknowledgement that such a common purpose is possible, would alter the face of world politics at once.' Wallas, p. 306.


*Imperialism*


587. 'Nations impelled with a desire to secure markets gradually absorb weak countries.' Bowman, p. 564.

588. 'If leaders can get their people to believe that they are hemmed in by enemies and that openings everywhere invite attack, and to become sufficiently 'jumpy' about

it, they can impose heavy taxes for large armies that are not meant for the defense of the country, but for the aggrandizement and the satisfaction of greed.' Bowman, p. 348.

589. 'Militarism strangles liberal political development and strengthens imperialistic tendencies.' Ross, p. 684.

### Diplomacy

583. 'Secrecy in the conduct of diplomacy is vital in a world where each nation is suspicious of its neighbors and obliged by its fears to try to discover their plans while concealing its own.' James Bryce, *Modern Democracies*, I, p. 54.

### Boundaries

449. 'War is often followed by a change in boundaries.' Semple, p. 183.

### International Trade

149. 'Famines, wars and scientific discoveries will make some trades expand and others dwindle.' Sidney Webb, *Industrial Democracy*, p. 745.

177. 'War often curtails the capacity to export goods and increases the demand for imports.' Ely, p. 353.

These generalizations constituted a clear departure from the predominant political emphasis on human conflict which characterizes much history textbook writing to this day. To the extent that Rugg was able to incorporate the generalizations in his textbook series, the multifaceted interpretations of historical process inherent in the generalizations on war conveyed to young readers that the importance of World War I in human history extended far beyond the assassination at Sarajevo and the political settlement at Versailles into the realms of international trade, imperialism, diplomatic relations and propaganda (p. 588).

Since Rugg was especially concerned with developing problems from contemporary history, it is not surprising that World War I, rather than earlier — wars, was the most frequently used time frame in which to communicate the war generalizations. Of the nineteen generalizations, seventeen were developed within the context of the Great War. Of the two remaining generalizations, Ellwood's statement (592) relating societal survival to population size was apparently not included in any part of the Rugg series. Ross's comment (594) on the influence of climate on invasion and conquest was integrated by Rugg in his brief account of Napoleon's defeat in Russia during the winter of 1812–13, but was not included in any section on World War I (Rugg, 1932, pp. 300–1).

Rugg's treatment of the Great War gave scant attention to portraying the details of battle strategy or even the names of the more well-known clashes. On the other hand, he did take considerable pains to list the financial and human costs of the war. Of all the texts, Rugg devoted the most space to World War I in Volume Two, *Changing Civilizations in the Modern World*. It was in this text that we find the greatest contrast in coverage between the military and cause-and-effect dimensions of 'the war to end all wars'. In a twenty-six page chapter entitled, 'The Interdependence of Europe in 1914', Rugg discussed the major causes leading to World War I. In the next chapter, 'How the World War Changed Europe', eight pages (363–71) were devoted to the military phase of the war followed by a much longer study of the costs of the war and the European recovery in thirty-nine pages (372–411). Furthermore, Volume II developed the highest number of war generalizations pertaining to World War I than any other text in the junior high curriculum.

The cause-and-effect dimensions of Rugg's interpretation of World War I, as evidenced in the generalizations, were incorporated in various degrees in three other texts. Invariably, some of these same generalizations were also expressed in connection with other historical conflicts as well (see, for example, Rugg's sections on the American Civil War in 1930b, pp. 226–58 and the Bismarckian Wars in Rugg, 1932, pp. 120–5).

In terms of coverage alone, the Rugg texts placed special emphasis on three interrelated causes of World War I. One (595), largely psychological, focused on 'hatred, rivalries, ambitions and the like'; the second (583) was predominantly political and involved secret alliances; and the third (587) grew out of economic pressures to secure markets. As complex and difficult as Billings's task was in imposing some kind of order on the multitude of generalizations, it should not be surprising that his classification scheme appears naive here and there in treating some factors as separate from the causes of the war, i.e., the competition to secure world markets and secret diplomacy. Nevertheless, Billings's work in extracting the generalizations from the work of leading social scientists and historians constituted the basis of Rugg's effort to the develop an integration of the social studies curriculum.

The meteoric rise to power by the fascist states in Europe and Asia prompted Rugg to reassess his treatment of the boundary provisions and war reparations included in the Treaty of Versailles (see the Semple generalization 149). Rugg apparently felt that the Treaty of Versailles was worth only two paragraphs in Volume Two, the first book in the series to introduce students to international relations. When the first edition of Volume Six was published two years later, in 1932, Rugg expanded his treatment of the treaty provisions to five pages. Some four years after Hitler's *Machtergreifung*, Rugg published his second edition of Volume Six, but this time he interjected a prologue to Versailles. One notes a tone of urgency in his writing: 'There seems to be no doubt that the great powers, backed by the largest peace-time armaments in the history of the world, are now lining up for a world struggle. In the midst of this tension, which seems to herald a Second World War ... democratic countries are asking: What will happen to our way-of-life? Can democracy survive?' (Rugg, 1937, p. 678).

The survival of democracy in Rugg's mind was directly related to the existence of an informed citizenry in both war and peace. The reality that political systems were prone to using false propaganda in order to garner support for the furtherance of war aims was an especially critical issue for Rugg. The Bowman generalization (588), which indicated that governments can manipulate their populations to support war, represented a major theme in the Rugg social studies curriculum. In his fourth volume, *A History of Government and Culture*, Rugg brought to his readers one of the most direct attacks on the conduct of the United States government in the days leading up to the American entry into the war:

The American people, accustomed to peace, were educated to support war. Thus, a people who had struggled for nearly 300 years for democracy, thus voluntarily gave up much of their liberty and many of their rights. How could such an attitude come about in a democratic country in which the rights and liberty of the individual were such sacred things? It came about because the government conducted a great campaign of

> education to convince the people that our country confronted
> a great crisis and that *while war continued* the government
> must be given complete power. So with the understanding
> that it should be only *while the war continued* the people
> submitted and gave the government dictatorial powers over
> their very lives. (Rugg, 1931a, p. 559)

There is in much of Rugg's textbook writing a kind of Jefferso-
nian distrust for government, especially those governments which
sought an increase in war powers at the expense of domestic policy or
improved foreign relations (Rugg and Mendenhall, 1930, pp. 226–
58). His social criticism also extended to the political institutions that
encouraged the headlong drive toward colonization and market
security without giving consideration to the implications for international economic competition and impending war (Rugg, 1930a,
pp. 244–5). From Rugg's standpoint, wars in textbooks could not
be dismissed merely as a result of only one set of circumstances. A
complicated interplay of social, political and economic forces were at
work. Billings and Rugg thought that by integrating the social studies
generalizations into the text series, students would be better able to
understand the nature of this complexity (Billings, 1929, pp. 7–17).

However, the seventeen generalizations related to war included
in the six volumes of the junior high schools series do not by
themselves convey a definitive notion of Rugg's outlook on the
long-term processes underlying historical change. Although not an
avowed Marxist or socialist, Rugg also integrated the concepts of
class struggle and property ownership into *Man and a Changing
Society* (see especially the social studies generalizations on poverty
and accumulation of capital in Billings, 1929, pp. 141–5). His treatment of the Industrial Revolution, for example, was based on this
kind of interpretation (Rugg and Mendenhall, 1929, pp. 84–102).
Indeed, the interrelatedness of class and property ownership remained for Rugg very much a part of his conception of war and
international relations even though the connection was not explicitly
made in the seventeen generalizations. What caused World War I in
Rugg's eyes was not an isolated constellation of political forces. The
basic causes for the 'war to end all wars' had historical antecedents in
much earlier generations, all of whom were tied to the struggle over
property rights and social class (Rugg, 1932, pp. 188–90).

The sixth volume of the series, for example, included a collection
of six drawings entitled, 'the age-long struggle for property'. The
reality of conflict over ownership was portrayed by a pack of wolves

competing for the carcass of a rabbit, followed by a confrontation between two cavemen over rights to a woman, the attack by ancient Persian armies, the Battle of the Spanish Armada, the overthrow of the British Crown and American Indians attacking a Conestoga wagon. In a related reading, Rugg summed up his view of historical process for readers with history being defined as 'the story of men settling the age-old question: How should property be owned?' (1932, p. 189).

Bagley and Rugg (1916) had asserted in their textbook study that the common person was usually omitted from the pages of a majority of history texts because of an undue emphasis on events and what they called 'Hall of Fame' personalities (p. 58). Rugg's series sought to redress that imbalance. In *Changing Civilizations in the Modern World*, Rugg introduced a section on the conditions in Europe on the eve of war in 1914 in which he stressed the essential unity of human interests. Most of the population from the belligerent countries, he wrote, did not want war and cared little for the schemes of the major power brokers in expanding foreign markets of hiking arms budgets. Although this interpretation might be regarded by some historians (cf. Fischer, 1967, pp. 29–37) as too simplistic, one can not deny that Rugg did challenge the social studies student to consider the impact of war beyond the treaty obligations and the state of contending armies. Never to be forgotten, if the research group at Lincoln School had anything to say about it, were the countless masses of humanity who 'were not especially concerned with the building of the British Empire, nor particularly excited about France's desire to regain Alsace-Lorraine, nor especially keen about Germany's growing control of trade. Most of the people,' according to Rugg, 'were interested in steady jobs, in good wages, in vacations and in good homes' (Rugg, 1930a, pp. 361–2).

With the memory of the Great War still fresh in his mind, Rugg challenged his young readers with the highly controversial historical problem of war guilt. After presenting statistics on the increase in expenditures for arms production in Russia, France, Great Britain and Germany from 1905–1914, Rugg stressed that the vast outlays in weaponry were made possible by the imposition of a staggering tax program 'upon the peasants and artisans' with the blessings of all four governments. Furthermore, the biggest enemy of international co-operation and economic interdependence-secret diplomacy — was practiced by the Great Powers and thus gave more credence to the notion that the responsibility for World War I was not rightfully placed in the German camp alone as the war guilt clause in the Treaty of Versailles suggested (Billings, 1929, p. 174; Rugg, 1932, p. 384).

In many ways, the Rugg textbook project build on the legacy of mass destruction that was World War I in order to warn about the likelihood of another, even more devastating, conflict. Rugg was especially inventive in terms of integrating controversial cartoons into his texts in order to make his points clear. In the 1932 edition of *Changing Governments and Cultures*, one cartoon illustrated public frustration with war as a perceived solution to the international chaos unleashed by unchecked nationalism. In the same volume, another cartoon suggested that the world of 1930 was largely out of touch with the lessons of the Great War. Seven years later, when Rugg published his second edition of volume six, the consequences of an unbridled arms race were brought to the fore by the increasing power of fascist states. One cartoon portrayed the end of civilization with a boat sinking under the ominous weight of armaments and carrying with it to the depths the dove of peace (Rugg, 1932, p. 670; Rugg, 1937, p. 15).

In no other segment of the Rugg Junior High School Program were students challenged to think about their own attitudes toward the legacy of the Great War more than in the workbooks accompanying the six volumes of text. The workbook for *Changing Civilizations* was especially noteworthy in this regard. In the very first problem, students were asked whether each item below elicited an agreeable or disagreeable impression (Rugg and Mendenhall, 1930, p. xiii):

'How Do You Feel About These Things?'
_____ 1. 'America First'
_____ 2. League of Nations
_____ 3. Germans
_____ 4. Army
_____ 5. Jews
_____ 6. Russians
_____ 7. Military preparedness
_____ 8. Disarmament
_____ 9. Foreigners
_____ 10. Free speech
_____ 11. American Legion
_____ 12. Interdependence
_____ 13. Tariff
_____ 14. European nations
_____ 15. World Court
_____ 16. Chinese

_____ 17. 'Asia for the Asiatics'
_____ 18. Negroes
_____ 19. Revolution
_____ 20. Philippine independence

In all of the teacher guides, Rugg and another one of his students, James Mendenhall, included a discussion of ten psychological principles of learning underpinning the entire program. According to the first principle, the pupil 'learns by active assimilation'. The keynotes of the 'older formal school' were rote learning, order and attention, they said. Students, Rugg claimed, were rarely asked what they thought about contemporary issues in this stultifying atmosphere. 'What does the book say?' was the dominant question of the school day. To Rugg and Mendenhall, restraint and repression in the social studies classroom would be replaced by 'guided growth in the ability to reason'. As the above list of terms illustrated, the intertwined issues of war and peace were very much a part of the active schooling advocated by Rugg in the workbooks. To reinforce this orientation, Rugg presented students with an opinion survey relating to issues they would later confront in the text. Among the questions in the survey were those dealing with student impressions of the German people, the lessons of World War I, the best way to settle international disputes and the war guilt problem. Clearly, an attempt was being made to involve the students in thinking 'beyond the textbook' about issues which were then and still are controversial (Rugg and Mendenhall, 1929, pp. 2–13; Rugg and Mendenhall, 1930, pp. xiii–xiv).

The seventeen social studies generalizations relating to war, colored as they were by the sweeping changes wrought by the collapse of thrones and empires in 1918, constituted an ominous warning for the future when framed in the Rugg curriculum. In one of the workbooks, an eerie cartoon by Hendrick W. Van Loon reflected Bowman's generalization on the manipulation of public opinion. Death is personified as a military drummer leading humanity to a great precipice.

Rugg (1931c) once remarked to his colleagues that 'the schools were indeed the chief contestants in the battle between humanitarian international cooperation and selfish nationalism' (p. 299). The seventeen generalizations on war and international relations, diplomacy, boundaries, international trade and imperialism which Rugg and his research group at Lincoln School integrated into the texts and workbooks of *Man and His Changing Society*, built on the historical friction between these two forces. Looking back on the generalizations yields a curious reflection on the legacy left by the Great War to some of the 'frontier thinkers' whose works were published in the 1920s.

Through Wallas's 'consciousness of a common purpose for mankind' (598) and Bowman's call for political coordination as a viable alternative to war in the international pursuit for vital economic resources (593), Rugg's drive for world peace through the League of Nations was delivered, a theme prominently expressed in at least three of his textbooks. The influence of Bowman's thought is apparent in the treatment accorded to the Treaty of Versailles, as well as Rugg's sharp attack on the American government's propaganda activities in galvanizing public opinion. The tensions arising out of the competition for markets and colonies also did not escape Rugg's attention. In his wholehearted support of President Woodrow Wilson's call for open covenants between nations, he included extensive text material on Bryce's observation concerning secret diplomacy, one of the long-term causes of World War I that Rugg especially wished to convey to his young readers.

## The Rugg Textbook Legacy

The Rugg series enjoyed a huge success for at least a decade. Between 1929 when the first volume was published by Ginn and Company and 1939, 1,317,960 copies of the text were sold and an astounding, 2,687,000 copies of the workbooks (Winters, 1968). Conservative opposition to the series gained some momentum in the late 1930s, and, ironically, America's entry into World War II late in 1941 made Rugg's criticisms of the Great War unpopular and perhaps even irrelevant. The post-war period, dominated as it was by the ill-fated life adjustment movement, marked a return to a social studies curriculum keyed merely to efficient functioning of citizens much as the early scientific curriculum makers had advocated. An undercurrent of social protest remained but did not enjoy the popularity it achieved in the pre-war depression era.

Once life adjustment education collapsed under the withering attack by academicians charging anti-intellectualism in the curriculum, the teaching of social studies like that of other subjects became more discipline than problem oriented, although the high-school course commonly called Problems of Democracy was accorded James B. Conant's prestigious endorsement in his *American High School*

*Today* (1958). The subsequent work of Edwin Fenton, while deploring the isolated teaching of facts, turned to a search for structure within fields like history as the basis of organizing the curriculum in the social studies rather than toward generalizations that cut cross subject-matter lines. In 1979, Frances Fitzgerald (1979) issued a strong indictment of the history textbooks then in use. In particular, she castigated social-studies textbook authors for the blandness of their treatment of critical social issues, one of the very problems that Rugg sought to redress in his own textbook series.

One would be tempted to conclude that the Rugg series and his incorporation of an indictment of the causes of war was merely an aberration in the development of the social studies over the course of the twentieth century. After a brief moment in the sun, Rugg's dream of an integration of the social studies around social science generalizations that embodied the thinking of major social critics seems to have evaporated leaving few vestiges. The fact, however, that Fitzgerald's book received such widespread attention is some indication that there may be a strong residue of sentiment for Rugg's position. The popular perception that so-called pendulum swings do occur in terms of educational ideologies sometimes obscures the fact that no single ideology becomes completely dominant even for a relatively brief period. Fundamental ideological positions, like Rugg's effort to tie the work of the schools to a new social vision, are not so much extinguished as submerged. Just as the Great Depression created a climate conducive to the idea that the social studies should focus on critical social problems, so may new social conditions such as the threat of nuclear war prompt a new consideration of the extent to which the social studies curriculum should become the forum for the consideration of the great problems that society faces.

## References

BAGLEY, W.C. and RUGG, H.O. 'The content of history as taught in the seventh and eighth grades: An analysis of typical school textbooks', *University of Illinois School of Education Bulletin*, 16, 1916, pp. 5–59.

BILLINGS, N. *A Determination of Generalizations Basic to the Social Studies Curriculum*, Baltimore, MD: Warwick, 1929.

CONANT, J.B. *The American High School Today*, New York: McGraw-Hill, 1958.

COWLEY, M. *Exile's Return*, New York: Viking, 1951.

FISCHER, F. *Germany's Aims in the First World War*, New York: Norton, 1967.

FITZGERALD, F. *America Revised: History Textbooks in the Twentieth Century*, Boston, MA: Little Brown, 1979.

REPORT OF THE COMMITTEE OF SEVEN. *The Study of History in Schools*, New York: Macmillan, 1900.

RUGG, H.O. 'Needed changes in committee procedures for reconstructing the social studies', *Elementary School Journal*, 21, 1921a, pp. 688–702.

RUGG, H.O. 'How shall we reconstruct the social studies curriculum', *The Historical Outlook*, 12, 1921b, pp. 184–9.

RUGG, H.O. *An Introduction to American Civilization*, I, New York: Ginn, 1929.

RUGG, H.O. *Changing Civilizations in the Modern World*, II, New York: Ginn, 1930a.

RUGG, H.O. *A History of American Civilization*, III, New York: Ginn, 1930b.

RUGG, H.O. *A History of American Government and Culture*, IV, New York: Ginn, 1931a.

RUGG, H.O. *An Introduction to the Problems of American Culture*, V, New York: Ginn, 1931b.

RUGG, H.O. Education and international understanding. *Progressive Education*, 8, 1931c, pp. 294–302.

RUGG, H.O. *Changing Governments and Changing Cultures*, VI, New York: Ginn, 1932 and 1937.

RUGG, H.O. *That Men May Understand: An American in the Long Armistice*, New York: Doubleday, 1941.

RUGG, H.O. and MENDENHALL, J. E. *Teacher's Guide for an Introduction to American Civilization*, New York: Ginn, 1929.

RUGG, H.O. and MENDENHALL, J.E. *Pupil's Workbook to Accompany Changing Civilizations in the Modern World*, New York: Ginn, 1930.

WILSON, H.E. *The Fusion of the Social Studies in Junior High Schools*, Cambridge, MA: Harvard University Press, 1933.

WINTERS, E. 'Harold Rugg and education for social reconstruction', PhD dissertation, University of Wisconsin, Madison, 1968.

### Books by Frontier Thinkers

BOWMAN, I. *The New World: Problems in Political Geography*, New York: World Book, 1926.

BRYCE, J. *Modern Democracies*, I New York: Macmillan, 1921.

ELLWOOD, C.A. *Sociology and Modern Social Problems*, New York: American Book, 1922.

ELY, R.T. *Outlines of Economics*, New York: Macmillan, 1920.

HUNTINGTON, E. *Principles of Human Geography*, New York: Wiley, 1921.

ROSS, E.A. *Principles of Sociology*, New York: Century, 1920.

SEMPLE, E. *The Influence of Geographic Environment*, New York: Holt, 1911.

STEARNS, H. *Civilization in the United States*, New York: Harcourt, Brace, 1922.

TAWNEY, R.H. *The Acquisitive Society*, New York: Harcourt Brace, 1920.

WALLAS, G. *Human Nature in Politics*, New York: Alfred Knopf, 1922.

WEBB, S. *Industrial Democracy*, New York: Longmans, Green, 1920.

# Notes on Contributors

**Marianne Bloch** is an Associate Professor in the Department of Curriculum and Instruction at the University of Wisconsin-Madison. She has done historical and cross-cultural research on changing family systems, women's labor, and child care. Her recent research has focused on historical and cross-cultural issues in the development of curriculum for young children.

**Rodger W. Bybee**, an associate director & senior staff member with the Biological Sciences Curriculum Study (BSCS), received his PhD degree in science education and psychology from New York University. He has taught science at the elementary, junior high, senior high, and college levels. Throughout his career Dr. Bybee has written widely, publishing in both education and psychology.

**Kerry Freedman**, Assistant Professor at the University of Minnesota, has been exploring the social and cultural origins of art education. She is concerned with the implications of conceptions of aesthetics and the uses of technology in modern curriculum thought.

**Herbert M. Kliebard** is a Professor in the Departments of Curriculum and Instruction and Educational Policy Studies at the University of Wisconsin-Madison. His major scholarly interests lie in the areas of curriculum theory, history of curriculum and American secondary schools. His most recent book, *The Struggle for the American Curriculum: 1893–1958* traces the evolution of the American curriculum from the time of the Committee of Ten to the passage of the National Defense Education Act.

**Michael Bruce Lybarger** is Professor of History at Edgewood College of the Sacred Heart in Madison, Wisconsin. He received his Master's degree from the University of Notre Dame and his Doctorate from the University of Wisconsin in Curriculum and Instruction. He has published articles in *Cithera, Theory and Research in Social Education*, and *History of Education Quarterly* concerning the early social studies curriculum. His current research interest lies in the early history of educational psychology in the United States.

**E. Jennifer Monaghan**, the author of *A Common Heritage: Noah Webster's Blue-Back Speller*, is an Associate Professor of Developmental Reading in the Department of Educational Services, Brooklyn College, City University of New York.

**Dorothy B. Rosenthal** is Coordinator of Science and Health for the Rush-Henrietta Central School District in Henrietta, New York. Dr. Rosenthal has taught science at the junior high and senior high level and science and science education at the college level. Her research interests and publications center on science and society education and the history of science education.

**E. Wendy Saul**, a curriculum generalist with a special interest in the social construction of language education, teaches children's literature, writing and reading methods courses at the University of Maryland, Baltimore County.

**Christine E. Sleeter** is currently an Assistant Professor at the University of Wisconsin-Parkside. Her research areas include sociology of special education, multicultural education, and education policy related to race, social class, and gender.

**George M.A. Stanic** is now an Assistant Professor of Elementary Education at the University of Georgia. His research focuses on mathematics education and curriculum history.

**Kenneth Teitelbaum** is an Assistant Professor in the Division for the Study of Teaching at Syracuse University. His research interests focus on curriculum studies, the social foundations of education, and teacher education.

# Index

*Index*

white middle class children
   learning disabilities 224–31
   school failure 212
white-collar labor, expansion 214
whole language approach, literacy
   instruction 113
Wiecking, A.M. 76
Wightman, J.M. 34
Wilderspin, Samuel 31
Williams, R. 239, 240
Wilson, President Woodrow 284
Wilson, E.B. 139
Wilson, G.M. 162, 163, 164
Wilson, H.E. 273
Wilson, S. 217
Wimberley, Mrs 193
Winters, E. 284
Wirth, L. 177
Wisconsin idea 13
Wishy, B. 96
Withers, J.H. 166
Witmer, L. 194, 199
Wittick, M.L. 108
Wolff, K.F. 140
Women's Christian Temperance
   Union 130
Woodring, P. 217
Woods, R.A. 185
Woods, R.O. 179
Woodward, A. 93
Woodward, Samuel 33
Woodworth, R.S. 149
Woodyard, E. 150
word attack skills 99
word blindness 196, 224
word lists, Thorndike 97
word processors 116
work, preparation for 66
*Worker, The* 244, 245, 249, 254
workers
   education 182
   living conditions 258

working class 6
   public schools and 241–2, 243–4
working class children
   early education 53, 57
   education 248
Workingman's School 39, 40
workplace codes 183
World War I 255, 274–84
writing 21
   definitions 87–91
   emphasis on 111–16
   research 100–2
   research 112–13
writing acquisition 113
writing crisis 111, 112
writing equipment 95
writing instruction 85–6
   educational theory and 95–102
   professionalization 102–5
   social control aspects 91–2
   social pressures 106–9
   teacher control 93–5
   tradition 86–7
writing instruments 87
written examinations 90, 102–3
Wygant, F. 77
Wynn, R. 127

Yonkers Social Democratic Party
   245
Young, J.W.A. 146, 153, 156, 159,
   160, 161
*Young Socialists' Magazine* 252
youth activists, socialist 247

Zigler, E. 26, 27
Zilversmit, A. 115
Zirbes, Laura 98–9
zoology 125, 128–9, 130, 133, 134,
   140

310